D1749146

SOCCER, THE LEFT, & THE FARCE OF MULTICULTURALISM

John Pepple

authorHOUSE®

AuthorHouse™
1663 Liberty Drive
Bloomington, IN 47403
www.authorhouse.com
Phone: 1-800-839-8640

© 2010 John Frederick Pepple. All rights reserved.

No part of this book may be reproduced, stored in a retrieval system, or transmitted by any means without the written permission of the author.

First published by AuthorHouse   6/3/2010

ISBN: 978-1-4520-0139-5 (e)
ISBN: 978-1-4520-0138-8 (sc)

Library of Congress Control Number: 2010904732

Printed in the United States of America
Bloomington, Indiana

This book is printed on acid-free paper.

Contents

1. Why Can't America's Leftists Be Open-minded about Foreign Sports?   1
2. A Shocking Experience   11
3. Soccer's Place in the World   25
4. A Useful Analogy   53
5. Soccer Is NOT Boring!   57
6. Is "Prejudice" the Right Word?   69
7. The Historical Roots of Soccer Prejudice   125
8. The Persistence of Prejudice: American Cultural Isolationism   151
9. The Ugly American Leftist   163
10. A Leftist Critique of American Sports   175
11. The American Left and the People's Game   201
12. The Reactionary Left   243
13. Being Hard on Soccer   251
14. The Farce of Multiculturalism   267

Preface

This book is about soccer, politics, and culture in America. In particular, it is about soccer and the leftist movement known as multiculturalism. I first got involved in soccer in 1972, but I had no thoughts back then about writing a book about soccer in the United States. For that, two events had to take place. The first was the coming of Pelé to America, for Pelé's presence here drew huge crowds to soccer games, something which in previous years would have been unthinkable. The second was the coming to my home state of a professional soccer team, the Minnesota Kicks. That was in 1976, and again the crowds which flocked to these games would, in previous years, have been unthinkable. The thrilling atmosphere of these games – the huge and enthusiastic crowds, the tailgate parties, and even the various Dixieland bands – led me to believe that supporting soccer in America was not a lost cause, and I was swept away.

But for me this was more than just getting caught up in a new sport, for a Kicks' advertisement declared that by following soccer one would "join the world." And I did. I started reading foreign newspapers, following the game overseas, and traveling to countries like Brazil that I would have never contemplated going to before. In addition, since I'm a philosopher I couldn't help speculating about why we Americans had resisted soccer for so long. But there was something even more important I needed to speculate about, namely why my fellow leftists were so reluctant to go to the games. These were the people who talked about respecting other cultures, yet they refused to respect the sports of those other cultures. Why? Going to a soccer game turned people upside down, it seemed, because those who were generally cautious about change showed up at the games, while those who wanted massive changes in society clung to traditional sports. This mystified me for years. In any case, the results of all these speculations are contained in this book.

I want to thank Pelé, the owners of the Minnesota Kicks, and the many Minnesota Kicks fans for changing my life and for helping me to "join the world." My life has been immeasurably enriched by your actions. I also want to thank my wife, Sarah Blick, and my sister, Kathy Pepple, for looking over some of the earlier drafts of some of the chapters of this book. Naturally, any mistakes and flaws herein are due solely to me.

Chapter 1
Why Can't America's Leftists Be Open-minded about Foreign Sports?

Liberals and leftists aren't as open-minded as they think they are. A few decades ago leftists here in America allowed themselves to be outdone in open-mindedness by frat boys. The issue was the sport of soccer, which at that time was just beginning to enter the mainstream of our culture. We Americans have been prejudiced against soccer and other foreign sports for more than a century, so in the 1970s when soccer began making inroads into American culture, it provided a sterling test of who was and who wasn't open-minded. Surprisingly, it was not liberals and leftists who passed this test, but (among others) frat boys, sorority girls, and people in the military. They were the ones who took the lead in overcoming this prejudice, while liberals and leftists did nothing.

The left's shabby record on overcoming the usual American prejudice against foreign sports is a fact that is little known today. I believe it is little known because one had to be in the right place at the right time in the late 1970s to see it. Most people weren't there, and so neither leftists nor conservatives talk about it. Of course, the reason most people weren't there is because of the very prejudice at issue. They weren't there to see what was happening because they were prejudiced against soccer and so wanted to have nothing to do with it. As a result, they failed to see who turned up at the games and who didn't.

Why would open-minded people be so closed-minded about soccer and other foreign sports? The fact is that they are. As a soccer fan, I find that speaking to a left-of-center American these days can be jarring, particularly if the person in question came of age in the 1960s or earlier. The person I am speaking to will often have a college degree, and maybe even an advanced degree. They will generally be well read. They will be cosmopolitan, having done plenty of international traveling. They will know about foreign cultures (especially non-Western cultures) in a way that leftists in the past did not. They will like listening to Indonesian gamelan music, studying the Tibetan Book of the Dead, reading South American literature, and admiring African art. But let the conversation turn to sports, and suddenly the person before me is transformed. Suddenly, all that cultural sensitivity flies out the window. I find myself having gone through some sort of cultural space warp because the person I am now talking to is (to use some liberal stereotypes) as traditional as a conservative, as provincial as an Appalachian backwoodsman, and as loutish as a Southern redneck. When I bring up the topic of soccer, the reaction I often detect is scorn. That is what a young postmodernist professor expressed a few years ago when I mentioned soccer. She sneered, as Americans are wont to sneer, that soccer had very little scoring. I am used to this objection and suggested that if she wanted scoring, she could try cricket instead. "Cricket?" she said, looking totally baffled at this unexpected turn in the conversation. Then recovering, she denounced me for not being American. That a postmodernist professor would denounce *anyone* for not being American, given that they are generally contemptuous of America, shows how reactionary leftists can get if the topic is international sports.

What does it mean to be a leftist? I don't mean what beliefs leftists have about particular issues, but what it is about leftists that leads them to take the stands they have taken on particular issues. Leftists today usually list a number of qualities that they believe distinguishes them from those further to the right. They consider themselves unprejudiced, open-minded, tolerant, and respectful of other cultures. They believe that people on the right seldom or never have these qualities, and they frequently accuse them of racism, sexism, and homophobia, all of which involve prejudice. But the point I want to make is that anyone can *claim* to be unprejudiced. Whether they truly *are* unprejudiced, whether they are unprejudiced in all matters, can be tested by challenging them on something new, on something they have not yet thought about, to see how they react. Ditto for anyone who claims to be open-minded. Ditto for anyone who claims to be tolerant or a multiculturalist. There are many people making these claims today, but as I shall argue in this book, when they are challenged, they fail miserably. Of course, when they are challenged on the matters they are expecting to be challenged on, they will do very well. But when they are challenged on something comparatively new, like soccer and other foreign sports, they do miserably.

Soccer, the Left, & the Farce of Multiculturalism

The American left's failure to be unprejudiced and open-minded about foreign sports is a very curious phenomenon which has almost never been commented upon, or even noticed. In fact, the whole topic of soccer in America is a very curious phenomenon, when considered from the standpoint of the rest of the world. For the rest of the world, soccer is simply a normal and natural part of life, even in countries (like India) where it is not especially important. Why are we so different? In this book I want to talk about soccer and sports in general, and I want to talk about soccer and sports here in America. I want to talk about how Americans have been prejudiced against soccer for generations, and to trace this prejudice (if possible) back to its roots in the nineteenth century, and to observe that it was not the 1960s when this prejudice began to be overcome but the 1970s, and that the people who overcame it were not the liberals and leftists who came of age in the 1960s, but other people. I want to talk about the educational movement known as multiculturalism and to argue that it is a farce. It is a farce for two reasons: first, because many of the educators who demand that students respect other cultures are themselves disrespectful of the sports of other cultures, and second, because the aspect of other cultures which Americans are least respectful of is their sports, yet foreign sports are utterly ignored by the multiculturalists. The whole movement is like a police force whose officers include a large number of criminals and which in any case ignores the worst crimes and concentrates on the lesser ones. Finally, I want to try to determine if the failure of leftists to overcome the traditional American prejudice against foreign sports was an anomaly on the left or whether this should be considered more or less normal behavior.

Let me ask, Why should overcoming the traditional American prejudice against foreign sports be so hard for leftists? I don't have an answer to that, but my purpose right now is simply to document that it is hard for them. It is not that it is intrinsically hard for everyone, for some young conservatives have overcome it. So, why can't liberals and leftists? It is true that many younger liberals and leftists have overcome the prejudice against soccer, but there is nothing remarkable in that since they have grown up with the sport. Test them on cricket and one finds that they are still prejudiced. But even if they had overcome the prejudice against cricket, the real question is why *all* liberals and leftists cannot overcome these prejudices.

Being a soccer fan in America involves many frustrations, trials and tribulations. Important games are often not televised. Or they are scheduled to be televised and then mysteriously are canceled. The media are indifferent at best. The other fans are fickle, or if not fickle, then uninterested in making waves. Important books and movies about soccer from other countries never make it here or are difficult to obtain. There is a dearth of people with whom one can have a conversation about soccer because so many people are ignorant or hostile. But for me the biggest frustration has always been with my fellow leftists. Leftists should be soccer's biggest supporters in this country, instead of which they are usually counted among its enemies. And even when they happen to be soccer fans, they rarely see soccer as a cause to be promoted. They simply see it as a sport that they like. They never seem to see the prejudice that keeps soccer down in this country, or the many reasons why leftists should be soccer fans.

Accordingly, this book is a rant against leftists. (And it is mostly a rant against *American* leftists, for leftists in other countries typically regard soccer as the people's game. My main gripe with foreign leftists is that they never chastised their American cousins for their prejudices.) It is true that soccer prejudice did not start with leftists, but it is also true that leftists have seldom said anything against it. Nor have they said anything against most of the inequities in our sports. Let me set the context here. When I was a child in the 1950s, the left had political power, and the right had cultural power. The 1960s reversed that. Today, the left has an enormous amount of cultural power, while the right has political power (though even that changed in the 2008 election). The left basically controls the media and the schools. I'm not going to get into a discussion of this because it is so far from my main topic, but let me just say that any leftist who doesn't believe it should read some conservative blogs and notice how frustrated they are by the situation. My point is simply that, seeing all that power, I couldn't help but be frustrated that it was never used on the prejudices against foreign sports and the inequities in our sports. So this book ends up being a rant against America's leftists. As I said, it is true that soccer prejudice did not begin on the left's watch, but it has continued on the left's watch.

What were my expectations here? I want to lay these out so there can be no mistaking what I expected from leftists concerning sports. These expectations were based on what I saw of leftist reactions to other aspects of our culture.

To begin with, I expected that every leftist would have abandoned the prejudices against foreign sports. This doesn't necessarily mean that they would have become fans of those sports, but at the very least I expected them to become "fellow travelers," that is, people who were willing to treat foreign sports with the same respect that they treated American sports and to defend them against their many American detractors.

I expected that some leftists would have gone further and become fans of those sports.

I expected that the vast majority of fans at soccer games would be leftists, simply because I expected that other people were too prejudiced against foreign sports to show up at the games.

I expected a great deal of questioning by leftists concerning the reasons why our society hated these sports so much.

I expected a great deal of bashing of those conservatives who couldn't get over these prejudices.

I expected a great deal of interest among leftists in learning about foreign sports.

I expected demands by leftists that our media cover these sports much more than they are now.

I expected that our own sports would have been scrutinized by leftists and that their many failings would have been condemned. I expected that radical changes would have been demanded.

I expected much bitterness from some leftists that all our major sports are of American origin.

I expected that those on the more radical fringe of the left would be chanting, "Hey, hey, ho, ho, America's sports have got to go," just as some radicals, annoyed at the emphasis on courses championing Western civilization in our schools, have chanted "Hey, hey, ho, ho, Western Civ has got to go."

I expected that, just as some leftists speak of America as "Amerika" to show its similarity to Nazi Germany, some leftists would denounce our sports as "Amerikan" sports.

Finally, I expected that some leftists would denounce all sports invented by dead white males (thus attacking both the American triad of baseball, football, and basketball, and the English triad of soccer, cricket, and rugby), preferring to support only those sports invented by others (such as lacrosse, which was invented by Native Americans).[1]

Anyone who knows what has been happening in the United States since the 1960s knows that none of these expectations of mine have been met. As far as I know, I am the only leftist in this country who is a radical about sports. There is no one else advocating radical changes. Oh, to be sure, there are a few people demanding what *they* think are radical changes. They want more women's sports or they want team names offensive to American Indians to be changed, but these people generally want everything else to stay the same. They have a few minor gripes, but otherwise are quite satisfied. I, on the other hand, want to turn everything upside down.

Instead of finding myself in good company in my expectations and desires, I find myself utterly alone. There are a few other leftists who are soccer fans, but they seem to have no interest in big changes. There are many non-leftists who are soccer fans, but their ideology has no effect on their choice of sports. They just happen to be soccer fans.

The prejudices of leftists on sports are so thick that nothing can cut through them. (One can say this about non-leftists, too, but then one doesn't expect them to be anxious to overcome their prejudices.) Consider the following. Elton John was a co-owner of the Lost Angeles Aztecs of the old North American Soccer League (NASL). Rod Stewart compares a lover to Celtic United. Jacques Derrida, the darling of postmodernist professors, was not only a soccer fan but according to one account actually played the game professionally.[2] One of the Spice Girls marries an English soccer star, David Beckham. He is so revered throughout the rest of the world that a Buddhist temple in Thailand has a shrine to him.[3] Colin Firth rises from obscurity by playing Mr. Darcy in the BBC *Pride and Prejudice* miniseries, and then plays an obsessed soccer fan in the (British) movie *Fever Pitch*. Most of the people in the Third World are soccer fans. There are no baseball-playing countries in either Africa or the Middle East, but there are plenty of soccer-playing countries.

None of these events or facts has ever been able to cut through the prejudices of America's leftists. (The movie *Fever Pitch*, for example, had to be remade as a film about baseball in order to make it appeal to Americans. No leftists complained about this.) It is useless recounting them to any leftist. Somehow, mentioning them just doesn't penetrate. I had many arguments with other leftists about this, and have written many letters to leftists and many letters to editors of newspapers (who are generally liberal or leftist), to no effect. That prejudice is just too strong.

Consider, for example, Garrison Keillor in his book *Homegrown Democrat*. He talks of living in Denmark and of how he took the trouble to learn the local language. That is certainly commendable. And he disparages the American ambassador as a cultural philistine who didn't bother doing this. And he is certainly right about that. I would expect any of our ambassadors to at least *begin* to learn the language of their host country. Keillor goes on to add that "Mark Twain, H.L. Mencken,

George Ade, Sinclair Lewis, and James Thurber had all beaten on this man for a hundred years and there wasn't a dent on him."[4] Likewise, I feel that I have been beating on leftists for many years, and there is no dent on them, either. When will we be rid of the American leftist who hates foreign sports? Keillor, after all, was in Denmark in 1992, which was a pretty special year for Denmark, soccer-wise. But he says nothing about this. He says nothing about soccer in the year that Denmark managed to win the European Nations' Cup for the first time, *even though they hadn't initially qualified for it*. Look at it this way. Soccer is to some extent an international language, and most Americans don't like learning foreign languages. While Keillor certainly tries to buck this tendency, he didn't go as far as he should have.

In addition, Keillor also talks about how one can talk basketball with black taxi drivers at our airports.[5] This of course assumes that all black taxi drivers at our airports are basketball fans, but I have found such people to be recent immigrants from Africa, where the main sport is soccer. Why assume, then, that they are basketball fans? Does he believe that all blacks in the world are basketball fans, or did he just fail to recognize that these people were from Africa? If the former, I suggest he take a look at the sports sections of some foreign newspapers (particularly those of the old British Commonwealth) to see how seldom basketball is covered in them. If the latter, if he didn't recognize them as immigrants, then I have to wonder about Keillor's perceptive abilities. If someone who is as bad at recognizing people as I am can figure out that these people are immigrants, I figure most culturally sensitive people should be able to manage this as well. Moreover, what would he do if he were to encounter immigrants from India? Since their main sport is cricket, shouldn't someone like Keillor have educated himself to the extent that he could discuss cricket with them intelligently? Yet, I doubt if Keillor has so educated himself. If he has, then he is a rarity, since almost no leftists in this country know anything about cricket.

The significance of soccer for my generation is simple: it was something so new they didn't know what to do about it. The big liberation movements of the Sixties were in fact covering ground previously covered. For example, women's liberation and black liberation – these had been talked about by others already. Others had traveled the road against sexism and racial prejudice already. What about multiculturalism, animal liberation and gay liberation? Pearl Buck had lamented our attitudes toward foreign cultures back in the 1930s. People have always loved animals, and some were vegetarians long before I was born, so animal liberation was nothing especially new. Gay liberation was new to a certain extent, but most educated people were familiar with ancient Greek attitudes to homosexuality. Accordingly, the big changes that Sixties leftists pat themselves on the back for were merely the intense resuscitation of things that had been latent for some time.

But overcoming the prejudice against foreign sports was something completely new. In this instance, there was nothing latent in our culture that could be revived by Sixties leftists. Our cultural icons knew nothing of foreign sports. F. Scott Fitzgerald talks a lot about football, for example, and Philip Roth goes on quite a bit about baseball in *Portnoy's Complaint* (and to an Israeli psychoanalyst, yet), but I just don't know of any American authors who were very familiar with soccer or cricket. James Michener talks a little bit about soccer in *Iberia*, but he clearly isn't immersed in the soccer world. Ernest Hemingway goes on about a foreign sport, but it is bullfighting rather than soccer. And one of our country's icons who did know about foreign sports, George Washington, is not known for this. Most Americans are quite unaware that he played cricket.

So, there was almost nothing in our culture to prepare those of us who came of age in the Sixties for the idea that we needed to outgrow these ridiculous prejudices. Accordingly, almost every leftist of my generation decided that clinging to our own sports was best. When millions of others have already traveled a road, it's not so difficult to walk it. But what happens when no one else has walked that road? When I got onto the road against soccer prejudice, I found that virtually no one had traveled that road before me. And I found virtually all leftists reluctant to join me. It's pretty easy to be against a prejudice when millions of others were against that prejudice before you came along. But what if no one before you had been against the prejudice? And what if all those who generally condemn prejudice refused to join you in denouncing this prejudice? This is soccer's significance for my generation. It was a prejudice that had not been denounced before, and apparently that was enough to cause my generation to find it unimportant to overcome such a prejudice.

Before moving on, let me make a couple of clarifications. First, I am calling multiculturalism a farce, but I need to be clear on what it is. Some blacks seem to have the idea that multiculturalism is nothing but a movement against racism. This is incorrect. It is a movement that, among other things, wants us Americans to respect other cultures around the world. Second, some conservatives seem to have the idea that soccer is being rammed down our throats by leftists. Nothing could be further from the truth. It is people in the middle or even on the right who are pushing soccer, not the left. Leftists have no or little interest in it. Finally, I am talking about leftists, but I really mean liberals and leftists. I'm talking about all those who think of themselves as left of center, but I'm using the word "leftist" rather than the phrase "liberals and leftists" merely as a matter of convenience. Nor do I think there is much point, as far as my purposes are concerned, in making a distinction between liberals and leftists since what I am talking about applies to both groups. I am talking about the people who generally consider themselves unprejudiced, open-minded, and so on, and who distinguish themselves from those further to the right by these qualities. People on the right usually think of themselves in different terms (traditional, freedom-loving), though they may also in fact be (contrary to what leftists think) unprejudiced, open-minded, and so on.

With these points clarified, let me close this chapter with the following question. How many prominent leftists in America can you name who are known to be soccer fans or at least knowledgeable about soccer? The answer is, mighty few. Jon Stewart is one of the few who comes to mind. And if one restricts the question to Sixties leftists, I can think of only one: Camille Paglia. But she is such a maverick I don't know that she deserves to be included. There is also Janet Lever, who has written a fine book about soccer in Brazil, but – sorry, Prof. Lever – I don't know that she deserves to be called prominent. The ones who are prominent just aren't soccer fans, and that is all there is to it.

Endnotes

1. I will discuss, and denounce, this potential reaction in Chapter 14.
2. I discuss this in more detail in Chapter 11.
3. *USA Today*, May 8, 2003.
4. Garrison Keillor, *Homegrown Democrat* (Viking, 2004), p. 216.
5. Keillor, *Homegrown Democrat*, p. 151.

Chapter 2
A Shocking Experience

The biggest political shock of my life came in the late 1970s, and it involved soccer. I was born in the early 1950s and grew up on baseball, football, and basketball. I knew little about soccer, except that it was big elsewhere. When I started college in the late 1960s, I was still ignorant of soccer, though every other American was, too. But in 1972, a group of us began playing soccer, and while I didn't learn much, I did notice that most other Americans were prejudiced against it. Meanwhile, we young people were trying to turn the world upside down, and one thing we hated was prejudice. So, when a soccer team came to town, I naturally expected that the only people who would show up at the games would be leftists. But a funny thing happened on the way to the stadium. Who actually showed up? Frat boys. Sorority girls. Military personnel. Families from the suburbs. None of these people struck me as particularly leftist or even liberal. Imagine being outdone in open-mindedness by frat boys.

Let me go through my reasoning here in more detail, because often people don't seem to understand what I find perfectly clear. First, the Sixties spawned three big liberation movements: black, women's, and gay and lesbian. People involved in these movements all talked about the societal prejudices against them, and they demanded that they be treated as equals. They demanded that people become more open-minded about them. There were also lesser liberation movements, involving the disabled, animals and even children. The idea spread throughout the left that one ought not to be prejudiced against anything whatsoever. This included not just people, but anything. It included long hair for men, but most especially it included drugs. To be free to use mind-altering drugs was a huge part of the Sixties, and once again the idea was that people ought not to be prejudiced against them. It extended to rock music, of course, which our parents and the Establishment hated, but which we liked.

But the idea of being unprejudiced and open-minded also extended to other cultures. Though the word "multiculturalism" hadn't been invented yet, the concept of it was in the air, and I had read enough and heard enough to have absorbed it. I knew that judging other cultures as inferior to our own was to take a narrow and prejudiced view of things. I even got into a big argument during this era with someone who, despite having some leftist views, insisted that the West was best and absolutely refused to be swayed about the value of other cultures. She was an anomaly, though, and soon enough multiculturalism swept through the left.

Being unprejudiced and open-minded sometimes went to extremes. One day I saw in a question-and-answer column in my local newspaper that someone had submitted a question that ran roughly as follows: "I think vultures would make good pets. I think people are basically prejudiced against them and that vultures have been getting a bad rap. Why shouldn't I have one as a pet?" The expert who answered said that vultures were carrion eaters, and he also seemed to imply that having a vulture as a pet was a crazy idea, which I'm sure simply confirmed to the letter writer that the expert was prejudiced.

Another strand of thought in the Sixties was the idea of reform. Just before starting college, I met a young woman who said she was interested in reform. She wanted "education reform, prison reform, military reform, reform reform." She didn't explain what "reform reform" meant, but I was pretty sure she meant that she wanted the very process of reform to be made easier. Her statement has for me always been a nice summing up of the Sixties. We young people saw unjust institutions around us everywhere, and we wanted them changed for the better. We wanted them reformed. For example, we railed against education at every level, and we wanted it reformed. During this period, some independent film-maker made a film called *High School* that showed that high schools were run by authoritarian and petty people. In college I remember a lot of talk about how what we were learning was basically irrelevant to the real world. Everything had to be relevant back then, and the education we were receiving was widely perceived as not relevant. In response, some people at my university organized a "graduation" ceremony in which anyone who wanted could graduate into what the organizers called the "university of life." They even made up certificates for us and had a planned ceremony with speakers and music. Another time I read an article about education in the student newspaper that talked about how terribly difficult it was to avoid having a master-servant relationship develop between the professor and the student. This idea is still around. When my wife first started her college teaching career, she was advised by an older professor to avoid this. The woman said, "I start my classes simply by saying, 'Well?' and letting the students do the rest." The idea was (and for some, still is) that the professor should not be "the sage on the stage," but "the guide on the side."

There were also demands for changes in what seemed at the time every aspect of our culture. People thought that criminals were essentially good people who were caught by the system, which of course was seen as unjust, and they felt that the whole system of criminal justice needed to be reformed. There are still many people who see criminal courts as hopelessly flawed, and there are plenty who believe that prisons should be eliminated. The number of people (not counting criminals) who believed this prior to the 1960s was limited to a few people who were isolated and invisible.

Another change that was demanded was in food and agriculture. The whole organic food and farming movement began at this time. Environmentalism started at this time. People started communes to grow their own food and to live the lifestyles they wanted to live.

People demanded reforms in religion as well. Catholicism went through a big reform with Vatican II, though not being Catholic myself I was not aware of it at the time. Many leftists my age wanted to reform their religions, though many more simply dropped out. Some decided that organized religion was always bad, so while remaining Christian they refused to go to church. Others took off for the East and became Buddhists or (if they were black) Muslims. Still others began investigating other possibilities, such as Wicca and other New Age varieties.

A third strand of the Sixties was the idea of questioning everything. We were supposed to look at everything critically and to wonder why we were doing things the way we were and not some other, better way. The role of blacks and women in our society was questioned, and the results of that questioning were evident in the last election, when the Democrats' two strongest candidates were a woman and a black. As we all know, not only did the black (Barack Obama) win the nomination, but he also won the election. Had the questioning that went on in the Sixties not happened, that probably would have been impossible. But many other things were questioned as well. Many people questioned the idea of fraternities and sororities, because they saw them as bastions of conservatism. They wanted them run off campus. I still hear such people talk this way. Such people in fact did often succeed in getting the military off of our campuses. And as I mentioned above, the role of teachers and professors was questioned, the necessity of prisons, and so on.

A fourth strand was the idea of America and how we ought to think about it. Many of us believed that our country was basically fascist and we thought of our president, Richard Nixon, as a sort of Hitler. We thought that the proper way to deal with our flag was not to display it in this way or that way, but to burn it. We hated the "super patriots" who never questioned anything about our country and allowed many racist and other horrid actions and practices to take place in it and didn't care what our country did to other countries. We hated the idea that America was the best and that everything America did was the best. We preferred to look at the bad things, because we wanted to make things better, for if one refused to look at the bad things, then one would spend one's life not realizing how bad things were for other people. We didn't think of ourselves as patriots in the narrow sense in which our parents and others on the right did. Instead, we thought of ourselves as a higher sort of patriot.

This was what coming of age in the Sixties meant to me. This was the milieu which I was part of in college. So far I've said very little about the war in Vietnam, but that was also a big part of that milieu. I participated in many protests and marches and even a riot against this war. But although many seem to look back and think the Sixties was all about protesting against Vietnam, that was only one element of the Sixties. There were other elements, too.

I'm writing about what I remember, though there were probably many other things I have forgotten. Keep in mind that those on the right vociferously and vigorously resisted all of this. They thought there was nothing wrong with our country and that no changes were needed. The right included our parents and college administrators, but it also included stuffy members of my own generation. I remember a radical friend in high school getting into an argument with someone our age about change, and this rather pompous fellow kept talking about "going through the proper channels." We thought the proper channels for change didn't work, which is why we wanted "reform reform." The conservatives also included people in fraternities and sororities, anyone in the military (unless they specifically said they were against the war in Vietnam), and anyone from the suburbs.

This was what my college years were like, a time of intense radicalism. A few years later things had quieted down a little. The Vietnam War had ended, and to our dismay the young people entering college – by this time I was in grad school – seemed more conservative. Some were even majoring in (horrors!) business, and pretty soon this became a very popular major, replacing sociology and psychology. The enrollment in philosophy classes began going down, as young people began deciding that this was not very practical. Still, although my generation was no longer in college and the war was over, we hadn't disappeared. Some of us had gone into grad school and others had become investigative reporters. We were slowly taking over all of academia and the media.

Then in 1976, a soccer team came to town. I earlier said I had begun playing soccer with friends in 1972 and that I had noticed the prejudice against it. It was evident in the feeble amount of programming that was allowed for soccer on television during the Olympics that summer. I remember sitting with my friends and watching all thirty seconds of it. It was also evident when we invited other people to join us, for they acted with disdain. A friend and I argued with another friend about this. He said that he had played soccer in junior high and that all it consisted of was people kicking a ball and running after it from one end of the field to the other. He just didn't see the point at all. As I will relate in this book, there's a lot more to it than that. Anyway, at that time almost no one was playing soccer. Occasionally, foreigners would see us playing and ask to play. It was pretty clear that they were desperate for anything relating to soccer. And of course, they could dazzle us with their skills. But the average American didn't want much to do with it. And this included radical Americans. Still, I assumed that progress in eliminating this prejudice would begin with the radical left and eventually work its way through to even the most prejudiced on the right.

But it didn't happen that way at all. Over the next few years people in the suburbs began starting soccer teams for their young children. I lived in the city, and I didn't have children, so I really wasn't aware of what was going on in the suburbs. None of my radical friends seemed aware, either. Then in 1975, just about the time that the Vietnam War was finally ending, Pelé came to America. This gave soccer a huge jolt in terms of visibility. Since there were no soccer teams in my region, his arrival didn't mean much to me, but the very next year a team came to town. My first reaction to the news that we were getting a soccer team (the Minnesota Kicks) was actually dismay. Of course, I liked the idea of a soccer team in town, but I also knew that it would be accompanied by all the disputes and arguments that we radical leftists had had with conservatives down through the years over so many issues (not just Vietnam, but hair, music, and so on).

Then I went to the games and was at first surprised to see so many people there who were not at all like me. But I thought, "It is so nice that they are able to overcome their prejudices and come to a soccer game and join with the Kicks' core audience, which of course consists of leftists like me." Gradually, as I went to more and more games, I realized that this impression was completely wrong. There was no core audience of leftists. These people – the frat boys, and so on – were the core audience. I wasn't part of the core audience at all. I was an anomaly.

What I saw at soccer games back then – and the attendances were huge; the first four games I went to had over 40,000 people in the stands – was a complete violation of everything I thought I knew about people. The people who were showing up were conservative or at best middle of the road. These people were the super patriots who liked everything about America. They were exactly the sort who would get angry about the intrusion of a foreign sport into our midst. And they were the ones who didn't want changes in our society, yet here they were opting for a change.

Likewise, the leftists who stayed away were the ones I thought would show up. I always thought of getting involved in soccer as a logical extension of my activities as a radical leftist, and I've always looked with wonder, and increasing disdain, at my fellow radicals for not getting involved. Let me run through their lines of thought again. If one believes that one ought to be unprejudiced and open-minded about everything, then soccer is one of those things about which one ought to be open-minded. If one thinks everything in our society needs to be reformed, then surely sports need to be reformed, too, and since leftists wanted huge reforms for other aspects of our society, then they should have wanted huge reforms for sports, too (such as dumping our sports in favor of foreign sports). If one ought to question everything, then one ought to question America's hatred of soccer as well. And finally, if one concludes that America is not the best at everything, then it stands to reason that we weren't the best at inventing sports, so there is no reason to cling to "our" sports and every reason to look at the sports of other cultures, which includes the sport of soccer.

There is nothing particularly difficult about any of this reasoning. It is just that nearly every liberal and leftist from my generation shied away from making these simple inferences. To put it in language that was developed later, when confronted with the sports of the "Other," my

Soccer, the Left, & the Farce of Multiculturalism

fellow liberals and leftists went whimpering back to the warm comfort of America's traditional sports.

So who were the fans who were actually showing up? The fans for the Minnesota Kicks consisted of two groups. One group consisted of the people my age who were from the suburbs who had young children and who had obviously decided that going to a soccer game represented a cheap form of entertainment. (The Kicks' management had made the tickets very cheap. They had a student discount as well, plus free parking.) The other group consisted of teenagers and college students, that is, people who were just then coming of age. As I already said, my generation had watched these people as they came of age, and we were somewhat disappointed that they were more conservative than my generation. Yet, here they were doing something radical, going to a soccer game.

Sometimes entire fraternities or sororities from the University of Minnesota would come to these games, and I know that students from the Reserve Officer Training Corps (R.O.T.C.) got involved, also. In addition, a former Marine I knew observed that soccer and rugby were very big in the military. My parents were conservative, and they were members of some sort of veterans' group that had a supper club. One day I went to their house and happened to see a newsletter from this club, and it contained an article about how the younger members were starting up a soccer league. Incredible. I never heard of any socialist groups starting up soccer leagues. As far as I could tell, socialists didn't want to have anything to do with soccer.

Not only was there prejudice against soccer in America, but to my very great surprise, it was the conservatives (or at any rate, the non-leftists) who were doing better at overcoming that prejudice than the leftists were.

So, here were these two groups of people, suburbanites with families and teenagers ten years younger than me, who were turning out in massive numbers to see soccer. I was part of neither group. (As a grad student at the University of Minnesota, I lived in the city.) I noticed that almost none of my fellow grad students were interested in showing up at these games (with the exception of a man from Trinidad and his American wife). This provided further evidence of what I was seeing at the games, that leftists just weren't involved.

Perhaps, though, what I was seeing was confined to Minnesota. Perhaps elsewhere in the country leftists were involved. But the national media suggested otherwise. And later on after getting my Ph.D., I had a series of jobs in various parts of the country, and I could see perfectly well the same pattern I had seen in Minnesota: leftists just didn't want to get over their soccer prejudices. For example, I spent a year teaching philosophy at Augustana College in Rock Island, Illinois. There were three of us in the philosophy department, and by coincidence perhaps, we were the only three faculty members to attend the college's soccer games. But while I was on the left, the other two were Republicans, which given the small number of Republicans in academia is quite astonishing. Another example is Kenyon College, where my wife teaches. I've been to many of the college's soccer games (both men's and women's), and I know who among the faculty shows up and who doesn't. In general, the Sixties leftists do not show up, and in fact generally the leftists do not show up.

For those who don't believe me, consider another pertinent fact on this issue: the spread of soccer in America. Did it spread from liberal regions to conservative regions? I can't see that it did. It spread from suburbs to both rural areas and cities. Nothing about this suggests it was liberals who did the spreading. It was not the working classes spreading it to the wealthy, but the other way around. Also, this spread happened in liberal and conservative states alike, with the result that soccer today is spread fairly evenly throughout the country. If this was a left-right phenomenon, then the right was remarkably compliant. And coverage in newspapers does not suggest that the left has been at the forefront of overcoming soccer prejudice. (Here and throughout this book when I talk about newspapers I will be referring to English-language newspapers; newspapers in other languages can be quite different.) Newspapers that are generally progressive do not do any better at covering soccer than those that aren't so progressive. For example, the *Columbus Dispatch*[1] is not especially progressive, but it does not do any worse than progressive newspapers like *The New York Times*, and it does far better than the more progressive Minneapolis *Star-Tribune*.[2]

Moreover, after I got involved with soccer, I looked for some leftist American, for any leftist American, in the past who had overcome this prejudice and had begun learning about the world of soccer the way I was doing. I found no one. The best I could find was that the liberal James Michener had written a little about soccer in his book *Iberia*.[3] But that was all. Think about all the liberals and leftists of the past in this country, people of whom one would like to think well, but who just couldn't manage to shake off that prejudice. It was a sobering thought, to say the least. It made me put the activities of leftists in perspective, a perspective that they wouldn't like but which I deemed necessary.

Soccer, the Left, & the Farce of Multiculturalism

What's more, despite a lot of rhetoric from the left urging us to respect other cultures, none of that rhetoric urges us to respect foreign sports in particular. Let anyone bash soccer and these same people are silent, while if someone bashes other aspects of other cultures (such as their religion or literature), then the left rises up in righteous indignation. This is why I call multiculturalism a farce, though I will go into this in detail in a later chapter. Moreover, there are people who are probably on the left who just never got involved or got angry at the prejudice and hatred directed against soccer, despite what would seem to be a strong reason for doing so. These include Anglophiles, Francophiles, cosmopolitans, and so on. Why wouldn't Anglophiles promote soccer in this country? If they are true Anglophiles, don't they like English sports and aren't they bothered by the mindless rants against them by the soccer haters of this country? Apparently not.

More evidence comes from asking, Who started the professional leagues back in 1967? Socialists? The Democrats? Hardly. Those leagues were started by American businessmen who had been in England during the 1966 World Cup tournament. They had seen all the excitement that that event had caused and wanted to bring it here to America. I've never heard what their political leanings were, but there is nothing to suggest that they were on the far left. I presume that, being businessmen, they were in the center or on the right. In 1975, some of the owners of the teams lured Pelé here to play. Again, there was nothing that suggested that this was done by leftists. And certainly no leftist groups have ever taken any credit for doing this, or have ever even wanted to take credit for doing it. Moreover, today when the national team plays, who are the advertisers? They are likely to be ordinary American corporations or the U.S. Army or the Marines and not anything associated with the left.

Many people sacrificed to make soccer important in this country, but almost none were leftists. Kyle Rote, Jr., sacrificed a career in football for a career in soccer. During the 1970s he also participated in a number of media-sponsored events pitting athletes from various sports together in general athletic contests (races and such). His purpose was to get Americans to see that soccer players were genuine athletes and that they weren't out there playing tiddlywinks. Other people sacrificed simply by spending time and money going to games. Maybe they didn't see it as a sacrifice, but there was always a certain amount of ostracism for those who supported soccer. They sacrificed when they tried to persuade their friends to come to games. Some rich people sacrificed by buying teams, and one or two sacrificed to the extent that they built stadiums. Even some people in our sports whom I generally think of as hostile to soccer sacrificed by doing things to help soccer. For example, the former Dallas Cowboys' coach Tom Landry worked to make Dallas a venue for the 1994 World Cup.[4]

I myself sacrificed by not only going to games, but by buying soccer magazines, buying a movie projector and films of old games, buying a VCR when they first came out (and were much more expensive than they later became) so I could record games, buying a shortwave radio so I could listen to soccer broadcasts from other countries, and eventually traveling abroad so I could see games in other countries. Much of this I did when I was a poor graduate student, too.

Another who sacrificed was Henry Kissinger, who worked to get the World Cup for the U.S. in 1994. Yet another who sacrificed was former Minneapolis mayor Charles Stenvig. Stenvig was a Republican who got elected on a law-and-order campaign in the late 1960s. In 1972 he sent police to the University of Minnesota to clear out some students (including me) who were demonstrating against the mining of Haiphong harbor. During the ensuing riot, a tear-gas cannister landed at my feet. At the time, I thought of him as a fascist, but what was I to think a few years later when he came out as a soccer fan? At the time, he was the only prominent Minnesota politician who was a soccer fan. I believe he is *still* the only prominent Minnesota politician ever to be a soccer fan. What a pathetic record for Minnesota liberalism.

Leftists generally sacrificed not at all. They did nothing to push society to overcome the prejudice against soccer. For some reason, they never saw it as part of the progressive agenda. Eventually, they began enrolling their children on soccer teams, but that was only because everyone else was doing it and not because they felt it was a progressive thing to do. While other people sacrificed to bring soccer to this country and to make it important, leftists did not sacrifice at all.

To sum up, there is no evidence that the left did much of anything to promote soccer or to overcome the prejudice against soccer and other foreign sports in this country.

Let me, though, consider some other opinions. There are conservative bloggers out there who rant against soccer and connect it with socialism. As far as I know, however, they have no particular evidence that the rise of soccer in this country is due to leftists in general or socialists in particular.

Another, more considered opinion, is that of Franklin Foer, who in his book *How Soccer Explains the World* insists that the rise of soccer was the result of liberal and leftist parents like his who have pushed young people into soccer for the past thirty years or so.⁵ This seems to be a mistake based on generalizing from one example. Moreover, Foer is younger than me and so didn't see all the things I saw. He didn't see the more conservative teenagers that I saw attending soccer games, or the lack of interest exhibited by most of the leftists I knew. Maybe the parents I had seen bringing their small children to the games were radicals, but they sure didn't dress like radicals. They seemed pretty mainstream to me. Moreover, a study has been done complaining that these people were and are racists.⁶ Plus, anyone who goes to a professional soccer game in this country has only to look at the bumper stickers on cars in the parking lot and then compare them with bumper stickers on cars in, say, a Whole Foods parking lot to see that there is virtually no overlap in bumper stickers. Leftists mostly remain aloof from soccer.

But mostly Foer's remark misses a big point, even if it is true (which I doubt). Overcoming the prejudice against soccer has never been a theme of the left's. Prior to the 1960s, the main interest of the left was the plight of the worker. Racial prejudice was a minor issue, and sexism was even less of an issue, while homophobia wasn't an issue at all. In other words, prior to the 1960s, a leftist could be a bit of a racist (especially by the standards of later generations of leftists), a sexist, and a homophobe without other leftists complaining. After the 1960s, none of these were possible. No leftist today is racist, sexist, or homophobic. But leftists today can be xenophobes about other countries' sports. No one on the left will chastise you for this (that is, no one except me, and my lone voice is too feeble to have any impact). And that is why Foer's claim is just beside the point. The rise of soccer in this country may be the result of the activity of leftists – and I say there is massive amounts of evidence that this is wrong – but so long as leftists can remain prejudiced against soccer, the record of the left on this issue is a bad one.

But what can one say about the suburbanites who decided to enroll their kids in soccer beginning in the 1970s, if they weren't leftists? Presumably, they were to some extent influenced by the open-mindedness of the 1960s, but one can still ask, Why soccer rather than rugby or cricket or lacrosse or any of a number of other sports? Probably, these people were looking for a summer sport that had some running in it. That same period was the period when jogging became big, after all. Baseball just isn't a sport that includes a lot of running, and cricket is no better. They weren't looking to replace football, so they generally didn't bother with rugby. They didn't think of lacrosse because, unless they lived in the East, they weren't even aware of it. But most of them had some dim awareness of soccer.

What it comes down to, then, is they chose soccer for the same reason I initially chose soccer: it had a lot of running in it, much more running than baseball or touch football. I saw it as a sport to play rather than one to watch. What converted me to also watching it was actually going to a few games and seeing the impressive skills that the pros had (as well as the thrilling atmosphere of the Minnesota Kicks games).

What can one say about soccer fans in America today? The most notable feature of soccer fans in America today isn't their political leanings but the year of their birth. There is no year that represents a sharp dividing point, but the year 1955 can be chosen as convenient. People born, say, five years before 1955 are extremely unlikely to be soccer fans, while people born five years after 1955 might well be soccer fans. There is a difference here of less than 1% of the population for those born in 1950 versus perhaps as much as 20% for those born in 1960.[7] This is a huge jump. And that jump was taken not by people who came of age in the Sixties, but by people who came of age in the Seventies.

One can also say that for those born after 1955, even if they aren't soccer fans they have some knowledge of the world game which their elders generally don't have. The difference between the years, say, 1970 and 1990 is instructive. In 1970, virtually no young Americans knew anything about soccer, and of course the idea of going to college on a soccer scholarship was almost unheard of. Nor were there any Americans playing abroad. By 1990, plenty of young people knew about soccer, and some of them chose their colleges based on the soccer team. And today, young people can look up to a number of Americans who are playing abroad or who have played abroad: Brian McBride, Brad Friedel, DaMarcus Beasley, and so on. Back when I first got into soccer, the closest I could find to an American player abroad was Felix Magath, a German player who grew up in Germany but who had an American soldier as a father. But his father (from Puerto Rico) abandoned him rather quickly, and so the American influence in this case was nil.

Now let me be quite clear about one thing. I'm saying that some conservatives in this country have overcome the traditional American prejudice against foreign sports, while most leftists (especially leftists my age and older) have not. That is surely an astonishing situation. But I am *not* saying that all or even most conservatives have overcome this prejudice. That would be going much too far. Not every conservative from the suburbs was converted. But consider the conversation I had during the 1998 World Cup with a Minnesota conservative who hated soccer. He sneered at soccer, and then pointed out that two columnists in the sports section of the Minneapolis *Star-Tribune* also hated it. What could I say? That the good liberals of Minnesota hated those columnists? That they thought of them as xenophobes and thus as no better than racists? No, I could not say those things. Obviously, the good liberals of Minnesota *liked* and still do like those columnists, or else they would have run them out of the state ages ago. Obviously, the good liberals of Minnesota *like* xenophobic columnists.

As I've already said, it is not a record that brings any credit to the left.

Endnotes

1. Full disclosure here: I have written some book reviews for the *Columbus Dispatch*.
2. Back in the late 1970s and early 1980s when it was two newspapers, the *Star* and the *Tribune*, the coverage of soccer was quite good.
3. James Michener, *Iberia* (Random House, 1968), pp. 356-60 and 625-7.
4. See Christopher Merrill, *The Grass of Another Country* (Henry Holt, 1993), p. 121.
5. Franklin Foer, *How Soccer Explains the World* (HarperCollins, 2004), pp. 273 ff.
6. David L. Andrews, Robert Pitter, Detlev Zwick, and Darren Ambrose, "Soccer's Racial Frontier: Sport and the Suburbanization of Contemporary America," in Gary Armstrong and Richard Giulianotti, *Entering the Field: New Perspectives on World Football* (Oxford and New York: Berg, 1997), 261-281.
7. I say 20% as a guess, simply because the percentage of soccer fans in the U.S. is about 10%, and since being a soccer fan is something generational, that means that later generations must be higher in terms of percentages to make up for the lower percentages of their elders.

Chapter 3
Soccer's Place in the World

In order to put what I'm talking about in perspective, I want to talk about soccer's place in the world, particularly as it exists in the rest of the world. Many Americans don't know much about soccer and try not to think about it very much, and so are very ignorant. Moreover, our media isn't much help here, for it tends to focus on our sports and to shield us from what is happening elsewhere. Much of what I'm saying, though, is pretty well known, at least to people outside of the U.S.

1. Soccer is the most popular sport in the world. There are lots of Americans who don't want to hear this, and who try not to say it, but it is true. Moreover, it has been true now for over a century. There are some rumors that it has been overtaken by basketball, but as the saying goes, one swallow does not a summer make, and a few rumors to this effect – and from Americans yet – are not enough to shake the conviction of most people outside the U.S. that soccer is still king. Some outside the U.S. have suggested that cricket is king, simply because it is so popular in the Indian subcontinent, which contains a billion people. Nevertheless, while this represents a substantial number, it still doesn't equal the popularity of soccer.

2. Soccer is the most popular sport in the Third World. This is perhaps more debatable, but it is still a good bet. Soccer is a very popular sport in most of Latin America, and the most popular sport in that area's southern region. Soccer is king in Africa. In most of Asia, soccer is king as well, though here we do run into a few other sports. Recently, basketball has taken off in China, which has of course a very large population. Likewise, India, which also has a large population, is mad for cricket. But even if soccer is not as popular in these countries as it is in, say, Brazil, in neither country is there the soccer prejudice that one finds in America. And even

if soccer isn't the most popular sport in the Third World, it is certainly closer to being so than, say, baseball is.

3. There are no baseball-playing or football-playing countries in Africa or the Middle East. I mention this because inevitably, when the facts are being trotted out, some prejudiced American will mention that baseball is played in Japan, as though somehow Japan represents the entire rest of the world and as though this one example makes up for its near entire lack of fandom on the part of most of the rest of the world. In contrast with the facts about baseball and football, there just is no region where soccer doesn't have some presence. Only here in America has its presence been somewhat lacking, and that has been changing in recent years. However, neither baseball nor football has much presence in Europe or Australia. Basketball has traveled the furthest of our sports, but its existence is practically unknown in most of the countries of the old British Commonwealth. Go to England or India and look at the sports pages of their newspapers, and you will see almost nothing about basketball. The sports will almost always be one or another British sport (whether soccer, cricket or rugby). For that matter, while baseball has no presence in either Africa or the Middle East, cricket has a presence in both places (in Pakistan and African countries like Zimbabwe). It also has a presence in the Americas (in the West Indies and Guyana).

4. For every baseball fan in the world, there are eight other people who are *not* baseball fans. Granted, this is a rough statistic. It is based on the populations of those countries that can legitimately be called baseball-playing countries. These are the United States, Canada, Mexico, the countries of Central America, Cuba, Venezuela, Colombia, Japan, Taiwan, and South Korea.[1] Of course, not everyone in these countries is a baseball fan, and likewise there are baseball fans outside of these countries. In particular, the descendants of Japanese immigrants to the state of São Paulo in Brazil are often baseball fans, but this list gives us a rough estimate. When we add up the populations of these countries and compare that figure with the entire world's population, we see that only one-ninth of the world's population are baseball fans. Which is not very many.

By contrast, cricket is more popular just because of India and its huge population. India alone puts cricket ahead of baseball in terms of world popularity, and when other countries are added in, cricket does reasonably well. (In fact, there are twice as many cricket fans in south Asia alone as there are baseball fans worldwide.) But soccer comes in far ahead of either of them. For every soccer fan in the world, there is less than one other

26

person who is not a soccer fan. That is, there are more soccer fans than people who are not soccer fans. (Again, this is based on countries where soccer is played. In any of those countries, there may well be many people who ignore soccer, or hate all sports, etc.) The situation with respect to basketball is unclear, but as I said earlier, there are many countries (those of the old British Commonwealth) where it is mostly ignored. As for football, it has traveled less far than either baseball or basketball. It is pretty much true, despite some leagues in other countries, that most football fans live here in America.

5. Everyone knows about the pyramids of Egypt. Most also know about the pyramids in Mexico and Central America. Almost no one in America knows about the pyramid in England. (This includes our multiculturalists, who think they know so much more about the rest of the world than other Americans, but who are just as ignorant as everyone else.) Our ignorance is partly due to its not being a physical pyramid but a conceptual one, so it is not a pyramid that one can see the way one sees, for example, Buckingham Palace or the Tower of London. This pyramid consists of all the soccer teams of adult males in the country which are officially registered with England's Football Association (FA). At the top of this pyramid is the top professional league (called the Premiership), consisting of twenty teams. Below this are three lower leagues (called the Championship, League One and League Two), each with twenty-four teams.[2] Below this are some five hundred semipro teams (called nonleague in England), and below this are thousands of amateur teams. (This is a theoretical grouping; in practice it has been found that amateur and semipro players are scattered throughout the "amateur" and "semipro" teams.) It has been estimated that there are over seven thousand teams total in this pyramid, which is a remarkable figure considering that England's population is about one-fifth that of the United States. In addition, there is a system of promotion and relegation of teams, so that the best teams at one level get promoted up a level at the end of a season, while the worst teams at a level get relegated down. Accordingly, there can be considerable flux down through the years regarding the teams in any one league. Moreover, below this pyramid of official teams are some unofficial pub teams, as well as people playing on a casual basis with friends or in pick-up games. Off to the side is another pyramid consisting of teams associated with schools – these are described to some extent by Nick Hornby in *Fever Pitch*[3] – but these teams have little importance for most English soccer fans.

The existence of this pyramid has been described in a humorous way by the British writer Lynne Truss as follows:

> I try not to think too hard about the so-called pyramid of football. The trouble is, it's becoming increasingly clear to me that the broad base of the football pyramid is actually the same size as the ground area of the United Kingdom. This is a scary thought, obviously. Beneath the four visible divisions, organized football just spreads out far, wide and vigorously like volcanic lava, knocking over tall buildings in its path. Call me paranoid, but look out, football is seeping under your front door! One day you will come home from work and find a small pets league has been formed in your living room![4]

Truss talks as though she herself as an adult was only just beginning to understand the concept of this pyramid, for she makes a mistake. She meant to say England rather than the United Kingdom, because Scotland has its own pyramid. Outside of the United Kingdom, the pyramid exists to a lesser degree. A German friend told me that there is a big gap in quality between professional and semiprofessional teams in Germany. In Brazil, based on what the sociologist Janet Lever has written, the situation is more informal, but it includes many amateur teams, especially those that play in Rio on the beach. The equivalent of minor-league teams scout those beaches and swoop in when they spot someone who seems capable of turning pro, while the major-league teams in turn poach from the minor-league teams.[5]

Getting back to England, let me observe that the existence of this pyramid (and the lack of similar pyramids in our sports) has several consequences, all of which add up to this: England has a better sports environment than we do. Here are the consequences.

I. Second-rate players who are not quite good enough to play in the top league (the Premiership) can still play at a lower level and thus make some sort of living.

Let me contrast this with our sports. It is true that baseball has minor leagues, but below them there are no or very few semi-pro teams where a player could get a little money. (It's because at that level everyone opts for softball, and softball is not a professional sport.) Basketball has very little in the way minor leagues, but the National Basketball Association (NBA) has been fostering a league below it called the NBA Development

League, which currently has 16 teams. By comparison, England has 72 minor-league soccer teams, even though it has a much smaller population. If we had the equivalent in minor-league basketball, then since we have five times the population of England, the Development League would have to have 360 teams. A mere 16 teams is nothing, and the result is that many players exercise a different option: playing abroad (generally in Europe). But how humiliating to have to go over to soccerland to have one's career. Football has basically nothing. There have been attempts to create minor leagues, but they have not worked very well. The league in Europe has died, while arena football did not have a 2009 season, so the second-rate football player who can't make the National Football League (NFL) has almost no career possibilities. Likewise, the NFL player who can no longer make the team must give up football instead of ending his career playing (and making some money) in a lesser league.

II. Any adult male who is willing, able, and has the time to play can probably find a way to play.

Again, let me contrast this with our sports. It is in basketball that we find the closest parallel to this aspect of soccer. Many people in America play basketball on a casual basis. There are many pick-up games to play in. What is missing is the large number of amateur teams that form the base of England's pyramid, but at least the amateur can play. With baseball, it is more difficult because people opt for softball rather than baseball. Playing watered-down baseball seems the best that baseball lovers can do in terms of playing their favorite sport. I once met a pathetic young man in a park who wanted to play baseball, not softball. No one else was interested. He said he had once rounded up a bunch of guys to play, but that after that one game no one else bothered. Maybe playing softball rather than baseball is satisfactory, but then again maybe it is not. Obviously, many people here in America think it is satisfactory, but these are people who have grown up with this situation and have warped views on the subject. They have never thought about it and have never imagined that there could be a pyramid of the sort that exists in English soccer. Why play a sport that is somewhat different from the one you watch? If you like the sport you watch, why would you want to play something else? My main point here will be discussed below (IV).

Football is the worst in that it is very difficult for the casual player to go out to a park and play. Because it is so difficult, most people don't bother, and those who do bother will play instead the very-much watered down touch football. Touch football compared to real football is quite pathetic, for it lacks the macho factor that makes football so superior to soccer in the eyes of the soccer hater. In England, the person who watches a professional game can go out afterward and play real soccer. Amateur soccer is real soccer. It's just at a lower level than professional soccer. Pick-up games are sometimes watered down a bit if there are no actual goals available. The players throw down some shirts for the goals and dispense with the goalie. Yet, this is much closer to real soccer than touch football is to real football.

Why is it so difficult for the casual player to go out to a park and play our brand of football? It's because our brand of football is so expensive and inconvenient to play. Let me enumerate the expenses and inconveniences. To begin with, there are uniforms. It is very cheap for a soccer player to buy a uniform, while it is very expensive for a football player to do so, what with all the padding and helmets that are required. I've heard it said that one can outfit an entire soccer team for the money it would take to outfit one football player. Then again, football is a rough, tough sport, so this means there is a greater chance of getting severely injured. Accordingly, one must have very good medical insurance to play this game, compared with soccer. An inconvenience with football is the comparatively large number of officials (seven) needed to referee a game, compared with soccer, which requires only three. (In 1991, a fourth official was added on the sidelines, but that official's duties are quite limited, and he or she may be easily dispensed with in an amateur game.) Moreover, to determine first downs, one needs a chain gang to measure whether a first down has been gained or not, and there are a great many timeouts for the officials to keep track of. And while a soccer team needs only eleven players at game time, plus one or two subs, a football team playing real football would require a huge number of people for the offense, the defense, and the various specialty teams. Of course, one can dispense with all these and make do with eleven plus some subs, but then it starts to feel less like real football. Finally, a football game lasts three hours, compared with the two hours that soccer takes. Adult amateurs at the lowest levels of the game have other things in their lives that compete with sports, such as families and jobs. That one extra hour is simply one more burden for the person trying to play football on a casual basis or at the amateur level (or even the semipro level). Adding up all of these factors leads to the conclusion that while it is easy to play a pick-up or amateur soccer game, it is very hard to play a pick-up or amateur football game. In fact, it's so hard that I've never actually seen anyone do it (other than juveniles). Adults who want to play football have to settle for the wimp sport of touch football.

III. The system of promotion-and-relegation means that, theoretically, a group of friends can start a team and get promoted up the pyramid at the end of every season until they are at the very top.

There is simply nothing like this in our sports. I admit that to move up the pyramid like this would be highly unlikely, simply because the best players get noticed very early and are quickly snatched up by the best teams. Still, that one can start up a team with some friends, have it be part of the official association, and slowly work one's way up the pyramid is enticing. But we don't have it.

IV. Since the game being played at every level of the pyramid is soccer, there can be open-cup tournaments involving both professionals and amateurs.

What is an open-cup tournament? Since these are so novel as far as the American sports fan is concerned, let me explain. (Even soccer fans here in America don't seem to understand what these are.) To begin with, let me note that England's open-cup tournament, called the FA Cup, is a separate competition from the league competition. Americans are quite unused to the idea that there can be several different competitions going on at once. When something other than a league game is played in baseball, for example, it is nothing but an exhibition game. College football has non-conference games, but these aren't part of a separate competition. But in soccer, there are generally several competitions going on at once. Most of the games a team will play will be league games. But some will be for these other competitions. So when Manchester United won the treble in 1999, this meant that they won the league competition and the open-cup competition and the European competition. All three of these competitions were going on at once, though as I said most of the games that were played were league games.

Now the open-cup tournament is a competition that is *open*, theoretically, to every team in the pyramid down to the lowliest amateur team, though in practice it is now limited to those with their own stadiums. It is a single-elimination competition that begins in the fall with the semipro teams battling it out while the professional teams have byes. Once a sufficient number of the semipro teams have been eliminated, the professional teams get involved, until at the end of the season in May, the FA Cup Final is played. Along the way there can be many upsets, with lower-division teams occasionally beating those of the Premiership, and with semipro teams occasionally beating the pros. The charm of this is captured in a book by Geoff Tibballs called *F.A. Cup Giant Killers*, whose back cover observes that "every few years a motley collection of carpenters, plumbers and roofers or a team of lowly-paid professionals, somehow contrive to defeat one of the fat cats of English football." Perhaps the most celebrated game of this sort since I have been following the FA Cup occurred in 1998 when the semipro team Stevenage was matched against a team in the Premiership, Newcastle. (For an equivalent in American sports, imagine a college football team – and by "college" I don't mean a big university team but a team from a small college – playing a team in the NFL.) It's true that Stevenage didn't win, but they held Newcastle to a tie, thus forcing a replay. And though they lost the replay, these games were televised (in several countries, if I remember correctly), thus giving some lowly semipro players a great deal of visibility.

Anyway, let me take the reader through the 2008-2009 season of the FA Cup by focusing on one semipro team and following it (or its winning opponents) through to the final. I'm going to choose a team called Lowestoft Town. Lowestoft Town began by playing a game in the Extra Preliminary Round on August 16 of 2008. It played St. Ives Town and won, so St. Ives Town was eliminated. On August 30, Lowestoft Town played AFC Sudbury in the Preliminary Round, and it won (though it had to play a replay, which then went to penalties before they were declared the winner). Then on September 13 it played Cambridge City in what is called the First Round Qualifying and lost, so Lowestoft Town was eliminated. So, now let's follow Cambridge City. On September 27, the Second Round Qualifying was played, and Cambridge City lost (after a replay) to Worthing, so they were eliminated. On October 11, the Third Round Qualifying was played, and Worthing lost to Bury Town, so Worthing was eliminated. On October 25, the Fourth Round Qualifying was played, and Bury Town beat Basingstoke Town, so Basingstoke Town was eliminated. At this point, there were 32 teams left of all the hundreds of semipro teams that had entered, and they were ready to take on the pros (though only those of the lower two divisions).

We are now at the First Round Proper, played on November 8, and Bury Town lost to Gillingham of League Two (that is, the fourth and lowest professional division), so Bury Town was eliminated. In the Second Round, played on November 29, Gillingham defeated Stockport County, which was in the next highest division, so Stockport County was eliminated. In the Third Round, played in early January of 2009, the teams of the top two professional leagues finally entered into the fray. Gillingham played Aston Villa of the Premiership and lost, so Gillingham was eliminated. In the Fourth Round, played on January 24, Aston Villa defeated Doncaster Rovers, a team in the Championship League (that is, the second division), so Doncaster Rovers was eliminated. The Fifth Round was played on February 14, and it involved teams from only the top two divisions. All the minnows, including two semipro teams that had made it to the Fourth Round, had been eliminated. Aston Villa lost to Everton, another Premiership team, so they were eliminated. In the Sixth Round, played on March 8, Everton defeated Middlesbrough, another team from the Premiership, so Middlesbrough was eliminated.

We are now at the Semi-Finals, played on April 19, and Everton faced Manchester United and won, though it came down to penalty kicks. Since Manchester United won the league for the season, they could be considered England's best team, so it was quite an achievement for Everton (with its American goalie Tim Howard) to eliminate them from the FA Cup. And so we come to the FA Cup Final, played on May 30 between Chelsea and Everton. Chelsea won this match, so they won the FA Cup for the season.

This was the 128th time that the FA Cup has been played, and over 700 teams entered the competition. There is nothing like it in our sports, except a similar competition with our soccer teams and the golf and tennis opens (which are open to amateurs, hence the name).

Now let me return to my discussion of the pyramid in order to once again contrast the situation in England with that here in the United States. Baseball is the closest of our sports to having a pyramid. At the top are the major leagues, and below them are the minor leagues. But below them there are very few semipro and amateur baseball teams (not counting the colleges), because everyone would rather play softball. Because everyone at the lower levels of the game opt for softball, and because softball is a little different from baseball, there can be no open-cup tournaments.

Basketball is next in terms of having a pyramid like England's. At the top is the NBA, and below that is their development league, which consists (so far) of a minuscule number of teams. Below that are perhaps some semi-pro teams, but most people simply play in pick-up games. There is nothing to prevent an open-cup tournament, except that it hasn't occurred to people, and since the average American sports fan is prejudiced against soccer and so refuses to see what other countries are doing, it is not likely that an open-cup competition will happen soon. Moreover, basketball is dominated by the colleges, which sop up a lot of demand that fans have for the sport, which in turn means that the minor league has a huge fight on its hands getting people to switch over to the sort of pyramid structure that England has.

Finally, football is the worst of our three sports in terms of having a pyramid. At the top, there is the NFL, but below that there is little or nothing. There are virtually no minor-league teams, though every now and then a league emerges; however, the latest league, arena football, has recently struggled, while another option, the European league, has died. But as I said, there are virtually no minor leagues, there are a few invisible semipro teams, and there are no amateur teams. There aren't even people playing in pick-up games. (I'm talking about full-fledged tackle football, not touch football.) Football is an expensive sport, and the expense for young men is generally born by colleges and universities, but they have a limit of four years during which a player is eligible, after which he is either signed by an NFL team or he is out of football permanently. So again, as with basketball, the colleges play the role of the minor-league teams, but they play them badly, with their limited years of eligibility together with the lack of pay. It is true that there are a few semipro teams around, but they are invisible. By contrast, semipro soccer teams in England can participate in the FA Cup, and thus have a high degree of visibility. They can wind up playing some of the lower-division professional teams, and on rare occasions even the top professional teams. But there is none of this in America.

Thus, we see that the pyramid of England is not replicated here in this country. Someone suggested to me that we do have a pyramid in football: there is the NFL at the top, the college teams below them, and the high-school teams below them. But there are big problems with this comparison, because the four points mentioned above simply do not apply to this pyramid: second-raters in football don't get paid, people can't play on a casual basis, starting your own team would be hard, and there are no open-cup tournaments. The pyramid of football teams in America leaves a lot to be desired.

Now I have talked about England's pyramid of teams and its FA Cup competition in order to ask one question: Which sports environment is richer in terms of opportunities for players and fans? It is England's rather than America's. To see this, contrast the lives of the football-loving American jock with that of the soccer-loving English jock. Here in America, lots of guys play football when they are boys, but most do not play football in high school. (I, the worst in my neighborhood, played on the sophomore team, but didn't get very far.) Since there are no other teams, they no longer play football. A sport that they grew up on, a sport that they consider their favorite, is now a sport they cannot play anymore, even though they haven't even reached their prime yet. Nevertheless, they are out. They are forced to quit. Their playing days are over. What about those who do make the high school team? Sadly, most of those who play in high school don't play in college. Since there are no other teams, now their playing days are over, too. And what about those who play in college? But again, most of those who play in college don't make it to the next step, the NFL. And since there are no other teams to play on, they are forced to leave the game. Despite the fact that they could be considered a few years into their career, they are forced to retire. Their playing days are over.

The sad truth about American football is that by the time a young man is twenty-two years old, he is either playing in the NFL, which is extremely unlikely, or he is not playing at all, not even in pick-up games. (The young man who is hurt most by this, in financial terms, is the second-rate athlete, the man who isn't quite good enough for the NFL. Because there are no minor leagues, he has no place to earn the modest salaries that his equivalents in soccer and baseball can earn.) And so he turns to other activities, such as golf or tennis or other team sports like softball or basketball, or the wimp sport touch football, or he simply becomes a couch potato, watching the game rather than playing it. This whole phenomenon might be called the tragedy of the American jock, because he has no chance to play his favorite sport, even though he's young and capable of playing. If he is lucky, he might find a semipro team he could join, but they are few and far between, and in any case, they are invisible. (There is no FA Cup competition, of course, to give him a chance to shine against the pros.) If he had any sense, he would play rugby, and he would find that playing rugby is better than playing football, for the simple reason that it is much cheaper, which allows most people to continue playing into adulthood. He might then urge everyone else to abandon football for rugby, but until everyone else sees how limited the opportunities in football are, this isn't very likely to happen.

Now consider the soccer-loving English jock. Like his American counterpart, he grows up playing soccer, but as he grows up, he sees no need to stop playing. He might play on a school team, but there are many other teams to play on as well. As I have been saying, for the adult male there is a huge pyramid of teams to choose from. If he isn't good enough to play in the Premiership, there are three lower divisions in which he can play as a professional. And if he isn't good enough for them, there are some five hundred semipro teams for him to play on, and if he isn't good enough for them, there are thousands of amateur teams for him to play on. And if he still isn't accepted by any of them, there are pub teams or playing with friends or playing in pick-up games. No adult male who wants to play, is able to play, and has the time to play is excluded.

To put all of this simply, football ends up being nothing but a spectator sport, while soccer is both a spectator and a participation sport. And what that means in terms of lifestyles is that the football-loving American jock has to give up playing his favorite sport while young, while the soccer-loving English jock can keep playing his favorite sport endlessly, so long as time and well-being permit.

But there is more. The best that the football-loving American jock can hope for, if he actually makes it to the NFL, is to be the best player or the most valuable player in the league. But the soccer-loving English jock can hope for more than that. Because soccer is an international sport, there is international competition, which means that the best soccer players in England will play for their country. Obviously, playing for one's country is a much bigger deal than merely being the most valuable player in a league. The idea of playing for one's country is so ingrained in the English psyche, it is so much a part of English life that when J.K. Rowling wrote the first Harry Potter book, she mentioned one person who was so good at her made-up sport of quidditch that "he could have played for England."[6] The best English soccer players play for England. They could play for England in the Olympics, but even more important, they play for England in the World Cup. By contrast, sadly, American football players never play for America because there is too little interest elsewhere to have any international competition.

And while the idea of playing for one's country is limited to the very talented few, the soccer-loving English jock who is nowhere near that level of play can still root for his country as a fan when it plays in international tournaments. I myself have attended games of the U.S. national soccer team (both the men's and the women's teams), and they are quite special. They are particularly special when played in Columbus Crew stadium, because in that venue most of the fans will be American, unlike places like Los Angeles, where the vast majority of fans are likely to be rooting for the opposing team. The games at Crew stadium draw people from many parts of the country. People paint U.S. flags on their faces, wear special colored t-shirts, and so on. The fan group called Sam's Army has been particularly dedicated to attending the games (wherever they may be) to cheer for the U.S. Sadly, football fans in America never get to enjoy this pleasure because football just isn't an international sport. There's too little interest in it elsewhere to allow for any international competition, and so rooting for one's country just never happens for the fan of American football. Despite this, those who love football and hate soccer think that soccer is a stupid sport and that football should continue to prevail.

So, what does the American jock have that English jock doesn't have? Well, there is the enjoyment of following college football or basketball. But this entails something that most Americans don't want to think about, namely that those athletes aren't getting paid, even though they should be. They are playing on what are essentially minor-league teams, but they don't get paid. They are being exploited. They get a college education, it is true, but shouldn't the decision of whether or not to go to college be a decision they make themselves? Lots of young men these days are choosing not to go to college, so why should those who want to become athletes be any different?

It is also true that the American jock can follow the playoffs in our various leagues, while the English Premiership simply awards the trophy to whichever team is at the top of the table at the end of the season. But this assumes that a playoff system is something valuable to tack onto the regular season. Is it? It would take me too far astray to get into this, so let me merely note that the lack of playoffs in English soccer is more than compensated for by having the FA Cup, as well as the European championship (the Champions League) to follow. In fact, the English second division now has a playoff system for deciding which teams get promoted to the Premiership, so it is conceivable that the Premiership could adopt something similar, if they thought it necessary.

Finally, the American jock has lots of statistics to ponder, while the English jock has few, since soccer doesn't generate statistics to the extent that our sports do. But lots of statistics are generated in cricket, so the stats-mad English jock can always follow cricket. But more important is that, given a choice between being a fan of a sport with lots of statistics which is only a spectator sport, and being a fan of a sport with few statistics which is also a participation sport, I'd take the latter. I'd rather be out there playing than poring over stats. I'm 58 years old, but I still occasionally play in a soccer game. How many fans of American football can make this claim?

To put all this in other words, the American soccer hater has a simple-minded view of the matter: According to them, soccer is boring, and that's all there is to it. But things aren't so simple-minded, and there is more to consider than the soccer hater thinks. A sport isn't just a sport. It's an environment. It's a lifestyle. A sport encourages a certain environment to grow up around it, and that environment encourages some lifestyles and discourages others. And there is a big difference between the impoverished lifestyle of the American jock and the rich lifestyle of the English jock. In fact, one could put it even more starkly. Even jocks in the Third World can enjoy the pleasure of playing on a team, while your average football-loving American jock can't.

And this entails a rethinking of the idea promoted by most soccer haters, that soccer will never make it here. Let me remind such people of the 1919 song "How Ya Gonna Keep 'Em Down on the Farm After They've Seen Paree?" This song came out after World War I and referred to the way that many farm boys who had hardly traveled outside of their state, much less to a foreign country, saw what life was like in other parts of the world. It was an eye-opener for them. Likewise, I saw "Paree," so to speak, and it was an eye-opener. For me "Paree" wasn't a city, but was instead the structure of soccer in England and the opportunities that it offered that we are missing here in the United States. (The "farm" was living here in the United States and being immersed in our sports.) Understanding what we are missing was the eye-opener for me. World Cups, playing for one's country, a large pyramid of teams, open-cup tournaments, a sport that is both a spectator sport and a participation sport – all of this and more is what I saw. Eventually, as young people begin to understand what I saw, that understanding will spread throughout our culture until even the dimmest of college football and basketball players understands that there is something wrong with the way that sports are structured here in America. These players now understand that if they aren't quite good enough for the NFL or the NBA, there will be few or no opportunities for them to play at a minor-league level. Since everyone accepts this, no one protests against it, and no one makes comparisons with other cultures where this isn't true. But as knowledge of what is happening elsewhere seeps through our culture, eventually these athletes will start to wonder why, since college teams are essentially minor-league teams, they aren't getting paid. Others with much less ability may decide that playing in casual games is too important for them to give up and will switch to soccer, or possibly rugby, so as not to lose such experiences.

Soccer, the Left, & the Farce of Multiculturalism

But we should also ask, Why did we end up in this situation? We ended up in this situation for reasons that I will explain more fully in Chapters 7 and 8 (namely, that we have been convinced of our own superiority and have been too culturally isolated and insular to see what was happening elsewhere), but one factor has been our insistence that we have college sports. We are so insistent upon this that we go beyond what others think of as reasonable. We make ridiculous problems for ourselves in the way we handle sports here, problems that no one else has. We insist that athletes in our schools be amateurs, and then go into paroxysms of rage when we find that – gasp! – one of those athletes may have received some money. No one in the rest of the world would care. They simply wouldn't see what the problem was. We also get upset when we learn that some high school student has decided to jump directly to the pros. We don't think they should be doing this. We think they should be in college taking classes. Since as far as their athletic development is concerned taking classes is a hindrance, no one else would care.

What I am saying applies particularly to football and basketball, though much less so to baseball, ice hockey and soccer. Each of those other sports has recognized avenues of advancing that do not include going to college. But with football and basketball, pretty much the only way to advance is by going to college. Accordingly, colleges serve as the minor leagues for those two sports, but since they aren't really minor leagues, ridiculous problems are the result. Recently, some college basketball coaches prevailed upon some National Collegiate Athletic Association (NCAA) officials to take a fact-finding tour to Europe to see what the structure of sports is over there.[7] The coaches complained that if they recruited players from Europe, they couldn't possibly follow the NCAA rules on recruiting because there were no good amateurs. Instead of basketball teams being attached to the high school, as we have here, teams were sponsored by private clubs, and often young players got paid. Under such a system amateurs would be like players in this country who hadn't made their high school team, and so would not be worth recruiting, while the players who were worth recruiting were all getting paid.

Accordingly, things are different elsewhere, but here in America we are stuck with this system where there are essentially no minor leagues in football and basketball, except the colleges. And right here we see the tragedy that I mentioned earlier but which is almost never pointed out. The tragedy is that, whereas a player can play minor league baseball (or ice hockey or soccer) indefinitely, the rules for college sports specify *four years*

39

only. The result is that many a football or basketball player who could be employed at the minor-league level has no chance of doing this because the only minor leagues available are the colleges. And once you graduate, you're out for good. In football, it's either the NFL or nothing. In basketball, it's either the NBA, the so-far puny development league, or nothing.

The most tragic case I know of is that of one Todd Shackleford, who grew up in Manchester, England. It seems that while his father was English, his mother was American, and she must have told him about sports here in the U.S. So, instead of being sensible and dreaming of playing soccer for Manchester United or Manchester City or of playing for some rugby team, Shackleford fell in love with our brand of football. After a stint in the Marines, he ended up playing football at Augsburg College in Minneapolis. The trouble was that after just one game, a close look at his record showed that he had already used up his four years of eligibility at some other school, and so he was forced off the team.[8] Apparently, no one had ever told him about this ridiculous rule, which is quite unknown elsewhere in the world. That tragedy could have been prevented if he had just been a normal English kid and had stuck with English sports.

I like to compare the American sports' environment to Chinese foot-binding. Foot-binding was something that the Chinese liked but that no one else could make any sense of, which is also true of our sports. *Why would anyone in their right mind set things up this way?* Once one realizes how stupid it is, why would anyone want to keep it going? Yet, people do want to keep it going. (Even when I point out to other Americans how stupid it is, they still want to keep it going.) However, I say it is like foot-binding. It's like shooting oneself in the foot. Why deliberately cheat your second-rate athletes out of a chance to earn a living?

6. Football will never be the world's most popular sport, at least not in the way that soccer is the most popular sport. Soccer is not just popular in terms of people following the pros, but also in terms of people playing it at the amateur level. And football is just too expensive for this to happen. We can't even afford amateur football here in America; how, then, could the Third World afford it? Ask yourself what comes to mind when you hear the term "amateur football player?" In fact, nothing comes to mind. One's reaction, after a bit of thought, will be to think instead of "college football player," for college football players are amateurs. But beyond the college teams, how many amateur football teams are there in America? The answer is that there are almost none. There's the occasional semipro team that one can find in rural areas, but that is about it. And they are practically

Soccer, the Left, & the Farce of Multiculturalism

invisible (unlike semipro soccer teams in England, which are given a decent amount of media coverage during their league games and huge amounts if they advance in the FA Cup). The fact is that there are basically only two kinds of football team in America, school teams and the top professional teams. No one else can afford to run a football team, because football is so expensive. And if we rich Americans can't afford adult amateur teams, you can bet that Africa cannot, either.

This brings up another point: Third-World soccer and its money problems. Lots of ignorant Americans imagine that soccer's worst problem is fan violence, but I am convinced it is money. Despite soccer's being a cheap sport, there are money problems, even in Europe. As for Africa, the money problems there become huge. So it is doubtful if football will ever sweep the world like soccer has. It would be a tragedy if it were to happen because the game would offer many fewer opportunities than soccer does.

7. In hardly any other countries of the world is an athlete's being above average in size so prized as it is here in America. Of our three favorite sports, two of them demand that the participants be either big (football) or tall (basketball). People of average size, to say nothing of the short and the small, are excluded. In most other countries the most important sport is soccer, which favors people of average size. In some of these other countries (such as Brazil), basketball is a distant second to soccer. And in others (such as England), there are three sports of which two (cricket and soccer) are for people of average size and of which only one (rugby) demands that people be above average in size.

Why do Americans have such an obsession with size in sports? And why is it that no American even notices this? To find other countries like ours, one must look at New Zealand (where rugby is supposed to be the only important sport), Australia (where rugby and Australian rules football are important), and maybe Canada (which has Canadian football and some rugby). Out of nearly 200 countries in the world, then, less than five have this idea that size matters a lot in sports. Most other countries have heaped praise on their athletes who happen to be average-sized or smaller or shorter than average. I will say more about this in a later chapter, but for now, it is simply something for the reader to keep in mind.

8. While Americans like to think of soccer as a descent into the irrational by foreigners, exactly the opposite is true. The reason for this is, first, that soccer is about kicking, which is a very natural action. Even American sports have not entirely banished kicking, for football uses it.

More important is that soccer is what I call a goal sport, and goal sports are more important (based on their prevalence) than other kinds of sports. By a goal sport, I mean the following. Take a rectangular playing area, and place some kind of goal at each of the narrow ends. Take two teams and place them on the field so that each team is defending one of the goals. The object of the game is to score more goals than the other team.

There are many goal sports, and while soccer is the most popular among them, it is just one in a big crowd. Some of the others are ice hockey, field hockey, basketball, netball, lacrosse, shinty, hurling, Gaelic football, bandy, team handball, polo, pato, water polo, and Australian rules football. (This last sport is unique in having a round playing area.) Most of these have players designated as goalies, but not all do. Basketball, Australian rules football, and polo do not. Generally, the game is played with a ball, but ice hockey has a puck. Generally, the ball or whatever object is used is driven into the goal by the unaided human body, but ice hockey and several other of these sports use sticks of some sort. Generally, there is some sort of offside rule to prevent a forward from simply stationing himself or herself down at the other team's goal, but this isn't true in basketball. Generally, the goal is on the goal line, but ice hockey is one of several goal sports in which the goal is not quite on the line. Some goal sports are low scoring, like soccer and ice hockey, and some are high scoring, like basketball.

The particular rules in a goal sport may vary. The method or methods of advancing the ball may vary – whether by kicking or bouncing or pushing it with a stick. But essentially these sports are the same. To see this, begin with soccer and allow the players to use their hands to advance the ball, mandating however that they must bounce it. Eliminate the goalie and replace soccer's goal with a basket up high. Lo and behold, we have basketball. Begin with soccer again, but replace the ball with a puck, put the game on ice, give all the players sticks, reduce the size of the goal and bring it out a few feet from the end line, and voila, we now have ice hockey. All goal sports are essentially the same, except in terms of slight variations in particular rules, the method of advancing the ball, the type of ball (or puck, as in ice hockey), and the type of arena. The most significant difference among them is between those with goalies and those without, so that Australian rules football doesn't look much like soccer and looks more like rugby or even American football, until they take a shot at goal, when it looks more soccer-like.

Another type of sport is the goal-line sport. Goal-line sports are also played on a rectangular field, with the two shorter sides designated as goal lines. In a goal-line sport the object of the game is to cross the goal-line with the ball (or whatever is being used). Whereas there are many sorts of goal sports, there are only a few goal-line sports: American football, the two versions of rugby (union and league), Canadian football, and the game of Afghan polo (buzkashi) described in James Michener's book *Caravans*.⁹ Notice that, of the goal-line sports just mentioned, all of them except Afghan polo have some element of goal sports in them. Take American football, for example. In our brand of football, although the primary way of scoring is by going into the end zone with the ball, one can also score by kicking a field goal or an extra point. The goal in this instance consists of the goal posts. As in basketball, there is no goalie. Both versions of rugby share this feature of being able to score a goal, just as in a goal sport.

Finally, there are sports like cricket and baseball, in which someone throws a ball at a player holding a stick. In baseball, someone called the pitcher throws the ball to someone called the batter, who holds a bat. Behind the batter is the catcher, who is there to catch the ball if the ball goes by the batter. In cricket, someone called the bowler throws the ball to someone called the batsman, who also holds a bat (though a differently-shaped bat). Behind the batsman is the wicketkeeper, who is there to catch the ball if it goes by the batsman. The object of the game is for the person holding the bat to strike the ball in such a way that the ball is difficult for the other team's players to retrieve. In baseball, the player who hits safely will run to first base, and if possible, further so as to end up back at the batting area, home plate. In cricket, the player who hits safely will run from the batting area he is in to the other batting area, and if possible, back again, and he will try to do this as many times as he can.

Call these bat-and-ball sports. In their fundamental idea, cricket and baseball are quite unlike other sports (except for derivatives of them, such as softball and kickball, or rounders, from which baseball was derived). They are not played on a rectangular field, they do not have a goal or a goal line, they do not have goalies, they do not have an offside rule, and so on. They are somewhat similar to each other in that there is pitching (or bowling) in both of them, there is a batter in both of them, and there are bases (or safe areas) in both of them. But there are a sufficient number of differences so that they end up being quite different. Cricket has two "bases" while baseball has four. In cricket, a batter has an entire circle in which to bat safely, while in baseball, the batter has only a quarter of a circle; batting it outside of that quarter circle is a foul ball. Cricket has two innings, while baseball has nine. And so on.

I have provided a classification for team sports that divides them into three types: goal sports, goal-line sports, and bat-and-ball sports. Most team sports fall into one of these three categories, though the goal-line sports have an element of goal sports in them. There are exceptions, of course. Volleyball isn't like these other team sports because it has a net running down the middle of the playing area. Thus, it is much closer to sports like tennis and badminton. Doubles in tennis is also a team sport that is not one of these three types. Nor is rowing nor a relay race. Nevertheless, the sports that are covered by the media throughout the world the most, the ones that get coverage in the media day in and day out, fall into one of these three categories. Sports like rowing are seldom in the news, except during the Olympics and other special occasions. Volleyball hasn't become as big as these other sports, either. Accordingly, the most popular team sports in the world can all be classified as goal sports, goal-line sports, or bat-and-ball sports.

Now classification is an odd, messy sort of business. I think it is natural to classify soccer and ice hockey together, yet some people feel that soccer is closer to football (and if they are American, they then go on to disparage soccer because in their minds it's not as good as football). The fact that soccer gets compared unfavorably with football as a wimp sport suggests that this classification is often made. It seems to me that the reason that soccer and football are often compared, though, is perhaps the belief that football developed out of soccer (though in fact it developed out of rugby and not soccer). Or perhaps it is because both are played outdoors on rectangular fields. But neither of these points seems essential to me. They are quite different sports. I admit that one can classify sports in all sorts of ways. One can classify ice hockey and football together as two sports in which the players wear lots of padding. Football and rugby can be classified together because of their use of oval-shaped balls. Both soccer and basketball use bigger balls, while baseball, cricket and field hockey use smaller balls. Both baseball and ice hockey use sticks, while soccer, rugby, football, and basketball don't.

But in spite of all these other ways of classifying, I believe that my way is best. The fact that ice hockey and baseball players both use sticks doesn't mean much. In no way can ice hockey be seen as baseball on ice. But ice hockey *can* be seen as soccer on ice, for both have goalies, both have wingers, forwards, and defenders, both have centering passes (which are generally called "crosses" in soccer), both have offside, and both have penalty shots (rare though they may be in ice hockey). By contrast, baseball doesn't have any of these things. It does have pitchers and batters, infielders and outfielders, balls and strikes, home runs, double plays, and stolen bases; and hockey has nothing like these. Hitting it out of the park in baseball has a completely different meaning from hitting it out of the rink in hockey. Hitting it out of the park in baseball corresponds closely to hitting it beyond the boundary in cricket; in both cases, it is something spectacular. In ice hockey, however, hitting it out of the rink means that the other team gets an advantage of position in terms of where the ensuing faceoff will be taken, which is definitely not something spectacular.

Now let me repeat the point I made earlier, in greater detail. Goal sports are the most common type of team sport. There are endless variations on goal sports, only a few variations on goal-line sports, and hardly any on bat-and-ball sports. The idea of the bat-and-ball sport just isn't a very fruitful one. Of course, many variations are *possible* with bat-and-ball sports, but few seem worth the effort of trying. One *could* play some kind of bat-and-ball game on the ice, for example, but few have ever thought it worthwhile to do so. By contrast, at least two goal sports have been invented for ice, ice hockey and bandy.

Not only are goal sports the most common type of team sport (in terms of numbers of such sports), but they are also the sort of sport that is the most popular in the most countries. Most other countries play at least one goal sport, generally soccer and occasionally basketball as well. (And in countries with cold climates, there is ice hockey.) Here in the United States, of our three main sports basketball is a goal sport. Even in India and Pakistan, where cricket is so important, there is field hockey. By contrast, many countries do not have either goal-line sports or bat-and-ball sports. Germany, for example, which is a great sporting nation, pays no attention to any of the goal-line sports or the bat-and-ball sports. France plays rugby, but neither cricket nor baseball.

Goal sports seem to be quite satisfying to the human race. Why? I can't be sure, but one reason may be the obvious symmetry of the field of play. More important is the idea of territory. Each side has a territory that it wants to defend, a concept which is present in goal-line sports, also. In both sorts of sports, each team gets half the field, and it is the players' duty to protect their territory from incursions by the other team. With goal-line sports, the idea is to protect any deep incursion into one's territory – that is, points are scored by crossing the goal line anywhere along its length – but for goal sports the focus is on a particular location deep in one's territory. The goal can be thought of as the most precious part of the realm: the palace for the king or queen, the house of the president, the headquarters for the supreme commander, or something similar.

This concept of territory is completely lacking in baseball and cricket. One team occupies the whole field at a time. There simply is nothing to defend. Perhaps it is for this reason that baseball in the United States, although for a long time the most popular of our sports, was never much of a school sport the way that football and basketball have been. Football and basketball, each of them with territory to protect, seemed more suitable for the adolescent and young adult passions of protecting symbolic territory. Likewise, soccer generates riots and hooliganism, but cricket (aside perhaps from games between India and Pakistan) generates nothing along these lines.

Goal sports, then, are a natural part of human play. As already mentioned, even most goal-line sports are to a small extent goal sports. So, even if soccer were nonexistent, there would be more goal sports than other types of team sports. And that suggests, to paraphrase Voltaire, that if soccer didn't already exist, it would be necessary for us to invent it. Kicking a ball is a very natural thing to do, and as I've said, it hasn't been totally eliminated from American sports, for it is used in football. That makes it likely that sooner or later someone would invent a goal sport in which the main thing was kicking the ball. Moreover, as already indicated, soccer is an inexpensive sport, and given the poverty that exists in much of the world, the only sport that is likely to have worldwide popularity is a cheap one. Being cheap also allows for plenty of amateur participation. Finally, soccer is geared towards people of average size. Unlike football and basketball, it is not for the oversized.

The challenge for the soccer haters of America, then, is to invent a goal sport that involves kicking a ball that has all of the advantages that soccer has and is also more appealing than soccer is. Many of them have offered various suggestions for soccer to have more scoring (larger goals or the elimination of the goalie), but those making these suggestions have not exhibited any actual inclination to support soccer under these new rules, so I don't count these as serious attempts to outdo soccer. Moreover, even if these monstrosities were appealing to them, would they appeal to anyone else? Given that so many are satisfied with soccer, these people would have to do a lot to get the rest of the world to switch to what they thought was better. Recently, some Americans have begun a kickball craze.

Would kickball work better than soccer as the world's sport? No. Kickball isn't even a goal sport, but is instead a variation of baseball. Moreover, it is basically a casual participation sport, but it is not ever likely to become a spectator or professional sport. The reason why is the same as for softball: there is no pitcher-batter duel that those who love baseball find so precious. Back in the 1970s, some people tried to make softball a professional sport, but it didn't work, and if softball won't work as a professional sport, neither will kickball. And if kickball cannot become a professional sport here, it is unlikely that it will become one elsewhere.

So, I am offering a challenge to our soccer haters: Invent a sport (preferably a goal sport that has kicking in it) that has soccer's advantages without what you see as its disadvantages.

9. Which is the premier international sporting event, the Olympics or the World Cup? This is like comparing apples with oranges, since the Olympics are basically a competition in individual sports, while the World Cup is a competition in a team sport.

Nevertheless, let me make some observations. The standard opinion back when I was a child was that the Olympics were the premier international sporting event. But back then none of us knew about soccer's World Cup. Like it or not, many outside of America think of the World Cup as the premier international sporting event. In fact, for most people outside of the U.S., there is so much international activity going on that the Olympics can get lost in it. My wife and I spent January and February of 1992 in England, and during that time each of England's three major sports had some international event. In soccer, there was a "friendly" (that is, an exhibition game) between England and France. In cricket, there was a seemingly unending international tournament in Australia. And in rugby, there was the Five-Nations tournament (involving England, Scotland, Wales, Ireland, and France). In my entire life there was never a time when so much international activity was packed into two months for our sports (because there just is no international competition in football and very little that we paid attention to in baseball and basketball). During those two months, there were also the winter Olympics, and while the British paid attention to them, they also paid attention to these other events.

Also, keep in mind that the World Cup is about a team sport that most people like, and team sports are the sports that throughout the world are the ones that get the lion's share of attention in our media, day in and day out. By contrast, the Olympics are mostly about individual sports, and these are mostly ignored, except when it is Olympics time.

In addition, soccer draws big crowds at the Olympics. Until the 1984 Olympics, I knew that soccer was the second-best draw behind the track-and-field events, but oddly enough, during a year when it was held here in America, soccer was the biggest draw. And this popularity is despite the fact that Olympic soccer is not very important in the soccer world. Olympic soccer has to be considered a competition for the "junior varsity" when compared with World Cup soccer, which would be like the "varsity." What all this seems to mean is that soccer doesn't need the Olympics, but the Olympics (because of the crowds it draws) need soccer.

Because of the emphasis on individual sports in the Olympics, many great athletes never participate in the them. In soccer, Pelé is one example of a great athlete who never participated in the Olympics. Our own sports of baseball and football are replete with great athletes who were never in the Olympics, simply because their sports were not Olympic sports. For a short time, however, baseball was in the Olympics, from 1992 until 2008. In 1992 when I was in England, I asked a sports journalist there the following question: since baseball's fans had managed to get baseball into the Olympics, would cricket's fans be trying to do the same thing? The answer: "Why bother?" Indeed, why bother when cricket has so much international competition already. What are the Olympics going to add? Almost nothing.[10]

Now let me turn to the concept of winning the Olympics. Given that the Olympics are about individual sports, people look at which country has racked up the most medals and declare them the winner. Yet, this doesn't really reflect the way people think about sports overall. Winning should reflect respect, and simply piling up the medals does that only up to a point. Team sports are more important to most people than individual sports, yet the Olympics favor the individual sports over team sports. A single person can amass a large number of medals in swimming or gymnastics, and while they will be respected for this, they will be respected only at Olympics time. During other times they will be mostly forgotten. Meanwhile, a great soccer player, or a great basketball player, is merely part of a team that might win one medal. There is something lopsided about this system, because a country that wins a lot of medals in very obscure sports can look like the winner, even though they haven't garnered much actual respect from the rest of the world. To rectify this, a system of giving the medals different weights could be applied (though no doubt how to do this would lead to many arguments).

Another aspect of the situation is that doing very well at some sports but miserably at others ought to be taken into account. Surely, a country that does very well at some sports and tolerably well at the others should garner more respect than a country that does very well at some sports and *miserably* at others; yet the medals count doesn't reflect this. We Americans win lots of medals in sports like swimming, but we have been very poor at other sports like soccer, team handball, and so on. To my mind the country that, during the time it existed, garnered the most actual respect in the Olympics was the old Soviet Union. Like us, they racked up a lot of medals, but unlike us, they also did tolerably well at all the Olympics sports. No one could sneer at them, saying, "Sure, they got a lot of gymnastics medals, but how good were they at field hockey?" This couldn't be said because they did moderately well in field hockey.

So, do I advocate making these changes in the scoring of the Olympics? No. I am suggesting them merely to get Americans to think carefully about what's going on and not to mindlessly imagine that this is the only way to think about these things. As I said above, the Olympics are basically about individual sports, so the current system works fine. The Olympics give the individuals who are swimmers, gymnasts, and so on their turn in the limelight. In fact, it's not clear to me why team sports are in it at all. Certainly soccer has never figured out what the Olympic soccer competition is supposed to be about. When only amateurs were allowed, the amateurs of the communist countries won most of the medals, but since these people weren't what the rest of us would call amateurs, the competition meant nothing. Beginning in 1978, the international soccer organization, the Fédération Internationale des Football Association (FIFA), flexed its muscles and demanded a change, saying that no one who had played on a World Cup team could play on an Olympics team. This led to various changes, including permission for professionals to play. The tournament is now run as an Under-23 tournament, so it competes for attention with all the other "under" tournaments (Under-21, Under-19, and so on). Since most of the communist countries have disappeared, perhaps the amateur tournament could be brought back.

Now as I said, determining which tournament is the premier tournament, the Olympics or the World Cup, is like comparing apples with oranges. One is mostly concerned with individual sports, while the other is concerned with nothing but a team sport, so comparing them is awkward. Certainly, the Olympics are the premier tournament for individual sports. Likewise, the World Cup is the premier tournament for team sports, beating out all the other soccer tournaments as well as worldwide tournaments in other team sports. My main purpose here is to get Americans to realize that the Olympics aren't the only game in town. There is a World Cup for soccer, and it draws enormous amounts of attention, whether the American sports fan likes it or not.

10. We didn't question everything back in the 1960s. (By "we" I mean American liberals and leftists.) We just never questioned our hatred of foreign sports. We never questioned the idea that we ought to have school sports (for we assumed that everyone in the world had school sports), and we never questioned the fact that those sports should be reserved for big and tall people (with others excluded). We simply didn't ask these questions, and those who insist upon the importance of questioning everything still don't want to ask these questions. I will be talking more about this later.

11. What is the dumbest thing said by America's soccer haters? It is, "Why do they call it football?" Why call a game played primarily with one's feet football? Just to ask it in this way is to see how dumb it is. Yet, I've heard even intelligent people utter this nonsense. And it doesn't make the question any less dumb when one learns that the original meaning of "football" was intended as a contrast with games played on horseback. Under that definition, soccer still deserves the name football, for obviously soccer players aren't on horseback.

12. We Americans live behind what is in effect an Iron Curtain of Sports. We talk about the "world" of sports, but we do not really mean it. Our media seldom reports on what is happening in sports elsewhere in the world, so most Americans know nothing of the facts I have been enumerating. Nor do our schools do much to rectify what our media omits. We are told by college administrators that our students ought to know about other cultures, but where exactly in our curricula do students learn anything about sports in foreign countries? Where do they learn about soccer? Where do they learn about cricket? Nowhere. We are behind the Iron Curtain of Sports.

Endnotes

1. My sources for population figures are *The World Almanac and Book of Facts: 2010*, pp. 735-6; *The New York Times 2010 Almanac*, pp. 487-9; and Wikipedia. There were slight differences in the figures given, but

not enough to affect the basic fact that these countries represent about 1/9 of the world's population.
2. These leagues used to be called simply the First Division, Second Division, Third Division, and Fourth Division.
3. Nick Hornby, *Fever Pitch* (Penguin, 1992), p. 244.
4. *Times* of London, May 16, 1997, via the Internet.
5. Janet Lever, "Soccer in Brazil," reprinted in John T. Talamini and Charles H. Page, *Sport and Society: An Anthology* (Boston, 1973), pp. 147-149.
6. J.K. Rowling, *Harry Potter and the Sorcerer's Stone* (Scholastic Inc., 1997), p. 170.
7. *Chronicle of Higher Education*, November 16, 2001, p. A44.
8. Minneapolis *Star-Tribune*, Sept. 15, 1992, 3c; and Sept. 22, 1992, 3c.
9. James Michener, *Caravans* (Random House, 1963), pp. 296-99.
10. Just a couple days before sending this book to the publisher, I learned that some people are in fact bothering to try to get cricket in the Olympics. I suspect that this won't do much for the sport.

Chapter 4
A Useful Analogy

The points I have been making can be more usefully communicated by means of an analogy. Let us suppose that a century ago one of the states here in America went its own way on sports. We can either imagine that they took our sports and made a number of rule changes which no one else accepted, or we can imagine that they simply invented their own sports. Either way, let us suppose that from that day down to our own day the residents of that state have ignored our sports, while we ignore theirs. We can suppose that their sports have much more scoring than ours do, and that our sports are criticized by them for that reason. We can suppose that in their schools they learn almost nothing about our sports and that as a result of that and of the orientation of their whole culture, which is hostile to our sports, they have many misconceptions about the character of our sports.

Let us also suppose that a college Olympics were to be set up, involving all colleges and universities in the entire country and including all the sports that a sufficient number of colleges compete in. It is likely that in this college Olympics the football and basketball competitions would be huge, but it is also likely that the residents of the oddball state wouldn't pay any attention. And since their sports weren't popular outside of their own state, the Olympic officials would deem that they didn't belong in the college Olympics. Accordingly, the citizens of this state unconsciously viewed the college Olympics as basically a track-and-field and swimming and gymnastics competition. Let us suppose that they do very well in these competitions and win lots of medals. Often, they win more medals than other states do, so they think they have won the Olympics.

I hope this analogy is clear: one of our states has its own sports, while the rest of America has baseball, football, and basketball. What's more, the inhabitants of that state are very ignorant of our sports, which they imagine to be inferior, just as we are very ignorant of the rest of the world's sports, which we believe to be inferior.

Now let us also imagine that one of their newspapers decides that it wants to be "America's newspaper," just as *The New York Times* considers itself the world's newspaper. In pushing to be successful in this quest, however, the newspaper in question refuses to cover our sports and continues to focus on their sports, just as *The Times* refuses to give much coverage to soccer and continues to focus on our sports.

And let us imagine that at some point, some of their more progressive educators decided that their students should learn more about the cultures of the other states in our country, and that in pushing for this program to be instituted in their schools, they called it "multiculturalism." These educators might say, "Our students will be doing business with people from the rest of America, and they need to know their culture to be successful." However, this multicultural program does nothing to inform their students about the sports played elsewhere in America. It focuses on other things, just as our own multicultural programs focus on other things.

What would we say about such a state and its attitudes?

First, the rest of us would be of two minds about the idea that they have "won" the Olympics. We would likely say that since they hadn't won either the football or the basketball competition, which were the two most important competitions in this college Olympics, their win was limited, that while they had won the Olympics in one sense, in another sense they clearly had been a horrible failure. After all, winning ought to convey respect, but no one is going to gain complete respect when they don't win in the most important sports.

Second, we would probably snicker at the idea that one of their newspapers could be called "America's newspaper," given that they refused to cover the sports that the rest of us followed.

Third, we would think that their "multicultural" movement was a farce.

Fourth, we would probably think of them as prejudiced. And even if we refrained from using that word, others would come to mind: "ignorant," "provincial," "insular," and "out of step with the rest of the country." But most of all, we would hardly think of the progressives among these people as being progressive about sports. Wouldn't we expect their progressives to know about our sports, even if they weren't necessarily fans? Wouldn't we expect them to express curiosity about our sports, to the extent that when they traveled outside of their state they would occasionally attend our sporting events? Wouldn't we even expect some of them to have become fans of our sports? Is it unreasonable to have such expectations?

Chapter 5
Soccer Is NOT Boring!

Americans think soccer is boring. What Americans don't know is that there are plenty of foreigners who think *our sports are boring*. (I will present some of their opinions in the next chapter.) In fact, the British press generally denounces a relatively high-scoring soccer game as mere "basketball." One point against those Americans who think that soccer is boring is that they insist that soccer is boring because soccer has so little scoring, and so they are always demanding rule changes that would allow more scoring. However, *they never give any indication that they would accept soccer even with these new rules*. For example, indoor soccer has more scoring than the outdoor variety, but these people are not flocking to indoor games. And lacrosse, cricket and rugby have plenty of scoring, but they don't like those sports, either. No, the soccer haters focus on the scoring merely as a way to express their hatred of soccer.

Is there more that can be said? Those of us who like soccer think soccer isn't boring while those who hate soccer think it is, but is one side right and the other wrong on this issue? Or is it just a matter on which there nothing more can be said? Is it like the topic of which foods are enjoyable to eat and which aren't? Some people like the taste of broccoli and some people don't. There is nothing more to be said on this topic. Is the disagreement about soccer's allegedly boring nature like that? I don't think so. A great deal more can be said.

(1) To say that something or another is boring is to make a value judgment similar to those made in the arts, and if there is anything that can be said about judgment in the arts, it is that they are subjective. Not many today would dissent from this view (especially the students I had when I taught an aesthetics class), and if that is the case, then saying that soccer is boring isn't much of a criticism. It's exactly like saying broccoli

tastes bad. Some will agree, and some will disagree, but there is no further truth to the matter. People who criticize soccer for being boring seem to imagine that they are saying something as objective as "1 + 1 = 2" or "Jupiter is the biggest planet in our solar system," but maybe all they are saying is something subjective like "Broccoli tastes bad."

I happen to disagree with the general view of art (and I think most art critics do, too). I prefer to follow the eighteenth-century Scottish philosopher David Hume in believing that there are universally valid judgments, even if they are subjective.[1] Hume's example is that Homer is just as revered today as he was 2,000 years ago. In other words, while such judgments are not as sound as judgments made by scientists, they are not as hopeless as statements made about broccoli. They are somewhere in between.

Hume believed that some people had better taste in the arts than others did, and we can trust their judgments more than we can those with worse taste. An obvious way one develops taste is by being exposed to as many art objects as possible, and the same general thing can be said about sports. People who grow up in soccer-playing countries have a greater exposure to a variety of sports than most Americans, for they see both high-scoring and low-scoring sports. In Brazil, for example, in addition to soccer there is basketball, and in England, in addition to soccer there are cricket and rugby. We in America are generally exposed only to high-scoring sports and are unfamiliar with the pleasures of low-scoring sports.

Similarly, being unfamiliar with soccer often means that people who are new to the game don't see what is actually happening. I've often brought people who are unused to soccer out to pro soccer games, and I would ask them if they had seen certain things. They hadn't. For example, I would ask them if they had seen someone head the ball *down*, because those unused to soccer might not think that players would ever do such a thing. And they hadn't seen it. The most recent time I brought some visitors to a game, there was a hand ball, and the people I had brought hadn't seen it, even though these were people who quite frequently watch sports (like football and basketball) that use the hands. Another thing that isn't seen is the play the English call "selling the dummy." This is when the intended recipient of a pass lets it go so that a teammate who is better placed can get it. Invariably, those new to the game see this as a mistake, while those of us more familiar with the game see it as brilliant (assuming the teammate does in fact get the ball).

Soccer, the Left, & the Farce of Multiculturalism

Another more important example of this sort occurred in 1977 at Pelé's farewell game, in which he took a free kick and scored a goal. The reporter for the *New York Times* described the shot as going "low and hard, a bullet keeping its line all the way to the left of the Santos goal."[2] The reporter for *The Times of London* described it as "a magnificent curling thunderbolt."[3] The American reporter implied that it went straight into the goal. He had had little experience with soccer and probably had never heard about how Brazilians had become masters at getting the ball to curve just right. The British reporter *did* have this sort of experience and so saw something quite different from what the American reporter did. Eventually, I saw a replay of that goal from an area behind the goal which showed that it indeed was a magnificent *curling* thunderbolt.

Yes, it's true that what many Americans are seeing on a soccer field is boring. But then what they are seeing isn't soccer. They are seeing something that is much duller than soccer.

(2) Isn't it possible that the soccer haters have it backwards? Maybe it's not that soccer has too little scoring, but rather that American sports have a great deal of scoring because, given that the action in our sports is so boring or infrequent, American sports fans need to be bribed by lots of scoring to keep paying attention. There is also the jab, which I believe comes from *National Lampoon*, that one could reform pro basketball by giving each team a hundred points and then letting them play for five minutes. And consider this: if baseball had more stolen bases and hot boxes, but a little less scoring, would that make it more boring?

(3) Many Americans think of soccer as boring because they are only familiar with *English* soccer. But English soccer isn't like Brazilian soccer, which is quite different. The Brazilian anthropologist Gilberto Freyre has said that English soccer is Apollonian, while Brazilian soccer is Dionysian: "Whereas the Apollonians have control over themselves, Brazilian football is a dance full of irrational surprises and Dionysiac variations."[4] I shall never forget going to Brazil back in 1981. Within an hour of reaching my hotel, I turned on the TV and began watching a soccer game that was in progress. At one point, the ball came to a defender who was right near his goal. Now I had watched quite a bit of soccer at that point, and I had two expectations for what he was going to do next. One was to pass it back to his goalie. (In those days the goalie was allowed to pick it up.) The other was to blast it upfield. Either of these was the smart and easy thing for this defender to do. But he wasn't going to do the smart and easy thing. No. He was going to make life difficult for himself by *dribbling* his way

out of danger. He began doing this and doing it well, well enough so that he didn't see any need to pass it to a teammate. Obviously, he just wanted to dribble. Eventually, he lost the ball out of bounds, but by that time he was thirty yards upfield. It is this sort of exhibition of flair that one can see from other cultures and which one seldom sees in English soccer.

(4) Soccer in America is hampered by the fact that many games are played on football fields, which are generally narrower than soccer fields. A narrow field is thought to restrict the scoring because on a wide field, the defensive players are forced to spread out more, and being spread out more means they aren't as effective, which results in more scoring.

(5) Marathons aren't especially exciting, yet how often do marathon runners have to put up with the "it's boring" criticism? Surely not as often as we soccer fans do, if ever.

(6) I admit that the opening of a soccer game is pretty boring compared with that of a football game. Football starts with a long kick from near the center of the playing field that goes deep into the other team's territory. The team kicking are all lined up with the kicker, and they all rush forward as a player from the opposing team attempts to catch the ball cleanly and run with it; meanwhile, his teammates block the opposing team from tackling him. By contrast, soccer generally starts with a little flick of the ball with a foot. There's not much excitement there. But a kickoff in football doesn't last very long, and what happens very soon afterward is one of the many, many stoppages in play. Meanwhile, soccer keeps going. Anyway, compare the start of soccer with other sports besides football. Basketball has a jump ball, and ice hockey has a face-off, and while these are somewhat more exciting than soccer's kickoff, they still don't compare with football's kickoff. And baseball starts with a pitch that is no different from any other pitch. So, these other sports also compare badly with football. Accordingly, the fact that the kickoff in soccer is comparatively boring is not much of a point against it.

(7) Those who criticize soccer because of its low-scoring nature should also be willing to say that ice hockey is boring because it is low-scoring, also, though not quite as low-scoring as soccer is. (Some soccer haters do indeed make this judgment.) Next on the list would be baseball, because it has more scoring than soccer or ice hockey, but less scoring than other sports. After baseball would come football and rugby, and after them would come basketball. Finally, there would be cricket.

Do the soccer haters make such judgments? Of course not. Baseball, football, and basketball are all judged uniformly exciting, while soccer and cricket are judged boring. (Where does rugby fit in? one asks.) Yet, why shouldn't baseball be judged more boring than football and basketball? The reason is simple: the people making this judgment are prejudiced.

Cricket, naturally, is judged to be boring because it is too slow. Apparently, then, we have not one but *two* features of sports that can make them boring or exciting. Soccer isn't slow, but it is low scoring. Cricket is not low scoring, but it is slow. Apparently, then, American sports have the right combination of quickness and high scoring. But do they? First, let us rank team sports in terms of their slowness and quickness. At the bottom would be cricket. Next to the bottom would be baseball. After that would be football (because football has a great many timeouts and stoppages in play). Next would come, in no particular order, rugby, basketball, soccer, and ice hockey.

Now recall the ranking I made three paragraphs ago for scoring (that is, starting from the bottom, soccer, ice hockey, baseball, football and rugby, basketball, and cricket). Once we consider both these rankings, something strikes us: *baseball is near the bottom of both rankings*. Baseball has *some* scoring, but not a lot compared with basketball and cricket. Baseball is *faster* than cricket, but much slower than the other sports. If the point is to have a sport that is both high scoring and fast, then baseball is the worst of all these sports. Soccer is often fast plus it has lots of action, and cricket at least has high scoring, but baseball has very little of either.

Look at it this way. We can try being objective by using numbers. Award up to fifty points for how much scoring a sport has. Award up to fifty points for how much fast action there is. Based on the rankings just made, we might award soccer five points in scoring, but forty-five points for speed and action. That gives it a total of fifty points. Ice hockey would get fifty points for speed and action and, say, seven points for scoring, giving it a total of fifty-seven. Cricket would get fifty points for scoring and one point for action, giving it a total of fifty-one points. Basketball might get forty each for scoring and action, giving it eighty points. Football might get thirty for scoring but just ten for action (because while the action of football is exciting, there are just too many stoppages in the play for it to deserve more). But baseball would get, say, twenty-five points for scoring, but only five points for action (since its action isn't as exciting as football's action is), giving it a total of just thirty points.

Face it, baseball is the most boring of the team sports.

Just to appease the baseball lovers, let us try to see it from their standpoint (which is more than they have ever done for us soccer lovers).

First, they would object to the idea that football gets thirty points for scoring, given that the amount of scoring in football isn't really more than the amount in baseball. It just looks that way because a touchdown is worth six points and a field goal is worth three. The result is that football looks like it has more scoring than baseball when in fact it doesn't.

This objection is valid, but it does nothing to raise the ranking of baseball; it merely lowers the ranking of football. So suppose we try juggling the numbers in various ways. Suppose we make the category of scoring have seventy-five points instead of fifty while action gets only twenty-five. In that case, soccer could score twenty-two in terms of action, but only (say) seven in terms of scoring. That would give soccer at most just twenty-nine points. Baseball, meanwhile, would get about thirty-seven points for scoring and another three for action. That would put baseball at forty points, ahead of soccer.

The trouble here is that cricket will get seventy-five points for scoring, putting it way ahead of baseball. If the lover of American sports wants baseball to come out ahead of both soccer and cricket, this method won't work. Likewise, making action count more than scoring will hurt cricket but help soccer. Neither way of juggling the numbers will let baseball end up ahead of both.

Some who actually have some knowledge of cricket will argue that while in cricket many runs are scored, it also takes many hours or even days to score those runs. But while there is something to this point, as far as I can tell the number of runs scored per hour in cricket easily exceeds the number of runs in an entire baseball game. Twenty or thirty runs per hour still means that cricket will be way ahead of baseball, if scoring is made more important than action.

Suppose we bend over backwards a lot more than we have been doing and look at it this way. It might be argued that there is a certain crucial *threshold* that must be reached in terms of scoring and action and that once a sport has reached that threshold for a category, it deserves all fifty points. Baseball, it will be argued, has reached that threshold in terms of scoring while soccer hasn't. Baseball has also reached that threshold in terms of action while cricket hasn't. What that means is that the three American sports of baseball, football, and basketball each get 100 points, while soccer and cricket each get only fifty.

I think that this is the best that one can do. For those American sports fans who think that soccer and cricket are boring, I think this is the best that one can do in the way of making their case. How persuasive is it? After all, the point here is not just to make a case that persuades *you* but to make a case that persuades *everyone.*

Obviously, this isn't going to persuade very many people because some dubious assumptions have been made along the way. If one accepts those assumptions, then of course the point follows. But if one does not – and there is no reason why one should – then it just seems like special pleading on the part of those Americans who hate foreign sports. For example, many foreigners – and I'm talking about those who come from countries where neither baseball nor cricket are very important – find baseball to be ridiculously slow. Many Europeans (ignoring the British) have grown up on soccer, basketball, and ice hockey, all high-action sports. For them baseball is hopelessly slow. For them, baseball won't have reached the threshold in terms of *action.*

But even if we accept this idea of a threshold – and most people throughout the world will not accept it – and accept it in such a way that both soccer and cricket are boring while American sports are exciting, we still have rugby to deal with. Is it boring or exciting? It has plenty of action, and it has plenty of scoring. Apparently, then, it is as exciting as American sports. But in that case, why isn't it acceptable to the American sports fan?

(8) People who have tried to get Americans to like soccer have suggested a number of silly things, such as enlarging the goals. Would such a thing work? Probably not. It would be like bringing the fences in much closer to home plate so as to make home runs much easier to score or enlarging the baskets in basketball so there is even more scoring than there is now. First of all, bringing the fences in closer would be worthless in the eyes of baseball fans. While it would result in many more home runs, the fact is that hitting a home run is a special sort of thing. Not everyone is known as a home run hitter, and to make it easier would make a lot of earlier records worthless.

More important is that most sports, except for races, are a mixture of a number of elements. Baseball has many elements besides home runs or even runs. It has double plays (and on rare occasions triple plays), hot boxes, stolen bases, strikeouts, outfielders making spectacular catches at the wall, and so on. Likewise, soccer has many elements, too. Aside from scoring, it has goalies making lightning quick saves, heading (which virtually no other sport has), dribbling, passing, give-and-go's, and a variety of feints and fakes. It also has players who are goal-scorers. Just as not every baseball player is a home-run hitter, so not every soccer player is a goal-scorer. To score goals regularly requires a special aptitude.

Soccer also has different national styles such as the Brazilian style, the German style, the Italian style, the English style, and so on. Soccer began as a dribbling game, a feature which it has never lost. There was no passing at all. It was the Scots who figured out that passing the ball was important. But even though passing was instituted, the passing was all short passing. At some point, long passes were instituted, which necessitated that new skills be acquired. Meanwhile, various tactical innovations were being tried. All of these and many other things are part of soccer, though dribbling remains the most important.

Making the goals larger, or eliminating the goalie, would change this particular mix. If we eliminated the goalie, then many more goals would be scored. But something would be lost, and that something would no doubt be dribbling. The way the game would go would be like this. People would try to get the ball upfield as fast as possible, and that would be done primarily by passing. Then once players were within range, they would take shots. Some dribbling would remain, but the mix of elements would be quite different, and dribbling would be much less needed. But dribbling, as Paul Gardner has pointed out, is soccer's *poetry*:

> Dribbling is ... a flowing, imaginative and colorful part of the game. It is England's Stanley Matthews shuffling the ball right up to an opponent, daring him to take it, then whipping it impudently away and accelerating past him. It is Brazil's Garrincha hovering over the ball with his bow legs bent almost double at the knees, tormenting defenders with his ravishing body feints, toppling them helplessly off-balance without ever moving the ball. It is Pelé impishly waltzing past opponents as he seems to bounce the ball off their legs, or George Best corkscrewing his way past man after man on a flexuous run of perfect balance and improvised brilliance.[5]

Changing the rules so as to reduce the amount of dribbling would mean that an extremely important part of the game would be lost. It's as though we were to change baseball by outlawing curve balls. The resulting game would be considerably less interesting.

(9) And speaking of dribbling, here is a story about dribbling and what it means to foreigners. When I got involved in soccer, it was at a big university that had many foreign students playing the game. Most of these

Soccer, the Left, & the Farce of Multiculturalism

students were from either Iran or Nigeria. Those of us Americans playing intramural soccer often found ourselves playing against and even with Iranians. One of the Iranians I had played with, named Hussein, called me up one day saying he had joined a new team and that they needed another player. Would I join them? "Yes," I said. When I got to the field, I noticed that all the other team members were Iranian, but even more important, they were all very good. I resolved to play a minor role in this game by simply passing the ball to a teammate whenever it came my way. After about twenty minutes, I was feeling pretty good. I hadn't lost the ball and my passes had been on target. But Hussein came up to me looking worried and said, "John, why aren't you dribbling?"

This story shows what soccer can mean to foreigners. Do you have enough skill to dribble around another player or at least to keep the ball no matter how hard you are pressed? It's not just one team against another. It is also how well each player plays against the people around him. This is something, of course, that the soccer haters know nothing about. A similar example could be given of baseball, in which the duel between pitcher and batter seems to be all important for the baseball fan. For foreigners unused to sports like this, it just looks quite boring.

(10) It's easy to get fooled ahead of time on what is boring and what isn't. A game described in a boring way may turn out not to be boring. One of the early criticisms I found of soccer was expressed thus: "It's not much fun watching grown men kick a ball up and down the field."[6] But one could also say that it isn't much fun watching grown men bounce a ball up and down a court, or watching grown men in pajamas hitting a ball with a stick, or watching grown men going up and down the field butting their heads together like goats.

A number of years ago I went to a game in West Germany, and during the halftime I watched some of the reserves playing a simple training game. I had played this game myself and had thought of it as not just simple, but simple-minded. Someone is in the center of a circle and the others pass it back and forth to each other, trying to keep it away from the player in the center. Yet, I watched spellbound as these players made it more than anything my friends and I had ever made it. They added so many fakes and feints and other tricks that I would have been willing to watch for hours. And this is what happens in soccer. Just kicking a ball up and down the field isn't very interesting, but then so much more is happening.

(11) Let me admit that there are on occasion particular soccer games that are boring. But so what? There are particular baseball, football and

basketball games that are boring, too. For people who like scoring, whenever the defenses are more powerful than the offenses, then such people (if they are consistent) are going to find the particular game in question boring. And there is nothing to prevent such games from occurring.

(12) Just for the sake of argument, suppose I acknowledge that soccer is boring. Is this enough to make me like our sports? Hardly. The frequent stoppages in play in baseball and football bore me to tears. The last time I watched a football game (which was in 1976), I sat there with stop watch in hand timing how much actual action was taking place. During a three-hour game, it came out to about fifteen minutes, which is hardly enough to satisfy me. Plus, both football and basketball have size requirements that I don't meet, while in baseball I was always shoved into the outfield as a kid, so why bother supporting them? In other words, even if I stopped supporting soccer, I wouldn't turn back to our sports.

And just to show how complicated things can get for the soccer hater, there are other people in the world who think that soccer is boring who nevertheless don't like our sports. Many Australians seem to agree that soccer is boring (because of the low scoring), but what sports do they choose to watch instead? Baseball, football, and basketball? Not at all. They watch Australian rules football, or some version of rugby, or else cricket.

(13) Saying that soccer is boring is to exhibit the typical, narrow reaction of the American sports fan. The American sports fan is a person who is primarily interested in *watching* sports. Such a person has forgotten that all sports had their roots in people *playing* those sports. American sports like baseball and football have grown beyond their roots in this respect. Very few adult Americans *play* baseball. Very few adult Americans *play* football. They merely watch those games. Once we consider that soccer is a game that is not just watched but also *played* – and I'm talking about adults here – the whole question takes on a different significance. Recall what I said in Chapter 3. Soccer is both a spectator sport and a participation sport, whereas neither baseball nor football are participation sports. But even if they were, to play soccer is seldom boring, unless perhaps one is the goalie on a side that is winning by a large margin. But playing American sports means spending an awful lot of time just standing around. To play baseball is often to be bored. There are long stretches where one is simply watching what others are doing. In particular, I always hated it after I had an unsuccessful time at bat because I knew that it might be another three long innings before I could bat again. And I especially hated it when I was the last one out in one of the later innings because there was no guarantee

that I'd get to bat again at all. It is true that there are times during a soccer game when one is watching what others are doing, but during this time one isn't usually just standing around. One is running to get into an open position or something similar.

Let me say again what I'm saying here and what I said in Chapter 3, but in different words. A sport isn't just a sport. It's a lifestyle. A certain environment grows up around that sport, and people adapt their lifestyles to it. Soccer has an attractive sports environment. It has plenty of international competition, and it has plenty of adult (even older adult) amateurs playing. It has open-cup tournaments between the best and the worst. Baseball, by contrast, has a less attractive sports environment, while football has one that is even less attractive than baseball's. There is little in the way of international competitions in either of them. Even the most stellar college football player never represents his country at the Olympics. And people who play football in college almost never play the game after college. Whereas there are plenty of young men around the world who are, say, twenty-five years old who are playing soccer, there are very few young men that age playing football. The reason, as I mentioned in an earlier chapter, is that football is too expensive.

So, even if soccer is boring – and I don't think so, and lots of people around the world don't think so – our sports have some severe limitations. Their environments and the lifestyles that grow up around them aren't as attractive as soccer's is.

On the other hand, I admit that *there are some things about soccer that ought to be improved*. I will discuss these in Chapter 13.

Endnotes

1. See his essay "Of the Standard of Taste."
2. *The New York Times*, Oct. 2, 1977, sec. 5, p. 3.
3. *Times of London*, Oct. 3, 1977, p. 8.
4. Cited in Paul Gardner, *The Simplest Game* (Little, Brown and Company, 1976), p. 13.
5. Paul Gardner, "Soccer, American Style," *New York Times Magazine*, May 4, 1975, p. 60.
6. *Sports Illustrated*, letter to the editor for September 11, 1967, p. 124.

Chapter 6
Is "Prejudice" the Right Word?

I am claiming that there has been prejudice against foreign sports in America, and in the next chapter I will try to trace the roots of this prejudice. I have also been claiming that most leftists are still in the grip of this prejudice, while some other Americans have been slowly overcoming it. But the big question at this point is, Is "prejudice" the right word for the attitudes I am talking about? Yes, it's true that there are feelings of hatred or indifference in connection with foreign sports, but that doesn't make it prejudice. After all, Jews hate the Nazis, but that isn't the result of prejudice. In fact, it's the other way around. Jews hate the Nazis for justifiable, historical reasons (because the Nazis were and are prejudiced and bigoted against them). Likewise, America's soccer haters think that their hatred of soccer (and cricket) is very much justified and that if it is justified, then it is not prejudice.

Against this, I am going to point out that people who are prejudiced have feelings of hostility, that these feeling are usually unjustified, and that they are based on ignorance. The prejudiced person uses bad or inaccurate stereotypes and bad arguments. Finally, the people least likely to be prejudiced are young people rather than old people. All of these features can be found among our soccer haters, including our leftists.

American Hostility towards Soccer

The first sign that people are prejudiced against someone or something is that they show hostility towards that person or thing. Americans generally (especially those who came of age in the Sixties or earlier) are *hostile* to soccer. This can be seen in many ways. It can be seen in the fact that the sports sections of American newspapers almost never treat soccer as the equal of our sports. Soccer seldom gets front-page coverage in the sports section, except for the most important games. Moreover, the coverage often includes critical comments about the sport, either in the article itself or in columns by the regular sportswriters. None of our sports are treated this way. While there may be some occasional sniping at one of baseball, football, or basketball, I've never seen any sniping at all three at once, plus the continued existence of any of these sports is rarely questioned by the staff of the sports pages. No one could legitimately claim that soccer is treated that way by the American media today.

One glaring example of this occurred in connection with our Major League Soccer (MLS) all-star game in the year 2000, which was held in Columbus, Ohio. While the *Columbus Dispatch* gave it decent coverage (though nothing compared to what it would have gotten if it had been played in Europe), the situation was totally different in Cleveland's *Plain Dealer*. The article was not put on the front page, and the reader had to endure page after page of articles and statistics about baseball before finding one small article about it. That article was hostile. It talked about the various problems that soccer faces. It ignored the fact that there are many soccer fans in the Cleveland area who might have wanted something better. The many articles about baseball refrained from mentioning any problems that baseball has.

Here is another example. After two academics, Andrei S. Markovits and Steven L. Hellerman, wrote a book friendly to soccer in America called *Offside*, *Sports Illustrated* responded with an article by Frank Deford, in which he explained that soccer was not an American game and that it was never going to make it here, never mind that it has been making it here and under conditions under which American sports would never thrive.[1] And then there is the comment made (I don't know when) by the sportswriter Dick Young, that soccer is a "game for commie pansies."[2] On the eve of the World Cup in 1994, David Letterman and Jay Leno made countless jokes against soccer.[3] I believe one of them said something to the effect that American soccer fans are wild about soccer, then pointing out that there were only ten such fans. Fortunately, events proved him wrong, for the games were well attended. Finally, there are the hidden insults, for example, the fact that I have never yet detected a kind word for soccer in certain magazines (such as *The Nation*).

The intelligentsia also gets into the act. The book *An American Looks at Britain* is chock-full of important information on the manners and ideas of the British. My wife Sarah and I read it before we went on our first trip to

England and absorbed some useful information from it. But when it comes to sports, its author cannot help himself. Instead of spending his time explaining the differences between the American sports environment and the British one, which would have been highly interesting and informative, he could do nothing other than talk about soccer violence.[4] Given all the other interesting things he could have said, this seems a rather strange thing to begin with. But it does reflect the American perception of soccer. His chapter on sports really tells us more about him than it does about Britain.

Here are some more examples, except that these are from ordinary sports fans and not from the media itself or books. The Columbus Crew originally used the stadium of the Ohio State University football team, but then had to leave because of planned construction. So it decided to build its own stadium. At first, it wanted what teams in our sports get to have: public funding for their stadiums. But a fuss was made about that, and so it managed to get a new stadium, a soccer-specific stadium, funded on its own. But that wasn't good enough for the soccer haters. Here is what one of them said: "Why not re-configure the new stadium on I-71 for baseball (Clippers) and send the Crew packing to a 'soccer-specific city?'"[5]

This letter was from a section of the *Columbus Dispatch* sports section called "rants." People could call in with a rant, and if it was deemed colorful enough, it would get printed. A number of these have to do with how boring soccer is and how those of us who like soccer had better remember that *the* sport of Columbus is Ohio State football. One rant said, "Well, we've gone from the sixth circle of hell – professional hockey – directly into the seventh – professional soccer."[6] In his book *Fever Pitch*, Nick Hornby says that being an Arsenal fan means having to put up with two or three insults a week from the British media.[7] The same can be said about just being a soccer fan in America. Often, the soccer haters smirk at the low ratings of soccer games on television, imagining that it shows what a poor sport soccer is, when of course all it really shows is the degree of prejudice against soccer there is in this country.

Another ranter said, "Is it just coincidence that the words soccer, sleep and snooze all start with the same letter?"[8] Still another one complained as follows:

> In an effort to understand my soccer friends, who are otherwise rational people, I have watched bits and pieces of a number of games

on TV the last several weeks. (In fact, one such viewing was well over an hour.).... Alas, I have yet to witness a single goal being scored.

The writer went on to say that soccer ought to eliminate the goalie so that more goals will be scored. To his credit, the editor, Danny Goodwin, responded by saying, "Then you could get away with only watching 15 minutes, eh?"[9]

I am not the only one who has noticed the exceptional hostility of Americans to soccer. Bob Hunter, who writes for the *Columbus Dispatch* and is one of the more enlightened sportswriters around, said, "I know a lot of people in this country don't like soccer, but I don't understand why so many of them seem so eager to see it fail. It's almost a crusade with some people."[10]

Now I don't intend this book to be a mere list of what people have said. I am only giving a sample of the hundreds and perhaps thousands of things that people have said that I have run across. I assume that readers who are soccer fans will have already encountered enough hostility to soccer so that they know what I am talking about. Still, every now and then I am surprised when I run across someone who is unaware of it. I mentioned this hostility recently to a woman my age, who seemed utterly surprised by it. But then she rarely talks about sports or goes to sporting events, so it is not surprising that she failed to notice such hostility. Anyway, my purpose in this chapter is to see whether this hostility counts as prejudice and then in the next chapter to see how, when, and where this prejudice arose.

Prejudice as Prejudging

The basic idea of prejudice is prejudging, which is making a judgment without knowing all the facts (and indeed without having any interest in all the facts). Mere hostility is not enough to show that someone is prejudiced. Something more is needed, namely an irrational hatred, which is exhibited when someone makes a judgement without looking at all the facts (and sticks with that judgement, even when new facts are presented to them). Let me, then, talk about how the soccer haters of America have prejudged soccer.

To begin with, I had encountered in others vague feelings of hostility toward soccer long before *any of us knew much of anything about the sport*. This hostility must have been passed down from parents to their children, who then passed it down to their children, and so on in a process that has lasted over a century. The result was that the grandchildren and great-grandchildren, while knowing nothing about soccer, knew that they were supposed to heap scorn on it. But that was all they knew. They didn't even know enough to say that it was boring. Yet, as the American public became more aware of soccer and its advantages, the soccer haters have continued their hostility toward soccer. Knowing, for example, that many people in the rest of the world, including people that they respect, love soccer doesn't sway the soccer hater at all. After all, almost all of us, except American Indians, are either immigrants or the descendants of immigrants, and it is a good bet that the people back in the old country love soccer. That means the soccer hater must either scorn everyone back in that country or somehow live with the knowledge that those people are soccer lovers. Many people of Irish descent are quite devoted to Ireland, and many Jews are quite devoted to Israel, yet the fact that the people of Ireland and Israel are soccer fans means nothing to those soccer haters who are of Irish or Jewish descent. In my own home state of Minnesota, many people are of Scandinavian descent, and of course there is interest in Scandinavia as a result. But that interest never extends to interest in the *sports* of Scandinavia. Obviously, there is some severe psychological repression going on here.

In line with what I say is prejudice, none of the soccer haters I have encountered, either in person or in print, has ever shown any special knowledge of the world of soccer. In fact, generally they are ignorant of the basic facts (such as which countries play soccer and which play cricket), to say nothing of the more complex facts. It is a fact that sports in the rest of the world do not have the same structure as sports do here. (Recall what I've been saying about England's pyramid of teams.) There are differences. It is not just that they play soccer and we don't. Rather, there are differences in the mindsets, the assumptions, the traditions, and the way sports are structured between our country and other countries. Not knowing about these differences immediately shows that the soccer hater is prejudiced. The Jews spend a great deal of time studying the Nazis and learning everything they can about them. By contrast, the soccer hater spends no time at all learning about sports in other countries. I feel that I am still learning about soccer in other countries (to say nothing of cricket and rugby). Even after years of study, I can still be surprised by some basic fact that previously, for reasons unknown, I had not happened to encounter. For example, I first began hearing about Manchester United in the late 1970s, but it wasn't until the early 1990s that I learned that they were associated with Catholics. Incredible! How had I never heard this before? How had that fact eluded me for so long? I don't know, but if that is possible for me, then it surely is likely for everyone else, especially the soccer hater who spends no time at all examining sports elsewhere.

Why should it be so important to learn about how soccer is structured elsewhere? *For the simple reason that it might be to our advantage to do so.* Learning about sports elsewhere helps us to see what is wrong with sports here, to see what flaws we have in our sports and our sports environment that need to be overcome. What is particularly pathetic about the American soccer hater is that, if he is an athlete, he may be treated unjustly in some way that is invisible to us Americans, because we assume that that is the way that sports are supposed to be structured. As I pointed out in Chapter 3, a second-rate football or basketball player could be earning a decent living playing in a minor league, but he cannot do so because there are no minor leagues for those sports in this country. Looking at sports elsewhere would be to his benefit, but of course being so hostile, he won't do it.

But even beyond any benefits that might accrue to us, any fair-minded person who encountered soccer for the first time and who knew, as soccer haters must know, that it is popular in the rest of the world would take the time to get to know it. This is the way that fair-minded people act. A parallel argument was once made by a fellow student when I first began studying philosophy. He argued that we ought to study Marxist philosophy because it is (or was at that time) a philosophy that much of the world was living under. In the same way, the fair-minded person will learn about sports elsewhere just because following soccer is something that most people in the world do. The fair-minded person – indeed, the multiculturalist – will want to know the reasons why this sport has become so popular. Such a person will want to acquaint himself or herself with the rather hefty chunk of human experience that soccer represents. He or she will also assume that, given that it may be impossible to understand America without understanding our sports, as Jacques Barzun has said somewhere, the same thing holds true of other countries, that we cannot understand them without understanding their sports. He or she will then endeavor to become educated along these lines.

It goes almost without saying that the soccer haters of America have no interest in treating soccer this way.

Unjustified Hostility

Is any of this hostility justified? I say no. The question comes down to this: Was there ever any full-fledged investigation by any American examining the advantages and disadvantages of American sports compared with English sports, an investigation that showed that our sports were superior to their sports either from a sports point of view or from a broader American point of view? The answer is no. For example, I've never seen any American talk about the pyramid of teams in England, and I've never seen any American compare the lives of American jocks and English jocks. It just hasn't been done. Instead, the comparison between soccer and our sports has been done on a very superficial level, a level that ignores the disadvantages of our sports as well as the advantages of soccer. Even intelligent leftists have engaged in this sort of comparison. (Recall the postmodernist professor I mentioned in Chapter 1.) If people disparage something without knowing any of its advantages, then it is reasonable to say that their hostility is unjustified.

Ignorance

The America that I grew up in was an America that was almost completely isolated from the rest of the world as far as sports were concerned. As I said in Chapter 3, we lived behind the Iron Curtain of Sports. Aside from the Olympics and a few tennis and golf tournaments, the newspapers never mentioned international sporting events, and only rarely did they mention any leagues for any sport that existed outside the U.S. Obviously, there was baseball going on in Japan, Cuba and other places. Still, these weren't covered. (In fact, they still aren't covered.) There was absolutely no interest in anything sporting outside of the U.S. The World Cup never received any coverage whatsoever in my local paper, or if it did, it was buried deep in the back pages. It wasn't until the 1970s that the World Cup began to get regular front-page coverage.

This monumental change was partly the result of Pelé's having come to America. At that time, many people were forced to pay attention to this sport which they had formerly ignored. People began to realize that sports like baseball and football simply weren't followed in the rest of the world, at least not in the majority of the other countries of the world. People began to realize that the following that soccer had was simply huge. Nevertheless, it was hard for many Americans to accept these things. Indeed, these facts are so hard for Americans to accept that some *still* don't accept them.

Here are some examples of what I mean. In the World Cup of 1994, Diego Maradona was stopped in the hallway of his hotel because some security people didn't know that he was a player.[11] Nowhere else would this have happened. In fact, earlier that year, only 20 percent of Americans even knew that it was going to be played in the U.S.[12]

Another example along these lines occurred during the 1998 World Cup. My wife met a man who seemed educated enough, but who was only just learning that the World Cup was a contest between different countries. Keep in mind that this occurred during the World Cup that occurred four years *after* the World Cup that was hosted in the United States. Another example was that of a young woman I knew who claimed to like "all" sports. When I had been in high school, I knew various jocks who said this kind of thing, but by the time I had gotten involved in soccer, I had lost track of them and so couldn't question them. Here was my opportunity to test the truth of such a claim. I mentioned soccer to her, and she replied with shock and dismay, "Soccer?" It was as though she hadn't previously thought that soccer counted as a sport. Or perhaps she didn't understand that claiming to like *all* sports committed one to liking soccer, cricket, and other sports that the American media didn't deign to cover. Examples like this could be repeated endlessly.

Another example of our ignorance of sports concerns professionals playing in the Olympics. For years Olympic soccer was rather uninteresting because of the way that the communist countries were allowed by the technicalities of the rules to field their best players while the capitalist countries couldn't. The result was that the communist countries always won. Then in 1978 the international soccer organization, FIFA, ruled that no one could play on an Olympics team if they had already played for their country on the national team. This was the first of a series of changes that eventually allowed some professionals to compete in the Olympics. That change spread from soccer to ice hockey and then to basketball. During the 1992 Olympics, a letter writer in Minneapolis complained about the way that professionals were now being allowed to play in the Olympics: "Is this just a plan for the United States to get as many medals as we can and maybe dominate the Olympics?"[13] Now I had been following this whole process right from the beginning, and what for me had been a series of international decisions beginning with soccer and so, given our unimportance in the soccer world, having almost nothing to do with the United States was seen by this person as something concocted in the United States to lord it over others in basketball. It was his complete ignorance of what had been going on in soccer that caused this ridiculous notion.

These are all interesting examples of our ignorance, but most other examples fall into certain categories. What I'm going to do is to examine five sets of statements, the first three by Americans, the last two by foreigners. The first set comes from Americans who think that foreigners avidly follow or even play our sports, the second set that foreigners have no sports of their own, and the third that foreigners are indifferent to or hate soccer. The fourth set comes from foreigners exhibiting their devotion to soccer. And the last comes from foreigners indicating what they think of our sports and of us in connection with sports.

(1) A few years ago *Time* magazine had a short statement about North Korea accompanied by a large illustration. The statement said:

> THROWING THE BOMB? Excited perhaps by his consolidation of power, or maybe by the start of a new football season, North Korea's unpredictable Kim Jong Il marked last week by firing a missile (carrying a satellite, he claims) over Japan.[14]

The accompanying illustration showed the North Korean leader holding a small missile as though it were a football and he were a quarterback. Now the idea that anyone in North Korea follows American football, and especially that the leader of North Korea follows American football, is thoroughly laughable. They are one of the most isolated countries on earth. Why would they pay attention to a sport played by capitalists? And the idea that the leader of North Korea was *inspired* by one of our sports, and in fact the very one of our three main sports that has traveled the least far around the world, just takes the cake.

Another example comes from an article in *The New York Times Magazine* about Red Smith, an American sportswriter. We are told that "he was the most widely read sports columnist of his time."[15] Now this is a statement that is almost certainly untrue, and even if it were true, it is very unlikely that the author of this article can prove it. Sportswriters live all over the world and write in many different languages. Are we really supposed to believe that the author had canvassed all of the sportswriters in all of these languages to be certain of his facts? After all, the most widely read sports columnist of that era might have been living in the Soviet Union and writing in Russian, or living in China and writing in Mandarin, or living in Spain or Latin America and writing in Spanish. How likely is it that the author even *considered* these possibilities? Or that he could name a single sports columnist outside the U.S.? Or that he has ever even looked at the sports pages of a foreign newspaper? Yet, he was convinced that Red Smith had an influence far beyond that of any foreign sportswriter.

I know what people are going to say in response. They will say that what was meant was that he was widely read by Americans. But it doesn't say that. And there will be plenty of Americans who will assume that he was widely read in other countries as well, which is very unlikely.

A third example is that of the *Newsweek* writer who, in the midst of an article on the British physicist Stephen Hawking, couldn't avoid talking about baseball. Hawking has amyotrophic lateral sclerosis, which in this country is better known as Lou Gehrig's disease. That was enough for the writer to say:

> Hawking, who is known to have a sense of humor about himself, might appreciate the irony that he managed to contract not just any terminal disease but one named after the greatest first baseman of his age.[16]

Why should we assume that Hawking had ever heard of Lou Gehrig? After all, Hawking is British, and as we learn later on in the article, the writer admits that Lou Gehrig's disease is known in Britain as "motor neuron disease." Why, then, assume that Hawking had ever heard of Lou Gehrig? Turn the situation around. If the English were to name a disease after a cricket player, how many of us Americans would recognize the name? In fact, how many Americans can recognize the names of *any* cricket players, whether English or not? One cricket writer describes the cricketer W.G. Grace as "arguably the most famous man in Victorian England."[17] But I've never heard any American refer to him, not even those who study Victorian England.

Now let me include some examples about myself. Once I got involved in soccer, I recalled at least three occasions when I had assumed that the word "football" had referred to our football when in fact it referred to soccer. One of these was in an obscure science fiction book written in England that few will have read, but most people should have at least heard of the other two. One of these was in Anne Frank's diary,[18] in which she related the story she had heard of two "football" teams that had played a game. One of these teams was composed of the police, while the other was composed of members of the secret underground. I remember being puzzled by this reference. It seemed unlikely that this was a game of professional football – I imagined that this was American football, of course – for it seemed highly unlikely that the players on such public and visible teams would be engaged in secret activities that the authorities didn't know about. So, I imagined it must have been a group of people playing *touch* football. I now realize that it was of course two amateur soccer teams.

The other reference was in Albert Camus's book *The Stranger*:

> At five there was a loud clanging of streetcars. They were coming from the stadium in our suburb where there had been a football match. Even the back platforms were crowded and people were standing on the steps. Then another streetcar brought back the teams. I knew they were the players by the suitcase each man carried. They were bawling out their team song, "Keep the ball rolling, boys." One of them looked up at me and shouted, "We licked them!" I waved my hand and called back, "Good work!"[19]

I didn't know quite what to make of this because it seemed so strange, but I now know that it was a soccer game. In fact, I now know that Camus himself was very fond of soccer and that he aspired to be a goalie, until ill health thwarted him and he became a philosopher instead. In both Frank's and Camus's works, the word "football" was used in the translation. Either the works were translated by British translators, or they were translated by Americans who didn't realize that their authors were talking about soccer and not our brand of football.

Still another aspect of our ignorance is that we impose our own sporting structure on the rest of the world. We imagine that sports in the rest of the world's schools are as important as they are in ours. As I've already mentioned, this has become a problem when recruiting college basketball players from abroad, because the structure of sports is so different elsewhere that there is no guarantee that such people have remained amateurs. As the *Chronicle of Higher Education* noted, two members of the NCAA were sent to Europe on a fact-finding mission. What did they find?

> That in Europe, amateurism and professionalism are often hard to untangle. In virtually all countries other than the United States, athletes participate in basketball, soccer, tennis and other clubs that have no affiliation with schools or colleges. Club-team rosters often include a mix of paid professionals and unpaid teenagers.[20]

One person was quoted as saying, "These kids don't have an option. They don't have a high-school team." This article did acknowledge that most American basketball coaches were aware of this. It was the officials of the NCAA who weren't aware. But we can also say that the general public here in the U.S. is not aware of it, either.

Another example of assuming an interest in our sports that doesn't exist comes from a column in the *Wall Street Journal* in which a writer wondered why, three summers after the American Olympic basketball team had won the gold medal in Barcelona, there was little trace of them.[21] No one seemed interested, he complained. This column, for the soccer lover, is quite unbelievable. The writer talked about many things in Barcelona. He talked about the people now living in the Olympic village. He talked about the American football team that was in residence there. He talked about a Spanish track and field star. He talked about the financial boon to Barcelona of having the Olympics in town. But he never talked about the Barcelona soccer team (or the other team in town, Español). He made the city of Barcelona out to be a sporting backwater. Yet, *Barcelona is one of the sporting centers of the world*. To talk about sports in Barcelona without mentioning soccer is like talking about sports in New York City without mentioning the Yankees. The Barcelona soccer team has a huge fan base that has a formal registry of 110,000; this registry is so prestigious that it included then Pope John Paul II, as well as then head of the Olympics Juan Samaranch (which may be why the Olympics were in Barcelona in the first place). It has fan clubs as far away as Tianjin, China, and it even sponsors an art competition which is, according to one writer, "so prestigious that Salvador Dali once submitted an entry."[22] To refrain from mentioning all of this is to see Barcelona through an American lens, but not as it is in reality.

Another very widespread example of our belief that others are following our sports is our tendency to call our sports champions "world" champions, as though everyone else cared about them. In baseball, the very championship is called the "World" Series. Yes, I know that this is called that because it was originally named after a newspaper by that name (though some have expressed some skepticism about this story). But how many Americans know that? I didn't know it myself until I started researching this book. Here is another quote:

> Though it is certainly conceivable that there are countless persons for whom the name Nebraska elicits absolutely no associations,

it is more doubtful that anyone who has heard of the state is not aware of "Big Red" football: the only game in town. It is an activity of sufficient impact to have attracted the attention of television (a special), magazines, (*Sports Illustrated, National Geographic*), and has been noted by "legitimate" authors (e.g., James Michener).[23]

Actually, there are probably many people in foreign countries who have heard of Nebraska but who have never heard of the University of Nebraska football team. Turn it around. Lots of Americans have heard of the English city of Manchester, but how many have heard of Manchester United? Almost none, despite the fact that they may be the most famous team on the planet. But our arrogance is such that we assume that everyone else knows about our teams, even though we know nothing about theirs.

(2) The next set of examples consists of those in which Americans assume that foreigners have no sports of their own that they follow. My first example of this sort is the best, but since I couldn't verify it, I hesitated to use it. But it's too good to pass up. The following is allegedly a quote from a speech by Congressman William Cahill made in the early 1960s to Congress:

> What better medium, for improving race relations in the United States and developing better international relationships through the world, than this great sport of baseball played as it is under ideal conditions prescribed by Little League baseball. Consider, if you will, the rare opportunity of bringing forcefully to the attention of some small South American community, or some village in France, or one of the industrialized cities of Germany, Poland, or even Russia, the rules of conduct, the spirit of fair play and sportsmanship, the competitive spirit and the overall good will of the great American game of baseball as played by their own sons in their own back yard under American rules.[24]

Even though I don't know for sure that Congressman Cahill ever uttered these words, I include them because they reflect so perfectly the ignorance and arrogance of the American sports fan that I want to expose and attack in this book. The typical American sports fan (including me when I was a kid) often sees the rest of the world as entirely bereft of organized team sports. In addition, they believe that the world would be a much better place if only foreigners all played our sports. They believe that we need to bring our sports to them, "forcefully" if necessary. The only qualification here is that sports fans who are also leftists would object to the use of force, but I have no reason to believe that our leftists would object to nonviolent ways of spreading baseball, even though they object to nonviolent ways of spreading other parts of American culture. But I will return to that theme in later chapters.

Another example comes from a conversation I once overheard. It took place between two Americans – in fact, two Minnesotans – in 1980, shortly after the United States had won the gold medal in ice hockey at the Winter Olympics.

> Person 1: "I think the U.S. win was the greatest sporting triumph of the twentieth century."
> Person 2: "Well, I don't know. How about Roger Maris's 61 home runs in a season?"
> Person 1: "I really think that the accomplishment of an entire team means more than the accomplishment of one person."
> Person 2: "Well, then, how about the Minnesota victory over Michigan back in 1977?"

The victory by the University of Minnesota football team over the University of Michigan was pretty much a fluke. It was an off day for Michigan rather than anything special by Minnesota, as far as I can remember. But that isn't the point. The point is that while the first person was probably ignorant of a great many athletes and teams throughout the world, he had at least picked an international event as the greatest sports accomplishment of the twentieth century. The second person couldn't even do that much. His two examples were both taken from American sports. One of these was so parochial that it was from his own home state. How many people today, outside of Minnesota, have heard of this victory? Yet, this person took it as an example that people *throughout the world* might agree with.

Many Americans, of course, have little knowledge of other cultures and no interest in them. However, there are some Americans who have at least some knowledge of other cultures, yet even these people are generally totally ignorant of those cultures' sports. Such people are the foreign correspondents and those scholars who are specialists in the culture of some other country. Such people can be entirely ignorant of the sports of that other country, especially if they came of age in the 1960s or earlier. For example, a number of years ago I read an article about the class

Soccer, the Left, & the Farce of Multiculturalism

distinctions in England, past and present.[25] Now in fact English sports were in the past divided in an interesting way along class lines, with the middle classes preferring rugby and the lower classes preferring soccer. But the writer didn't mention this. Another example comes from a professor at Indiana University who was frustrated trying to keep up with the many changes that occurred in the old Soviet Union when it was on the brink of breaking up. He said, "I've begun to wish that everyone over there would play baseball for a month or so and give me some time to rethink things."[26] It didn't seem to occur to him that they have their own sports that they play over there such as ice hockey, soccer, and even our own basketball.

Some statements are so stupid and bizarre that it is hard to know what to say in response. Consider this, for example:

> While American minds turn to baseball in early autumn, the French think Bordeaux and Burgundy. On each side of the Atlantic, a long season of nurturing quickens into a few decisive days that will bring victory to savor or defeat to nurse through winter's murk. The World Series and the harvest in France's vineyards give each society autumn rituals that span and bind seasons and generations.[27]

As though the French don't have sports of their own starting up in the fall! Anyway, I thought it was during the *spring* that American minds turned to baseball and not early autumn. There was also the State Department official who remarked that "the Soviet game is chess.... Our game is baseball."[28]

Finally, consider the following statement: "The hottest ticket in London isn't a smash West End play or an international tennis match. It's the Chelsea Flower Show." This statement appeared in the *Columbus Dispatch* on a Saturday one May.[29] By coincidence, that Saturday happened to be the very day of England's FA Cup, which the author of the article apparently knew nothing about. By an even greater coincidence, one of the teams playing in that year's FA Cup – and in fact the eventual winner – was Chelsea! How could an American in London on that day not know about this event? Yet, that sort of thing happens all the time. Countless Americans have been in England and for all I know in the suburb of Wembley on the day of the FA Cup and have been utterly oblivious. Of course, the *Dispatch* makes no pretensions to being a sophisticated newspaper, but one can find such howlers even in those newspapers that are more sophisticated. For example, the movie reviewer for *The New York*

Times admitted he had never heard of David Beckham before the film bearing his name reached America.[30]

(3) Now let me take up those examples showing that Americans assume that soccer isn't widely followed in the rest of the world. At the start of the 1998 World Cup, an American bond trader dealing with foreign investments talked about how suddenly, "The market just died.... Traders just weren't reacting."[31] It had died because everyone in the foreign markets had left their desks to go watch the first game. But in America that hadn't happened, and this trader couldn't understand at first what was going on.

Even with the rise of soccer in America, there are still many people who are totally ignorant of how widespread and popular soccer is in the rest of the world. My wife Sarah has a younger relative who decided to do a report for school on the city of Cambridge, England. She was about ten or eleven at the time, and when I told her that the most popular team in town was the Cambridge United soccer team, she exclaimed with amazement, "A soccer team!?" Apparently, nothing that she had ever been told before had prepared her to accept this information. For her, soccer was a minor sport compared with our sports and that was true not just in our country, but everywhere in the world. If this had happened in the 1960s when no one in America knew about soccer, her ignorance would have been understandable. But many books had been written about soccer for Americans in the meantime, plus we had had Pelé come to our country as a soccer missionary. By the time this conversation took place (the 1990s) Americans should have been past such ignorance. Yet, such ignorance still existed. (What was she being taught in school?)

Another example occurred when I was on a first date with a woman I had met at a party. She seemed particularly interested in learning about foreign cultures and she seemed interested in me. It seemed like a nice combination. At some point on this date, I was starting to tell her about Brazil's tragic loss to Uruguay in the 1950 World Cup. She interrupted me and said, "And no one showed up at the game. Right?" Any hope that this would be a viable relationship went out the window at that moment. And this ridiculous comment came from a woman who bragged about how she respected other cultures, yet she couldn't respect Brazil enough to understand that soccer is highly popular there.

One of the big themes today is globalization. One complaint about globalization is that the same American culture is emerging everywhere. There are McDonald's everywhere, there are the same American television shows everywhere, and so on. In fact, though, this process first began with soccer a century ago. Within a few short years, there was soccer just about everywhere. Only Americans ignored this siren call, with the result that now Americans tend to say the process has just begun, instead of acknowledging that it began at least a century ago with soccer.

Another example occurred after the 2002 World Cup from a writer who said, "I have no idea what the most popular sport is in the Muslim countries.... Soccer is popular in some African countries."[32] Where was this writer in 1998 when the U.S. played Iran in that year's World Cup? Didn't he read anything about that match and how much it meant to the Iranians? And as for the idea that soccer is popular in *some* African countries, which African countries is it *not* popular in?

Then there is an example from *The Nation* written back in the 1960s. The writer complained about plans to bring some soccer teams to America. He observed that soccer is "played, believe it or not, in 131 nations."[33] It is true that this writer knew about soccer's widespread popularity, but I include it because he talked as though he expected most Americans to be ignorant of this fact. In fact, he talked as though he expected Americans not even to believe it if they didn't see it in print. He adds that soccer's popularity is due to the fact that "literally anybody is smart enough to kick a large ball." This sneering comment, of course, takes us back to the usual prejudice I have been talking about. More important for my purposes right now, though, is that he assumed that Americans were ignorant of soccer's worldwide popularity.

Finally, the last two examples I'm going to give are ones that I run across all the time, but for this particular type of example nothing is actually said one way or another about soccer and other foreign sports. It is just that one *expects* them to be mentioned. The first example comes from a long article in *Time* magazine about the millions of Latino immigrants who have come to America and the culture they are bringing with them.[34] The article has photographs of some kids playing basketball and someone else getting ready to jog. Nothing is said in the text about soccer (or for that matter, baseball). And this is what is so strange. Isn't the immigration of millions of soccer fans to this country going to affect our sports scene? After all, there are so many immigrants from Mexico that Mexico's national team often plays home games in Los Angeles. But the writers of this article (and many others just like it) were in denial about that.

The second example is an article on Pakistan in *National Geographic*. Now there are only two references to sports in the whole article. The first is a photo showing a movie theater with a poster advertising a martial-arts movie, and the second is a photo of some boys at a boys school engaged in a tug of war.[35] Nothing is said about the main sport, which is cricket. Why? Either the writer didn't notice it, or if he did, he didn't think it was worth mentioning, or if he did think it was worth mentioning, his editor thought it wasn't worth mentioning. Whatever the case may be, the result was that Americans were not informed about an important part of Pakistani culture.

(4) Now I want to mention what foreigners say about their own sports. Foreigners, of course, write many books on soccer and other foreign sports. Only a small fraction of these books ever make it into our bookstores and libraries. On those occasions when I have a chance to travel abroad, I make a point of picking up those books that are impossible to obtain in the United States. With the rise of Amazon.com and more particularly of Amazon.co.uk, we aren't so cut off anymore. But it is still nice to actually look at a book in a bookstore before you buy it.

Probably the most famous soccer book (in the English-speaking world) in recent years has been Nick Hornby's *Fever Pitch*. In fact, this was his first book, and it was followed by others such as *High Fidelity* that Americans are more familiar with. Most Americans who have heard of Hornby seem unaware of his status as the most famous soccer fan in the English-speaking world and talk of him in completely different terms. That, of course, is just another instance of our ignorance.

There are any number of quotes about soccer that one can find from foreigners, but the following perhaps is the best. It comes from an article in the *Economist* entitled, "God falls, grown men weep" and it began as follows:

> As news of the disaster spread, men and women hurried to the scene. Surely it could not be true? But it was true, horribly true. From the several hundred fanatical followers who gathered on January 8th at the gates of their shrine, St. James' Park, there came a terrible lamentation at the rending asunder of their dreams – Kevin Keegan's resignation from the job of God, a post sometimes mundanely described as manager of the Newcastle United soccer team.[36]

In the midst of this amusing hyperbole, we also learn that "Tony Blair, who rates a kickabout with Mr. Keegan the best photo-opportunity of his career as Labour Party leader, issued a statement of regret."

Soccer, the Left, & the Farce of Multiculturalism

Most movies shown in America are made in America, so there is little to misunderstand. But occasionally foreign films come here, and the situation changes. I never saw the movie *Trainspotting*, and I only read part of the book, but I didn't have to read very far into it to realize that the narrator had a Catholic background. You could tell it simply by noticing what soccer team he was rooting for. If you understand Scottish soccer, this is easy to discern, but how many other Americans picked up on this? In the movie *Gregory's Girl*, the main character is shown in his bedroom at one point, and he has a poster for the team Partick Thistle on his wall. Partick Thistle is a neutral team as far as religions go. In Glasgow the Protestants favor Rangers and the Catholics favor Celtic, but Partick Thistle is neutral. Perhaps we are also supposed to recognize that the main character is a bit of a loser, but on that point I am less certain. (One soccer fan from Scotland told me that when he was growing up, he thought that Partick Thistle's name was "Partick Thistle Nil," because the word "nil" was always mentioned when its scores were being given.) The movie *Fever Pitch*, based on Hornby's book and which is about a crazed Arsenal fan, for the longest time didn't even make it to America, despite the fact that it starred Colin Firth. It eventually made it to New York, but I don't believe it ever got to where I live. In fact, it had to be remade as a baseball film in order to become successful in America.

Another foreign movie that relates to soccer was *The Marriage of Maria Braun*. During the last five or ten minutes of this film, the main character and her husband are sitting in their living room while a soccer game blares on the radio in the background. I myself didn't recognize initially that this was a soccer game, because my German was not good enough, and in fact from the frequent references to "Deutschland" I thought it was some kind of political rally. It wasn't until a goal was scored that I figured it out, and at that point I began listening more closely, and from one of the names mentioned (Puskas) figured out that it was the World Cup Final of 1954. The movie ends with a freak gas explosion killing the two, just as the radio announcer shouts out that West Germany has won the World Cup. But here is how it was described in a review in *The New Yorker*:

> Also a radio voice ... rises near the film's end to an authentic epiphany ("*Der grossartige Fussballspieler aus Budapest!*"), of soccer scores.[37]

The reviewer understands what most Americans seeing it perhaps didn't understand, that somehow the end of the film has some link to soccer, but she thinks that the rise of the radio voice is associated with the mere recitation of soccer scores. Instead, it was just one score that was being announced, for the voice was excitedly telling the audience that the West German team had defied the odds in beating the better team, Hungary, and so had just won the World Cup. In the television series *Red Dwarf*, the computer Holly at one point insists that something said was hogwash; only he says it differently. "That's a lot of Tottenham, that is. A steaming pile of Hotspur."[38] How many Americans understood that this referred to a soccer team?

Let me leave movies and TV shows and get back to ordinary statements. Here is one about South Africa: "However much South Africa humbles West Indies at cricket, whatever the pride in the Springbok rugby team, it remains football that liberates the sporting lives of the overwhelming majority of South Africans."[39] Nor should any Americans be unfamiliar (though I assume many nevertheless are unfamiliar) with Osama bin Laden's references to soccer in the transcript of a video he made which was published everywhere on Dec. 14, 2001:

> Abu-Al-Hassan Al-(Masri) ... told me a year ago: "I saw in a dream, we were playing a soccer game against the Americans. When our team showed up in the field, they were all pilots!" He said, "So I wondered if that was a soccer game or a pilot game? Our players were pilots." He ... said the game went on and we defeated them.

And as part of the video, a speaker named Sulayman Abu Guaith said:

> Do you know when there is a soccer game and your team wins? It was the same expression of joy.

Actually, although the transcript of this video was published everywhere in the U.S., I can't remember anyone commenting on the soccer aspect of it.

Of course, foreigners are also thrilled about other sports, such as cricket. Here is a clue about how Australians feel about perhaps the best cricket player ever, their own Donald Bradman. "The cricketing legend Sir Donald Bradman is seen by many Australians as their country's ideal first president if the Queen is rejected in the November 6 referendum."[40] This was despite the fact that he was 91 years old at the time. In addition,

Nelson Mandela's first question of an Australian after being released from prison was whether Bradman was still alive.[41]

Finally, the *Economist* once did a long survey of relations between India and Pakistan. The first page was nothing but a photograph of two cricket players, a Pakistani batsman and an Indian wicketkeeper.[42] Cricket is so much a part of these two countries that it was thought appropriate to represent them this way. Contrast this with the treatment of Pakistan mentioned above in the article in our *National Geographic*.

(5) Finally, I want to present statements from foreigners talking about our sports and about us in connection with our sports. A sportswriter from Israel, where soccer is the main sport, once referred to softball and cricket as "oddball sports."[43] Umberto Eco is an Italian who wrote the best-seller *The Name of the Rose*. In another one of his books, *Foucault's Pendulum*, the (Italian) narrator refers to the "senseless waits of baseball."[44] An Englishman, Geoffrey Wheatcroft, in an article about the BBC, says that "an Englishman doesn't suppose that every American recognizes LSE or QPR."[45] (I instantly recognized both, though I doubt if many other Americans my age would be able to do this.) Another Englishman, sportswriter Hugh McIlvanney, says:

> If insularity were a sport, it would be America's game. Rigid isolationism may have fallen out of favour with most politicians, but the majority of the population often behave as if the world begins and ends at their country's borders. And nowhere is that tendency more persistent than in attitudes to sport. How else do we explain the fact that people who played host to the World Cup finals less than three years ago, and to the Olympic Games ... as recently as last summer, can blithely describe the Super Bowl as the greatest sporting event on earth?[46]

Perhaps the most amusing such example, in the novel *Charters and Caldicott* (which in turn was based on a BBC television series), is about two ardent English cricket fans. They are intended to be the same cricket lovers who appear in Alfred Hitchcock's movie *The Lady Vanishes*, except that they are now in their old age. At one point, they are talking to an American businessman who lives in England, but who makes the mistake of calling cricket "association cricket."[47] The two cricket lovers are horrified by this blunder, but this shows that the English take it for granted that an American will be confused about whether the word "association" goes with football or cricket.

Very rarely, our own media gives us a clue about how our sports are received elsewhere. For example, when Johan Cruyff came to town to play against the Minnesota Kicks of the old NASL, here's what he said about the city of Barcelona, where he had previously played:

> There are six magazines like *Sports Illustrated* that come out every day. There are six other newspapers with five or six pages on sports, and it is mainly soccer. There are 75,000 season ticket holders and 200,000 on the waiting list. In Barcelona, soccer is so terribly big.[48]

Another example occurred during the Winter Olympics of 1992. The *Washington Post* reported on what it regarded as the strange behavior of a European sports newspaper: "One of the biggest sports dailies in Europe, *L'Equipe*, refuses to put the Olympics on its front page."[49] The article goes on to state that the editor planned to devote no more than 15 percent of its space to the Olympics. "We can't sell papers with the Olympics," he said. "The Olympics are not that interesting to most people, especially if France does not have good results. The Olympics are suicide. The people would much rather read about soccer."

The *Columbus Dispatch* has had a couple amusing items along these lines. One of them appeared during the 2000 Olympics. One of the sportswriters began asking Australians about the upcoming Ohio State-University of Michigan (football) game.

> "Never heard of that one," said Adrian Condon of Windsor, Australia. "Is it basketball or football?" The OSU-Michigan game? *The Game?* "Never heard of it," said Mark Johnston of Alstonville, Australia…. Isn't anyone getting excited about the Buckeyes and the Wolverines? "No," said Glenn Bosward of Sydney. "What's that? Gridiron? We get to see some gridiron on TV here. Mainly guys don't understand it."[50]

Here is another example:

> It takes just one very long distance phone call to give you the fleeting feeling that the impact of Notre Dame football might not be quite as large as a lot of people think.[51]

The writer of this article had a cousin in Ireland, where Notre Dame was traveling to play an exhibition game. He called his cousin on the phone and asked him about the game. "What's that name?" his cousin asked. "Notre Dame," I said, "the Fighting Irish." "Oh?" said his cousin, and since he was in the Republic of Ireland army, he added, "Maybe they'll be staying in our barracks."

The phone was then handed from his cousin to someone else, who was slightly more knowledgeable. His comment on the whole affair? NFL football had once been shown on Irish television (on a feed from a British channel). "But they don't show the Super Bowl anymore and the interest has dropped. I think there's very little interest in college football."

Another example comes from a writer in Britain, who gives his somewhat quirky view of our sports:

> Everybody knows that basketball, like the two other main American sports of baseball and gridiron football, is indescribably dull, which is the main reason why none of them has yet made a successful transfer across the Atlantic. The other reason is that we already have perfectly good versions of all three sports: netball is a more than adequate substitute for basketball and avoids the distraction of having to bounce the ball; rounders is superior to baseball and require no 80,000-seater stadium; differential equations satisfy the desire of some people to do difficult sums, which is the only appeal of American football.[52]

Admittedly, this person is a little naive, for basketball has crossed the Atlantic, just not to Britain. But it is popular in places like Spain. And this business about differential equations and sums I can't quite figure out. One would have expected him to mention rugby here. But aside from these quirks, what is so striking is *his claim that our sports are dull*. We Americans are so used to saying that soccer is dull that it simply doesn't occur to us that other people might find our sports dull. But if one considers the matter fairly, one has to realize that saying something is dull is generally a very subjective judgment, which leaves open the possibility that others may have a different opinion on the matter. However, our "Iron Curtain of Sports" prevents us from hearing such heretical opinions expressed very often.

One such occasion when our media did allow us to hear such opinions was after baseball had been allowed into the Olympics. The Soviet Union sent over some observers to see what the game was like, and one of our sports columnists had this to say on their visit: "Ever try talkin' baseball to someone who has never seen it? Or scarcely heard of it?" He reported that one of the Russians said, "To me it seems as though only two (the pitcher and catcher) are having fun. The others are standing around, freezing." After an inning, the Russians decided they had seen enough.[53]

Another example was one I watched on television in which an English soccer player (Alan Merrick of the Minnesota Kicks) who had come to the United States to play professional soccer commented on our version of football, which he was seeing for the first time. He indicated that he liked it, but he then added that he had seen not an actual game but a tape and that all the huddles and time-outs had been edited out. This suggested that he had been used to hearing criticisms of our sports that complained about all the time outs and stoppages in play.

Then there was the recent remark by a manager in England who claimed that using technology to determine whether a goal had actually been scored would lengthen the game to four hours and turn it into American football. This would make it boring, he said.[54]

Finally, an article in one of our newspapers commented on how many baseball bats are sold overseas, even though no one actually plays the game. The bats are used instead to commit crimes or to protect against burglars. One salesman at a store in Northern Ireland, where they sell plenty of bats, said, "Funnily enough, I don't know of any baseball teams [in the area]."[55]

These are a mere selection of the many thousands of statements made by people, both Americans and foreigners, that could be used. I have used only those I happened to run across, but obviously any thorough researcher who went through all of the newspapers and magazines published in the last thirty-five years (which is how long I have been collecting such statements) would find many more such statements than I have. Notice that most of the observations in the fourth and fifth sets were in the foreign media rather than ours. Only a few of them could be found in our media, which shows how rigid and impenetrable that Iron Curtain of Sports is.

The fact is that American sports exist in a critical vacuum. Fans of American sports are coddled by the American media. Typically, the American media doesn't allow much in the way of any fundamental criticisms of American sports to be published. Soccer has managed to survive in America in spite of the hostility of the American media and most

American sports fans. But how long would baseball or football last if they had to put up with such hostility? My guess is, not very long.

One result of this critical vacuum is the stifling of our curiosity. At the time when I first got involved in soccer, not even the most sophisticated and intelligent of our citizens knew a single thing about foreign sports like soccer and cricket (a statement which is still largely true today). If you wanted to find an American who had learned Swahili, you could probably have found an American who had learned Swahili. If you wanted to find an American who had learned to play the Indonesian musical instrument called the gamelan, you could probably have found an American gamelan player. And if you wanted to find an American who had studied Ukrainian film, you could probably have found an American with expertise in Ukrainian film. But if you wanted to find an American knowledgeable about soccer or cricket, you weren't going to have any luck because such people weren't to be found. Our curiosity had been stifled. We had learned not to see certain things when we went abroad and not to be interested in them if we didn't go abroad.

Another result of the critical vacuum is that Americans often sound terribly naive when it comes to sports. When I first got involved, I began talking to people about our national team. People would hesitantly ask, "Are you talking about an Olympics team?" Of course I wasn't talking about an Olympics team! An Olympics team, like it or not, is the equivalent of a junior varsity team, while the national team is the varsity. The national team consists of the best players, no matter what their amateur status or their age is. How many people throughout the world do not know what a national team is? Besides Americans, it is limited to young children and those who live in isolated jungles in the Amazon or New Guinea. Everyone else knows.

Another example of this naivete is that Americans typically talk about how obsessed we are with sports, without ever making any cross-cultural comparisons. Are we more obsessed with sports or less obsessed than people in other countries? When Americans make this sort of statement, they typically have no idea. James Michener was one American who took the trouble to find out. After investigating sports throughout the world, he divided countries into four tiers based on how obsessed they were with sports. In the first tier were countries like Brazil that he said had levels of sports obsession that Americans would find hard to comprehend. Significantly, he placed the United States in neither the first tier nor the second tier, but way down in the third.[56]

Another aspect of the critical vacuum is the naivete about quintessentialism. American baseball fans are always talking about how baseball is the quintessential American sport. The English used to do that with cricket, but the fact is that today the best cricket players are no longer English. Likewise, the best soccer players are no longer English, but Brazilian. I vividly remember the ice hockey series between Canada and the Soviet Union in 1972. A friend and I were roommates, and we discussed the series before the first game. Actually, I was reluctant to voice an opinion because I knew that he was much more versed in sports than I was. I felt that the Soviets would do well, but he predicted that the Soviets would hold their own for a period or maybe two, after which the Canadians would blow them away. Instead, it was the Canadians who were blown away. Not only was my friend totally shocked by this result, it caused a huge nationwide shock in Canada (where it was thought that hockey was quintessentially Canadian).

A somewhat similar event, though much more subdued, occurred to the United States in the 1998 Winter Olympics that took place in Japan. The U.S. ice hockey team, because it had happened to win an international championship the year before, was convinced that it was going to do extremely well in this Olympics, that it was in fact going to win the gold medal. In the event, it not only didn't win the gold, but didn't even come close to winning *any* medals. How did this happen? The reason it happened is familiar to anyone who follows international soccer. There are no guaranteed wins, not even for Brazil. Moreover, the international tournament that the U.S. had won the previous year involved games that took place solely in North America. In soccer's World Cup, only one country has won this event outside of its hemisphere: Brazil. No one else has done this. Consequently, when the U.S. team went to Japan, there simply wasn't any guarantee that they were going to win, no matter how well they had done the year before.

To get back to my point, people who say that a certain sport is *quintessentially* their sport are almost bound to be disappointed. If no one else takes up their sport, then they will be disappointed for that reason. But if others do take it up, then sooner or later some other country is going to regard that statement as a challenge, and they will do everything they can to beat you. In fact, this has happened in baseball, even if only at the Little League level. Taiwanese teams have won many championships in the Little League World Series. Because it *is* only the Little League, most Americans pay no attention.

To see how people in soccer look at this matter of what is quintessential, consider the example of the Dutch. Holland has produced many fine teams over the past forty years. Several of them should have won the World Cup, for they were in the final game twice, in 1974 and again in 1978. But they lost both times, and they have managed to self-destruct on numerous other occasions. All they have to show for their sporting excellence is a single European Championship (in 1988). No doubt if the Dutch had invented soccer and were virtually the only ones playing it, then they too would be talking about how soccer was a quintessentially Dutch game. Instead, they must say something else, and to see what that something else is, one can do no better than to look at the excellent book *Brilliant Orange*, by David Winner. *Brilliant Orange* is a study of Dutch soccer and Dutch culture, and Winner says that Holland's unaccountably poor record given the number of stars they have exhibits "a quintessentially Dutch combination of ill-discipline, complacency and lack of nerve."[57] This is what Americans might be saying about American baseball if it were ever to become the world sport that soccer is and if, as would be likely sooner or later, we began losing big matches.

Incidentally, Winner also reports that for the Dutch, the loss to West Germany in the World Cup of 1974 represented a catastrophe as large as the assassination of President Kennedy was for us.[58] In other words, a sporting event that most Americans have never even heard of had an enormous effect on the Dutch psyche. This just goes to show how ignorant we can be about other cultures.

To conclude this section, let me quote an immigrant to the United States (Andrés Martinez) on the eve of the 2002 World Cup:

> For New York City, World Cups can be an awkward time, a rare instance when the city's claim to be the world's capital is belied by the uneven level of interest in the matches. "We are so removed from this global festival here," laments Inocencio Arias, Spain's ambassador to the United Nations, who just wrote a book about the Real Madrid, Spain's most venerable team. I agree – though otherwise adjusted to American society, I feel as if I've been exiled to the ends of the earth every four years.[59]

Although this was published in the prestigious *New York Times*, how many *Times* readers were influenced by these statements to pay attention to soccer? One suspects, not many.

The Use of Inaccurate and Harmful Stereotypes

Another characteristic of those who are prejudiced is that they gleefully accept inaccurate and harmful stereotypes. The stereotype in America of the overseas soccer fan is that he is violent. The American media loves to hate soccer, and what it loves in particular is to report upon soccer violence in the rest of the world. Of course, this violence is never looked at with any sort of perspective. The only thing that makes the editors of American newspapers gleeful is that it is occurring. That is all that is necessary for them to consider it newsworthy.

Yet, a great deal more could be said about soccer violence. To begin with, there was very little soccer violence when I was a child, and to the extent that it existed, it was associated with Latin America. The soccer violence that began to afflict England in the 1980s was rare. Soccer had existed rather peacefully in England for over a century without this sort of behavior becoming a problem. But suddenly it emerged, and the American media lapped it up. The reasons for its emergence are complicated and are little understood, even by the English. For example, Nick Hornby in *Fever Pitch*, imagines that this violence automatically came from lower-class young men.[60] Yet, such men had participated in soccer for generations without exhibiting that kind of behavior.

Another thing to be noted about soccer violence is that our soccer haters imagine that it occurs all over Europe on a frequent basis when in fact most of it occurs in England, and when it doesn't it is often incited by English fans. There have been games between Croatia and Yugoslavia unmarred by violence, but this is ignored by those who hate soccer. During the 1994 World Cup here in America, the police in the New York/New Jersey area deployed a huge number of police officers to control the crowds at the Ireland-Italy game. As an exasperated editorialist in the *Irish Times* put it, "One peep out into the big world to ascertain what was happening in the spheres of politics, or even soccer, over the last half decade or so would have told them that Ireland isn't England, that Irish soccer fans aren't English soccer fans."[61] Even soccer violence among the English hooligans has largely been brought under control by the British government, and now it is only when the hooligans travel to other countries that they can engage in their violent behavior, yet Americans act as though hooliganism is *still* a problem at games in England. To be blunt, those Americans who attack soccer because of the violence it engenders are xenophobes who know nothing very specific about what is going on in other countries.

Thirdly, one of the most persistent objections against soccer made by the soccer haters is that it is boring, but why would a boring sport incite violence? This is never explained by the soccer haters. No one expects a riot at a golf tournament, with which soccer has sometimes been compared. Why, then, would anyone expect soccer to produce such violence? It is obvious that the people who attack soccer *both* because it is boring *and* because it incites violence wish to attack soccer any way they can. The soccer hater might object, "I'm not being inconsistent here. The fact is that anyone who likes soccer is already so stupid that they can't tell that soccer is boring." Of course, such a statement shows an abysmal attitude towards foreigners, and no doubt should count as hate speech, but even this defense won't work. The reason is that if foreigners are that stupid, we can still ask why they don't also riot at golf tournaments. Many foreigners like both soccer and golf, and if they are stupid enough to believe that soccer is so exciting that there is cause to riot, then why wouldn't they make the same mistake about golf? The soccer hater in America never wants to be fair to soccer. Anyway, even if foreigners are stupid about sports, we Americans can be just as stupid. We put up with games that have frequent and pointless interruptions in the action. And only in America do people voluntarily support sports that spit on them for being the wrong size (more on this point later) or that cannot be easily played on a casual basis.

Fourthly, our media tends to ignore the occasional soccer violence that has a point to it. They prefer to focus on mindless violence, but sometimes soccer violence has a political point to it that people in the United States can relate to. For example, in the late 1980s, there was a sudden flare-up of violence between Dutch and German soccer fans, a flare-up related to anger over World War II. One might wonder why it flared up over forty years after the war ended, but I leave it to the reader to investigate that topic. The point is that it happened and that Americans could probably relate to it. For that very reason, perhaps, it went largely unreported in our media.

Fifthly, we have our own occasional violence after sporting events. There have been riots in recent years in connection with the NBA championships. Somehow, the soccer haters don't imagine that our own sporting violence puts our sports on par with soccer. Mostly, too, our own sporting violence goes unreported nationally. There is frequent violence after the football games at big universities, but any outrageous behavior that the fans engage in is something that makes the local news only.

To digress a moment, let me note the inconsistent views of Americans concerning ice hockey. People who don't like ice hockey are always putting the game down because of its violence. It is true that something could be done about the fighting in the NHL, something that is done in the high schools and colleges (namely, penalize it as harshly as possible). Likewise, every time there is a boxing match one can be sure that there will be letters to the editor denouncing this "barbarian" sport. However, it is ridiculous for people who love football to talk about the violence in *other* sports while ignoring the violence in their own sport. James Michener, in his book *Iberia*, recounts an argument between an American and a Spaniard about bullfighting. The American denounces bullfighting because of the death of the bull, but the conversation takes an unexpected turn for the American when the Spaniard points out that every year in America there are a number of people who die playing football.[62] Generally, these are people playing football on high school teams, but such deaths are largely unnoticed by the general public, except in the locality where the death occurs. Not only do people die, but there are also the people who are maimed for life. Most of the time, the media ignores stars who have retired, but occasionally the newspapers run articles about past football stars and what they are doing today. Often, these stars took such a beating during their playing days that they can barely walk, even though they are only in their thirties or forties. Nevertheless, the controlled violence on a football field is acceptable for the soccer hater, although the riots in conjunction with a soccer match aren't.

Sixthly, much of the violence in soccer is the result of the fact that it is easy for people in England to travel to an away game. It is so easy and such a part of life there that entire sections of the stadiums are reserved for visitors. I have been to many soccer games in America, and when I was growing up I went to numerous other athletic events. Except for high school games, there were hardly ever any opposing fans in the stadium, and if there were, they came in such small numbers that there wasn't much point in segregating them. But it is completely different in England. I once attended a soccer game at Wembley between England and France at which there must have been at least five thousand French fans in attendance. I have seen nothing like this in the United States in connection with our sports (except at some U.S.-Mexico World Cup qualifying matches). Perhaps it happens in the Northeast and middle Atlantic coastal areas where the population densities and short distances can support such things, but where I grew up it was unknown. Since the presence of large numbers of opposing fans is a factor (although just one such) that is likely to incite violence, then such violence is much more likely to occur in Europe than it is here.

Moreover, so what if there is soccer violence in Europe, *given that Europe is considerably less violent than America is*? So what if our own sports don't incite violence among fans, given that our society is so much more violent in general? When I have traveled abroad, whether to Rio de Janeiro or Cairo or the cities of Europe, I have generally felt safe, whereas there are many American cities where I have traveled where I haven't felt safe, especially at night. Perhaps, then, these facts are related. Perhaps the violence of soccer fans is what makes those societies less violent, the soccer violence acting as a sort of safety valve which dissipates the even more violent behavior that we experience here in America. For that matter, soccer is very much a sport for the lower-classes in Europe. The stadia often have cheap tickets to reflect that fact. Here in America, sporting events are geared toward the middle classes. Every ticket is for a seat, unless a game is sold out, in which case standing room tickets are sold. But in England many of the stadia have entire sections reserved for standing. In the wake of recent violence, many of these stadia were redesigned, and it is sometimes said that there are no more standing-room sections in England. That is false, because I have stood in some of them quite recently. But my point is that we manage to keep the class of people who are more likely to be violent out of our stadiums. Is it any wonder, then, that our games are more peaceful than foreign soccer games?

Occasionally, a soccer hater will mention a war in Central America that was touched off by a soccer game back in 1969. What this is supposed to show is that soccer is this dreadful sport that no one ought to support. Perhaps it does show that soccer is a dreadful sport, but this example also shows something else, something that the soccer basher doesn't want to hear, namely that in order to be up on current events, in order to understand international affairs totally, you have to follow certain international sports like soccer, even if you despise them.

Down through the years, I have noted a number of international incidents in which soccer played a part, though Americans were often ignorant of this fact.

(1) The short truce in the Biafran War in Nigeria in the late 1960s, which was declared so that both sides could get to see Pelé play.

(2) The dissatisfaction that led to the Hungarian Revolution of 1956 began with Hungary's loss in the World Cup Final of 1954, a game that

everyone agrees they should have won. This was told to me by a woman of Hungarian descent who lived through this revolution and is now a professor of sociology.

(3) A transfer of payments made by Argentina to Peru in the 1978 World Cup that allowed Argentina to beat Peru by at least four goals, which meant they could go on to play in the final of that year.[63]

(4) The loss by Labor of the 1970 election in Britain, which was blamed on the elimination of England four days earlier from the World Cup, according to one source.[64] Another source adds that "some historians speculate that England's football defeat was responsible for the death of British socialism."[65]

(5) The trauma the Dutch felt in 1974 when they lost the World Cup to West Germany, which has been compared to the trauma we Americans felt after the assassination of President Kennedy.[66]

These are the incidents that I learned about on my own. Franklin Foer in his book *Soccer Explains the World* adds many more.[67]

One last point about the stereotype of soccer violence. While those Americans who hate soccer, and even those who are indifferent, imagine that this is the worst problem that soccer faces, as I already argued earlier the worst problem is in fact money. But those who are prejudiced don't want to think about such things.

Bad Reasons for Hostility

People who are prejudiced generally give bad reasons for their hostility. The Jews obviously have very good reasons for hating the Nazis, namely the six million Jews that were killed by the Nazis in concentration camps in World War II. During the Cold War, we Americans had good reasons for our hostility to the Soviet Union, namely that they wanted to "bury" us. They wanted to take us over and impose their totalitarian system on us. By contrast, people who are prejudiced often have very bad reasons for hating what they hate, reasons that are easy to see through. The same thing is true of the soccer haters. Their reasons for hating soccer are easily demolished, are easily seen to be freighted with massive self-contradictions or else stupidity.

Traditionally, there have been three reasons given for hating soccer. The first reason is that it is a wimp sport. One doesn't hear this reason as much these days as when I first got involved, though I still detect it on occasion. Yes, it is true that soccer is a wimp sport, at least in comparison to football. Obviously, football is a much rougher sport than soccer is. But why must the comparison be made with football *only*? Why not compare soccer, in terms of wimpness, with baseball and basketball? The truth is that baseball and basketball are just as much wimp sports in comparison with football as soccer is. In fact, truth be told, they are probably *more* wimpish than soccer is. If soccer is worthless because it is a wimp sport in comparison with football, then baseball and basketball are worthless, too. If, because soccer is worthless, it doesn't deserve any coverage in our media, then baseball and basketball, because they are also worthless, don't deserve any coverage in our media, either. Of course, the soccer haters would never dream of drawing such a conclusion, which helps to show that they are prejudiced.

(Incidentally, one of the ways in which Americans show their ignorance of soccer is that often when they see it for the first time, they are astonished at how rough it is. "I thought this was supposed to be a non-violent sport," one such person said.)

But what about football itself? Isn't it a wimp sport in comparison with some other sports? American football is more wimpish in comparison with Canadian football, where fair catches aren't allowed. It is arguable that American football is more wimpish in comparison with rugby as well. Football players are protected behind a great deal of padding, whereas rugby players aren't. Doesn't that make football players more wimpish than rugby players? (I once found a comment on the Internet from a rugby fan who sneered at football for being nothing but soccer with pads on.) One can find even more macho sports, if one cares to look. In his novel *Caravans*, James Michener describes a game that he calls Afghan polo, a game in which it is not unusual for people to be killed during the action.[68] For that matter, the gladiators of ancient Rome often fought to the death. Why shouldn't our sports be the same, if wimpishness isn't going to be allowed? How rugged is football really, if people never (or, remembering Michener's Spaniard, rarely) die when playing it?

It goes almost without saying that those who have advanced the argument that soccer is a wimp sport have never demanded that we eliminate football in favor of something even less wimpish. Denigrating soccer because of its wimpishness, then, is just a feeble excuse to attack it.

Another point here is that those who denigrate soccer because of its wimpishness are comparing the playing of soccer versus the playing of football. *But most people don't play football.* They watch it. How hard is it to watch football? Almost anyone can watch a football game. Only the most delicate and fragile of personalities will find the violence of football too brutal even to watch. So why is football considered such a macho sport when most people aren't actually playing it? By contrast, lots of people *play* soccer. I am 58 years old, but I still occasionally play. How many guys my age are playing football? None. I agree that playing football is more macho than playing soccer, but playing soccer is more macho than merely watching football, which is what most people are doing.

The second objection to soccer is that it is boring, and it is supposed to be boring because it has low scoring. I have already devoted a whole chapter to this topic, but for my purposes now let me make two points. If soccer is supposed to be dull because it is low-scoring, why is it that those who make this charge pay no more attention to indoor soccer than they do to outdoor soccer, *even though indoor soccer has more scoring*? Indoor soccer, for whatever reason, usually has more scoring than regular soccer does. In fact, it reaches the levels typical in a baseball game, yet the whiners aren't satisfied. The second point is that those who denigrate soccer because of its low-scoring quality *aren't any happier with cricket and rugby, which are high-scoring sports*. Rugby has about the same amount of scoring as football does, yet it has even less of a following in this country than soccer does. As for cricket, it is the highest-scoring of all the sports I have been talking about (that is, the American sports of baseball, football, and basketball and the British sports of soccer, cricket, and rugby). Scores in a cricket game easily get above two hundred points, which puts it way ahead of basketball as far as scoring goes. Yet, the soccer haters of this country like cricket no more than they like soccer. In fact, they probably like it even less.

Low scoring, then, has nothing to do with their hostility. It is just a handy way to attack soccer while hiding their prejudice.

The third objection against soccer is that it is not "our" sport. It is a foreign sport. It was invented elsewhere. To be sure, soccer *was* invented elsewhere. But of our three main sports, only basketball was truly invented here out of nothing. (And it was invented by a Canadian who was living in America.) Both football and baseball have roots in English sports. Football was invented from some form of English football (probably rugby rather than soccer) that crossed the Atlantic and that we tinkered with until we got something we liked. Baseball probably emerged from the English game of rounders. We imagine that baseball was invented in America, but it wasn't until I got involved in soccer that I found out that the English insist that it is nothing but their game of rounders, a game whose origins are lost in the mists of time. For that matter, baseball is mentioned right in the first couple pages of Jane Austen's *Northanger Abbey*, which was originally written in 1803, and 1803 is long before the alleged invention of baseball by Abner Doubleday. It is true that her novel didn't get published until 1818, by which time it may have been revised, but even that date precedes the alleged invention of baseball by at least twenty years.

But the most important point here is that wherever soccer was invented shouldn't matter a whit to any true, unprejudiced sports fan. No American golfer cares that golf was invented in Scotland rather than America. And no American tennis player cares that tennis was invented somewhere else. Millions of Americans play these sports. Moreover, the same sports pages that turn up their noses at covering "foreign" sports like soccer and cricket think nothing of covering golf and tennis. Finally, ice hockey was invented elsewhere, yet no one shuns it for that reason. Many readers of this book may not remember the excitement that was generated when the United States won the gold medal in hockey in the 1980 Olympics. No one at that time, even those who criticized soccer for its foreign origins, felt any need to attack hockey, despite its having been invented elsewhere. Most Americans, whether they knew it or not, felt the same way that many people in soccer-playing countries do when they are up against a country that is known to be highly skilled at soccer: they feel that they have something to prove and that they are going to beat the other guys at their own game.

In short, we find the same sort of inconsistency about this reason that we find with the other reasons.

In addition, attacking soccer because it was invented elsewhere isn't very bright. The other reasons given at least made some sort of sense, because they had something to do intrinsically with sports. But rejecting a sport because of where it was invented is just plain dumb. No true sports fan cares where a sport was invented. If it is an exciting sport, then why deny yourself some of that excitement just because it happens to have been invented elsewhere? On the other hand, if it is a dull sport, then that alone is sufficient reason to avoid the sport in question. If it is somewhere in between, then one will be devoted to it to the extent that one finds it interesting and exciting. Whatever the case may be, the sport's origins ought to have nothing to do with whether a true sports lover likes a sport.

Look at the matter from another angle. What would the soccer hater do if it turned out that some archeologists discovered that one of our three sports had been played ages ago in some lost civilization? Suppose that football had been played in central Africa five thousand years ago. Wouldn't that mean that football was no longer an American sport? Would the soccer haters then give up on football? You can bet your life they wouldn't.

Look at it from still another angle. Lovers of American sports want me to love those sports simply because they are *American* sports, but why shouldn't some other geographical area matter more to me? Since America is part of Western civilization, then why shouldn't I care about every sport invented in Western civilization? If I am told that I ought to care more for my country than for Western civilization, then I will point out that my country's highest ideals are the products of Western civilization. I will also point out that even if I hated the rest of Western civilization, that is not a good reason for rejecting their sports. If it is, then consider some other examples of hatred. Americans who live in the South have adopted the Yankee sports of football and baseball, even though they used to hate (and for all I know, still do hate) those areas. Why, then, shouldn't I like soccer, even if I were to hate the English? And if I am still supposed to hate soccer because I hate the English, then shouldn't Southerners hate football and baseball because they were invented by Yankees? I just don't see any reason why I should care for our sports, just because they were invented by us.

Instead of choosing my favorite sports on the basis of my country, I might want to choose them on the basis of some *smaller* geographical unit. "If I am not allowed to like foreign sports because they were invented by foreigners, why stop there?" I ask. Why not go further? The rules for football were mostly invented at Harvard. As a Midwesterner who didn't go to Harvard, why should I care about it? The rules for baseball were mostly invented in New York City (and England). Since I'm not from New York City and have never lived there, why should I care? Basketball was invented in Massachusetts, and again, I'm not from there and have never lived there, so why should I care? I could insist that I will play only those sports invented by Midwesterners. In fact, I could go further and insist that I will play only those sports invented by Minnesotans, or by Minneapolitans, or by those who went to my high school, or by those who grew up in my neighborhood, or by those who lived in my household, or (finally) by me. The sort of nativism that American sports fans favor leads, ultimately, to everyone inventing a sport and playing it by themselves. There simply is no stopping nativism, once you get going. It is the sort of argument that we philosophers call a slippery-slope argument because once you get on it, you slide all the way down to some absurdity. The absurdity in this case is that if everyone invented their own sports and played only those sports, no one would be playing a sport with anyone else.

Look at it from yet another angle. If I am supposed to reject all foreign-invented *sports*, why shouldn't I reject all foreign-invented things, *whatever they may be*? Take business suits, for example. These were invented by the same people who invented soccer, the English. The business suit goes nicely with the English climate, which is never especially hot, but here in the United States it is often perfectly ridiculous. I lived in Houston briefly, for a couple months in the summer, to be exact. There is no point in wearing a business suit in Houston in the summer, yet men in Houston voluntarily endure this kind of torture every year. The same can be said of men in New York and Washington, D.C. Many of the men in these cities are the same sort of people who are adamant that I not follow foreign sports.

About twenty-five years ago, there was a big fad (recently revived) for Rubik's cube, the little toy block that could be twisted in a number of different ways. It was invented by a Hungarian. Should I have avoided playing it because it was of foreign origin? One can say the same thing about chess, or many card games. (Poker, it is true, was invented in the United States, but as with baseball, its roots lie elsewhere.) Most ballroom dances, such as the waltz and the tango, were invented elsewhere. Many Americans avoid these dances today because they think they are too unhip, but must we *also* avoid them because they were invented elsewhere?

Many modern inventions were invented by Americans, but not all of them were. Radio was first theorized by James Clerk Maxwell, a Scot, and actually invented by Guglielmo Marconi, an Italian. Better throw out your radios. Since TVs and cell phones depend upon radio waves, better throw them out as well. Automobiles depend upon the internal combustion engine, which was developed by a number of Europeans (such as the German Niklaus August Otto), so better chuck them out, which leaves most of us in a rather desperate situation, given the fact that America is now based on the automobile. The first photographs were done in Europe, so let's chuck out all of our cameras. Many other inventions such as airplanes, while invented here, could not have been invented if foreigners hadn't invented vital parts or come up with crucial ideas.

And what about foods? Pizza comes from Italy. Why should I eat it? Likewise, tacos come from Mexico, so why eat them? If a food wasn't invented right here in good old America, why should I eat it?

Democracy itself is strictly speaking of foreign origin. It was invented in ancient Greece. Better avoid it, then, because it was invented by foreigners. Our own Declaration of Independence relies heavily on the musings of the English philosopher John Locke. Better burn all copies of it and denounce it. Americans have a variety of religious views, but most of them were developed elsewhere. Apparently, we must believe in only those religions that were invented by Americans. No more Catholicism, Judaism, Lutheranism, Presbyterianism, Islam or Buddhism.

What would seem the very height of absurdity is that the very language that we speak was developed by foreigners. Here in America nearly everyone uses English, the language that was developed by the very people who brought the world soccer. (And the people who don't use English are newly arrived immigrants, who have an annoying tendency to play soccer.) Of course, American English is slightly different from English English. They say "flat," and we say "apartment." They say "lorry," and we say "truck." But there is much that is common to both American English and English English, especially basic words such as "the" and "and." Better ditch the English language, then. No more using the words "the" and "and." Anyone who tries to give up English will be hard pressed to find a better language, though, for they were almost all invented by those hated foreigners. I suppose one could take up an American Indian language. Or one could take up Japanese because the Japanese love baseball as much as we do (though lately they have been playing soccer). But every other language is tainted because its speakers play one of those dreadful foreign sports. Again, we are on a slippery slope down to absurdity.

Finally, what the soccer haters don't realize is that their attitudes are very similar to those of the English whom they hate. The English invented soccer and gave it to the rest of the world. Then they turned their backs on that world. The World Cup was invented not by the English but by the French. The English were invited to come, but they turned up their noses at it. The European Cup (now called the Champions League) was also invented elsewhere. The English were invited to join, but again they refused. In addition, they also ignored new tactics that other countries developed. They arrogantly assumed that because they could always beat these other countries, they didn't have to worry about the newfangled ideas. It wasn't until they were beaten 6-3 by Hungary in 1953 that they changed their minds.

Likewise, we didn't invent soccer and the other "foreign" sports, and we turned our backs on the rest of the sporting world. Where did such a reaction come from? Didn't it come from England, the very country that gave the world soccer? Perhaps not, but it is something to think about.

Soccer, the Left, & the Farce of Multiculturalism

Also, contrast our situation with that of Ireland. Ireland has its own sports (hurling and Gaelic football), but it also plays soccer, even though it has some pretty good reasons to hate England. Most other countries simply accepted soccer and joined in with the rest of the world. But we in the United States refused to accept it. England, having invented the sport, refused to accept the new developments in it that happened outside of England. The phrase that best characterizes this is the phrase "insular Englishman," a phrase invented ages ago to describe this aspect of the English character (which applies to other aspects of life besides sports). Accordingly, the best way to describe the typical American who follows sports is to say that he or she is the insular American sports fan. It is true that things are changing, but not so fast as to affect the sports pages of our newspapers.

Another way of looking at this issue can be gleaned from thinking about which country it is that gave the world soccer. As I have been saying, it was England. And England is rather close to us, culturally speaking. Yet, from the animosity I have seen and heard in connection with soccer, anyone would have thought that soccer had been thrust upon us by the old Soviet Union at the height of the Cold War. Instead, it was England that gave us soccer, England, not the Soviet Union, Red China, or Nazi Germany. It wasn't an odious combination of Joseph Stalin, Adolf Hitler, Saddam Hussein, and Osama bin Laden who gave us soccer, but England. It is true that at one time we felt some antagonism towards England, but that was way back in the nineteenth century. That antagonism looks rather laughable today, in light of the conflicts that America faced in the twentieth century and that we face today. Nazi Germany, Imperial Japan, the Soviet Union, Red China, North Korea, North Vietnam, the Taleban, and al-Qaida are all quite distant culturally from both America *and* England. Of course, as America gains more immigrants from Asia and Latin America, our feelings of kinship with England will fade. I myself, although I am of northern European extraction, have no English blood in me. Nor do I even think of myself as an Anglophile. Yet, England has an attraction for us that will doubtless continue. But even if it didn't, the fact is that the America of the twentieth century, which had turned its back on soccer as a foreign sport, had to cope with cultures that were much more distant from us than England was. Hating soccer because of its English roots is just plain pathetic.

It might be suggested that soccer is foreign in terms of the *values* it espouses. However, I think it would be surprising if sports as different as baseball, football, and basketball *all* expressed American values. What is it that they have in common that other sports don't have? It can't be high scoring, because that would mean that cricket and rugby would also count as American sports. It can't be that they allow a certain position to dominate – the pitcher in baseball, the quarterback in football – because this isn't true of basketball. (Anyway, what would such dominance have to do with American values? It seems more reminiscent of the values of those societies that prefer absolute monarchy or a dictatorship.) And it can't be because these sports are faster than other sports – as we shall see in the next chapter, some nineteenth-century Americans believed this about baseball in relation to cricket – because ice hockey is faster than all of our sports.

One letter writer explained that American sports

> emphasize leadership, initiative and teamwork, the "big play," and most importantly a measure of progress – moving the ball down the field, or players around a base.[69]

But if emphasizing leadership simply means that one position gets to dominate, then basketball, as already mentioned, doesn't count as an American sport because it has no such position. Nor is there any reason to believe that soccer is lacking in emphasis on initiative, teamwork, and "big plays." As for a measure of progress, it is certainly true that in soccer the ball is moved down field, so why reject soccer? I take it that he means something in addition, that after the ball has been moved down field, play stops. Likewise, after a hit in baseball, a player is on one of the bases, and the play stops. The progress is consolidated, as it were. But if this is what he means, again he has excluded basketball because basketball doesn't have this business of stopping play anymore than soccer does. So, these reasons won't work.

One of the most popular reasons linking American values with our sports refers to individualism. Baseball, it is commonly said, is an individualistic sport, and since individualism is so enshrined in American life, that would seem to make baseball an American sport. But does it? The reason why baseball is generally considered an individualistic sport is that the batter faces the pitcher alone without the help of teammates. But that is something that can also be said of cricket, so if this is what makes baseball quintessentially American, *then cricket is also a quintessentially American sport*. And how many baseball fans in this country would want to admit that? Almost no one. Moreover, the one I find who admits it, after a fashion, trips over his feet in another way:

> In those nations where, in various forms, individualism and personal honor and the dignity of a man alone are deeply cherished, baseball elicits a responsive chord: in Latin nations, in Japan, in the United States. (Cricket is, one supposes, the British equivalent.)[70]

In this quote, Michael Novak cautiously allows that cricket is also individualistic (though he fails to explore why we reject it). But what savages his thought in this passage is his idea that Japan is individualistic! Perhaps at the time that Novak's book was written (in 1976) this mistake was excusable, but today when we know more about Japan, it just seems the height of idiocy. Japan, free in theory, is one of the most conformist nations on earth. And so Novak's statement, far from proving that baseball is individualistic, if anything helps prove the exact opposite.

He continues this passage by wondering why France doesn't accept baseball and decides that they are "too anarchic, too passionate, to accept the rules, boundaries, and coolness of baseball." I leave it to others to critique such thoughts.

But in any case, one's moment of individualism in baseball takes place in an instant. The pitcher can pitch whenever he wants to (within limits), but the batter has only a split second to exercise his individualism. (It's rather like always having to receive the serve in tennis and never being allowed to do the serving.) By contrast, in soccer it often happens that one receives the ball when everyone else is many yards away. At that time, the ball is your own and you can do what you like with it. You can pass it, you can dribble it, you can take a shot, you can execute a fake, you can just stand there, you can run away from it, you can even sit on it. You have, relatively speaking, a long time to make up your mind about what to do with the ball. There is nothing like this in baseball, except for the pitcher pitching the ball (and the catcher returning it if there is no one on base). The alleged individualism of baseball is an illusion.

Anyway, suppose baseball is individualistic. What about football? If there is anything to be said about football, it is that it is *not* individualistic. The offensive lineman in football are hardly indicative of individualism. They are nothing but anonymous peons who simply help out the quarterback and the other backs. So, if what makes baseball American is its emphasis on the individual, then football's failure to do this would seem to imply that it is a foreign sport.

Moreover, even if baseball is individualistic in one way, it also has another quality. The basic structure of the defense in baseball is purely hierarchical. The pitcher and catcher get more action than the infielders, the infielders get more action than the outfielders, and the right fielder gets the least action of all. Why should baseball, given that it has this hierarchy, be thought of as quintessentially American? Why shouldn't baseball's hierarchy incline us to think of it as *quintessentially Asian*? India has (or had) a caste system. China and Japan were and to some extent still are very hierarchical societies. In several Asian languages (including Chinese and Japanese), it is impossible to speak of a brother or sister. One must always speak of an older brother or a younger brother, an older sister or a younger sister. Even with identical twins, one must learn which is the older and which the younger in order to speak about them and to them appropriately. This kind of hierarchical thinking may be why people in Japan and the non-communist part of China, Taiwan, have adopted baseball, while countries that try to avoid hierarchies, such as Sweden, ignore it.[71] So, why not think of baseball as a quintessentially Asian sport? Moreover, if baseball is quintessentially American because of this hierarchy, then where does basketball fit in, given that it doesn't have such a hierarchy?

There just doesn't seem to be any specific value that is shared by all of and only our sports.

Suppose, then, that only one of our sports exhibited American values. Wouldn't that be sufficient for the American sports fan? Not at all. For since the other two didn't exhibit that value, yet were accepted by Americans, then there is no reason why soccer shouldn't also be accepted by Americans, even though it didn't exhibit American values. So long as one of these three didn't exhibit American values, then there is no good reason to reject soccer.

Incidentally, the objection that soccer is foreign is probably befuddling to foreigners who are used to hearing that soccer has historical roots in many cultures and seeing soccer take on the clothing of the local culture. Everyone in soccer knows, for example, that countries like Brazil and England play soccer in radically different ways, that Brazilian soccer is individualistic and uses flair, while the opposite seems to be true of English soccer. The idea that soccer is "foreign" must therefore seem wildly idiotic to them. Compare it to dancing. While there are some religions which ban dancing, every culture has had dancing in some form or another. Imagine

Soccer, the Left, & the Farce of Multiculturalism

if an American said that dancing was a foreign activity. Those who dance would be puzzled because every culture has some sort of dance. The dances vary from culture to culture, but dancing is still present. Likewise, soccer varies from culture to culture, so how can one say that it is foreign or that it has any particular essence to it?

At any rate, these are the three main reasons that are usually given why soccer doesn't deserve a place in our sports pantheon. Yet there is nothing especially intelligent or insightful about any of them. They are laced with obvious contradictions or stupidities.

The Real Reason

It seems to me that the real reason why soccer is rejected here is the third reason, that it is not American. Historically, this is correct, as I shall show in the next chapter. In addition, the third reason does a better job of explaining why Americans like the sports they do than the other two reasons. The first reason, that soccer is for wimps, doesn't explain why Americans love baseball and basketball. The second reason, that soccer is boring because it is low scoring, doesn't explain why Americans are indifferent to rugby, cricket, and indoor soccer. But we can explain Americans' indifference to those sports as well as their love of our sports by appealing to the foreign-origin reason. Americans love baseball, football, and basketball because of their American origin. They hate or ignore soccer, rugby and cricket because of their foreign origin.

It is true that this doesn't explain why such people love golf, tennis and ice hockey. But golf and tennis are individual sports. As a result, they don't evoke national loyalties to the degree that team sports do. As for ice hockey, this is the fourth most popular of our team sports, which puts it pretty far down the list. Many people still don't accept it. My parents, for example, in spite of being Minnesotans, never pay any attention to it, and I'm sure the same is true of many other people their age, or for that matter, my age.

Finally, if Americans are prejudiced against soccer, then it makes sense to say that the real reason is based on the foreign origin of soccer than on any of the other reasons, which are mere excuses. That is because most prejudices go back to what are called primordial sentiments. These are mentioned by Janet Lever in her book about Brazilian soccer, *Soccer Madness*.[72] She was talking about sports rivalries, but in fact what she said – she relies upon the anthropologist Clifford Geertz here – applies to any sort of prejudice. Primordial sentiments are the sentiments that concern our group, whether we identify with our family, or our race, or our language group, or our country. Prejudices are associated with these primordial sentiments.

Although neither Lever nor Geertz explains why this is so, the explanation is simple. When you are young, the people who love you the most in the world are your parents. (Of course, this is a generalization; there are parents who are indifferent to their children and abuse them to death.) They are the ones who care for you. As you grow older and become more self-reliant, that tie loosens. Still, you need to provide for yourself, and that depends upon getting a job, or for the traditional woman, getting a husband. The best way to do these things is to rely on connections formed through family ties or ties that are similar to family ties (ties based on one's school or religion or neighborhood or race, and so on). Relying on something other than connections is much riskier. I was foolish enough to think that ability meant everything and connections meant nothing, with the result that I have experienced years of unemployment.

And that is what prejudice relates to: who will help you survive? Who among the many billions of people in our world will actually care if you don't get a job and die of starvation? Not many. Almost no one, in fact. And so people often prefer to move in social circles based on their own group. Uprooting oneself can be a daunting experience. Most of the people from my high-school class live within fifty miles of where we grew up. The primordial sentiments are too strong to allow them to move away.

Under certain circumstances, these primordial sentiments spill over into prejudice. People begin to feel that it's not just that those other people are different, but that they are inferior, or if not inferior, at least to be hated and feared. The idea that soccer is of foreign origin fits in easily with these ideas. As I shall explain in the next chapter, we Americans felt that we had the best political system in the world, that we represented a fresh start from all the tired ideas that Europe had to offer, so it was natural to imagine that *everything* we did was wonderful and that everything Europeans did was miserable.

Refusing to See the Advantages

Another reason for thinking that American hostility to soccer counts as prejudice is that those who hate soccer enjoy talking about soccer's alleged flaws, but they will never talk about soccer's advantages. This is typical of those who are prejudiced. But what are soccer's advantages, or to look at it differently, what are the disadvantages associated with the supposedly superior American sports?

Take the three big objections raised against soccer. Each of these three has another side to it that soccer haters don't want to consider. The *disadvantage* of having a sport that isn't for wimps is that such sports usually *exclude on the basis of size*. Both football and rugby aren't for wimps, but how many average-sized or undersized people play these sports? Not many. For those who favor the democratic ideal, the ideal that says that all ought to have the same opportunities, football presents a problem because it violates this ideal. Many soccer players (such as Pelé) have been undersized people. If one likes the idea of macho sports, then one faces a difficult choice: one can either demand that society choose only macho sports, like football, or one can allow society to choose sports that give most people an opportunity to play, like soccer. Like it or not, avoiding wimp sports has its disadvantages.

The disadvantage of high-scoring sports is that there isn't any point in having competitions between amateurs and professionals. Games between amateurs and professionals are usually one-sided affairs. Obviously, the professionals are going to be much, much better than the amateurs. Consequently, a baseball game between a professional team and an amateur team is going to be a blowout. The same thing can be said for games between professional and amateur football teams and professional and amateur basketball teams. Take any NBA team and imagine it playing against a college basketball team. I'm not thinking here of "colleges" like the University of Michigan, but of actual colleges like Kenyon College (where my wife teaches) or Augustana College in Rock Island, Illinois (where I once taught). What is the score likely to be? 150-30, perhaps? Similar blowouts will occur in football.

The same sort of thing can happen in soccer, of course. If there is a mismatch between the two teams, the weaker team can get blown away. But that isn't always the case. If the weaker team has a well-organized defense and a good goalie, they can hold the score to something manageable, like 2-0. There have even been many times in which the much weaker side has won the game, and because of this, pro-am soccer tournaments are possible and enjoyable.

Because there are no pro-am tournaments in America's sports, our sports have become – one has to face this – elitist. This form of elitism is taken for granted here, except in sports like tennis and golf, where it is acceptable for amateurs to compete against the professionals. But in our team sports, elitism reigns. It is so common, so much a part of our sports atmosphere that we don't even notice it, just as fish aren't supposed to notice that they are in the water. This form of elitism means that the professionals never play against any teams but the other professional teams. Elitism means that major league baseball teams never play even the minor league teams. Or rather it means that when these contests *do* occasionally take place, they are nothing but exhibition games that don't mean anything. The implication is pretty clear: if you are an amateur, you don't have any business playing in a serious tournament against the professionals. Accordingly, we have missed out on the pleasures of pro-am tournaments.

In England, this attitude, if it exists, is tempered by the existence of the FA Cup. The FA Cup, as I explained in Chapter 3, is open to all comers. There is no elitism. But we in America have voluntarily allowed our professionals to hold elitist attitudes, and I say this is partly because we have adopted high-scoring sports.

Finally, there are disadvantages to following and playing only American sports. While there can be a great deal of pride in adopting only those sports that were invented by us, there are enormous drawbacks to this, too, drawbacks that Americans seldom notice. If we prefer only those sports invented by us, then if we want international competition, we have to hope that others won't follow our example because if others decide that they, too, will prefer only those sports invented by themselves, then there will be no international competition. Each country will have its own sports that it follows and prefers, but since no one plays anyone else's games, then there will never be any point to having an international competition like the World Cup.

Look at it this way. As I have already said, not only do Americans like American sports because they were invented here, it is often said that they capture America's essence as well. (I don't agree, but let that pass for the moment.) Yet, the more that these sports capture America's essence, the less they will appeal to others. Most people simply aren't going to be interested in some sport that seems foreign to them (just as many American are uninterested in soccer because soccer seems foreign to us). Why should people who are indifferent to America, or even hostile to America, care about sports that capture America's essence? They have their own countries and cultures that they care about and are proud of. It is true that some foreigners will be interested in our sports just because they happen to like

America. But international competition cannot be built out of the small percentage of foreigners who feel that way.

Of course, it might be argued that Americans have gotten along just fine without international competition. We have done just fine with our own competitions in baseball, football, and basketball. We don't need international competitions because our athletes are the best anyway. Yet, if that is true, why do we make such a fuss about the Olympics? Anyone who has seen our country go mad at Olympics time knows perfectly well that we *crave* international competition. And anyone who has watched the way *other* countries deal with the Olympics knows that we probably crave the Olympics more than anyone else. What I'm going to say will be anathema to most Americans, but everyone else has other international competitions to follow in addition to the Olympics, and as a result, the Olympics just don't have the importance for most foreigners that they do for us. (Recall the quote above from the editor of *L'Equipe*, who insisted that his readers didn't want to read about the Olympics and preferred reading about soccer.) We alone must get our international-competition fix via the Olympics and the Olympics alone.

Finally, not playing or following the sports of other countries can hurt us in war. Our insularity means that we know little or nothing about other countries. Not many Americans care about soccer games between Iran and Iraq or cricket games between Pakistan and India, yet following such games helps us to understand those cultures.

Preferring macho sports can mean excluding people who are smaller, preferring high-scoring sports can lead to elitism, and preferring one's own sports to all other sports means no international competition and a sometimes fatal ignorance of foreign cultures. As far as I know, no American has ever pointed out these disadvantages before.

The Young

Another indication of prejudice is that the people most likely to be free of it are the young. And that is definitely true of soccer. Few Americans my age pay any attention to soccer. Soccer first made a big splash in this country when I was in my mid-twenties, but that was still too late for my generation (because, apparently, we were already set in our ways). It was people who were a good ten years younger than me who began following it and going to games.

This phenomenon is typical of prejudice. My generation has come to grips with homosexuality, but my parents' generation still has not, and given their advanced age, it is unlikely that they ever will. I've heard that in South Africa, the people who were opposed to the old racist system of apartheid were the young. Even in science, it seems that the people who are most likely to accept new theories are the young. The physicist Max Planck has said that new theories get accepted not because everyone changes their minds, but because the old guard dies off and a new generation takes over believing in the new theory.[73] The same will be true of soccer. Eventually, the people who didn't grow up with it will die off and those who have known it all their lives will take over. They will make changes in society in soccer's favor that would have been unthinkable for earlier generations.

Those who are hostile tend to be older, and those who are not tend to be younger. Go to any professional soccer game in this country, and you will find mostly young people. In the year 2000, I went to see a Columbus Crew friendly (i.e., exhibition game) against Hamburg of Germany and was surprised to see a number of old men in the bathroom after the game. Who were they? I had never seen such fans before at Crew games. It wasn't until I heard them speaking German that I realized they were Hamburg fans who had followed their team to America as it went on tour. Soccer has long been accepted in Germany, so it wasn't surprising that old people in Germany would be interested in soccer. But old people in America today (that is, my parents' generation) reject soccer and no doubt will never be converted.

To what extent others have observed this hostility in older people, I do not know. A few years ago, I was talking to a young woman who had been to Chile as part of a junior-year-abroad program at her college. She happened to be there during the 1998 World Cup, and after one game that Chile won, she took pictures of large crowds of Chileans celebrating in the streets. When she got back, she displayed these photos in a local coffee house. I told her that thirty years earlier, few Americans would have thought to take pictures of such a celebration, to say nothing of displaying them in a coffee house. But she didn't seem to understand what I was getting at, which not only shows the huge changes in the attitudes of young Americans over the past thirty years, but also perhaps the lack of awareness among young people that attitudes were quite different in the past.

Prejudice in Favor of American Sports

I have been arguing that most Americans have been prejudiced *against* foreign sports like soccer, but the opposite side of the coin is that they are prejudiced *in favor of* American sports. I already mentioned that newspapers here in America seldom present criticism of American sports while dumping criticism onto soccer with a steam shovel. In fact, the people who criticize American sports are few and far between. George Will has made a name for himself by criticizing football, complaining that it encapsulates the two worst features of American life, violence and committee meetings. But he is also a firm lover of baseball. A few feminists have complained – in a very mild fashion, in my opinion – about football and how women are excluded from it. Yet, as far as I know, no feminist has ever demanded that it be de-emphasized in our schools. In Woody Allen's *Annie Hall*, a woman asks about basketball, "What is so exciting about watching some pituitary cases bounce a ball around?" But it is made clear that her criticism is decidedly unhip.

What is strange is that there is so little by way of criticism in the mainstream media or in our schools of our sports, which are otherwise so critical of anything traditional in our society. These sports have become our civic religion, and support for them is more widespread than support for Christianity. They are sacred cows which must never be attacked. Not even the most rebellious of rebels dares rebel against them. Not even the most radical of radical leftists wants them eliminated. Not even the most avant-garde of artists, willing to spatter images of Christ with feces, would do the same for the image of an athlete in one of these sports. The people who want to shock have limits beyond which they dare not go, limits which they don't even seem to realize exist.

All of this embodies a prejudice in favor of our sports. Just as racists are not only prejudiced *against* blacks but also prejudiced *in favor of* whites, so the soccer hater is prejudiced against soccer and other foreign sports and also prejudiced in favor of our sports.

Foreigners Who Hate Soccer

Some are going to object, "What about foreigners who hate soccer? Aren't they prejudiced as well? And if they are prejudiced, then why is it bad if Americans are prejudiced?"

It is true that there are some foreigners who hate soccer. But foreigners who hate soccer have grown up with it and know it through and through. Accordingly, they aren't generally prejudging and so aren't prejudiced. They will have definite reasons for not liking soccer that are reasonable, even if I and most soccer fans disagree with them. Foreigners who hate soccer generally fall into a small number of categories. (1) Some hate all sports or all team sports, and as such they don't count as prejudiced against soccer in particular. (2) A very few have decided that America's sports are better than soccer. These are people who know all about soccer, but who generally know nothing about sports in this country. Just as Americans know none of the advantages that soccer has, so typically foreigners who like our sports are aware of none of their disadvantages. It's easy to watch a game of football on television and to think that you are somehow understanding football culture. It isn't until you realize that there are no minor leagues, very few semi-pro teams, no amateur teams, and no pick-up games that you understand how limiting this sport is. So the foreigners who hate soccer and who like our sports are still prejudiced because they are prejudging before having all the relevant information.

(3) Finally, some hate soccer because they prefer some other foreign sport (like rugby). These are like, say, football fans here in America who hate baseball. Again, they are not prejudiced because they aren't prejudging. But let me point out something about those, whether foreign or American, who think that soccer is a wimp sport: they are a strange and pathetic club. We soccer fans are a huge club, but what is distinctive about us is that we are united. It's not as though England, Germany, Italy, Brazil, and so on, play by different rules. They play by different *styles*, yes, but by different rules, no. However, those throughout the world who think soccer is a wimp sport are not united. Imagine a convention in which they try to agree on a sport to play. The moderator asks, "Should we play American football?" "YES!" shout the Americans. "NO!" shouts everyone else. "Should we play Canadian football?" "YES!" shout the Canadians. "NO!" shouts everyone else. "Should we play Australian rules football?" "YES!" shout the Australians. "NO!" shouts everyone else. "Should we play rugby league?" "YES!" shout the fans of rugby league. "NO!" shouts everyone else. "Should we play rugby union?" "YES!" shout the fans of rugby union. "NO!" shouts everyone else. What this means is that there is little in the way of international competition. And this illustrates what I was talking about earlier. If you prefer a game that was invented by your countrymen, you will almost certainly be playing with and against your countrymen only. If you refuse to compromise with foreigners, then out goes international competition And that is why I say that this worldwide club is pathetic. We soccer fans have a huge World Cup, but those who think soccer is a wimp sport don't have much of anything. There is no World Cup for American football. Nor is there one for Canadian football or Australian rules football. There is a World Cup for rugby union, and another smaller one for rugby league, but neither one is watched by

Americans. It is true that soccer's World Cup isn't generally watched by Americans, but then soccer doesn't need Americans because it has such a huge following already. Those who think soccer is a wimp sport need every fan they can get to watch their World Cup in order to have a respectable rival, and that is why Americans (and Canadians and the Australians who are fans of Australian rules football) are so important. But the American fan won't budge. He refuses to make any compromises on what he sees as the best sport in the world, and to hell with all those who disagree with him. And so his chances for significant international competition are almost nil. The American who is a soccer fan can either play for his country or at least cheer for it in international competition, while the American who is a football fan cannot. That this problem is never mentioned by those Americans who hate soccer is just another way of exhibiting their prejudice.

Conclusion

Soccer prejudice exists in America. It is nowhere near as harmful as other sorts of prejudice, I grant. But it still counts as prejudice. Perhaps most important is that it is virtually invisible, except to some of us who are soccer fans. But I have seen quite clearly how America's soccer haters act. They have never acted in an unprejudiced way. They have simply attacked what they didn't know anything about, have continued to attack it since its introduction, and will not cease to attack it even into their graves. They talk as though the only thing dumber than a soccer fan is two soccer fans. Yet, I look back upon my pre-soccer days as the period when I was dumb, because (as I shall explain later) I supported sports that treated me shabbily. This sort of stupidity is true even for those that our sports treated well, for such sports didn't treat them as well as they could have (as I argued back in Chapter 3). Occasionally, too, the soccer haters say really stupid things. There is the question that I mentioned in Chapter 3 and which I call the dumbest-question-asked-by-a-soccer-hater, namely "Why do they call it football?" Obviously, a game that people play with their feet ought to be called football. Aside from being able to amuse oneself at their stupidity, there is not much else that one can say to such people, as I learned long ago.

There will be some who will be disconcerted and upset by my calling hatred of soccer "prejudice." That is a strong word that one shouldn't use lightly. Of course, some people are so used to hearing about how they are prejudiced that they don't even listen anymore. They just tune out. But leftists, who aren't used to this, will probably be angry. Yet, what else am I supposed to say? I've never heard any leftist denounce others for such prejudices (or, if you wish, hostile attitudes). I've never heard any leftist denounce the bad reasons for hating soccer held by other Americans. I've never heard any leftist denounce the stereotype about soccer violence used by other Americans. If it isn't prejudice, what is it? If it isn't xenophobia, what is it? Isn't this all related rather pathetically to our national pride?

Assuming, though, that it is prejudice, why did it emerge in the first place?

Endnotes

1. July 2, 2001.
2. Cited in *Utne Reader*, Nov/Dec. 1996, p. 27.
3. Cf. Andrei S. Markovits and Steven L. Hellerman, *Offside: Soccer and American Exceptionalism* (Princeton University Press, 2001), pp. 211 and 262.
4. Richard Critchfield, *An American Looks at Britain* (Doubleday, 1990), pp. 189-199.
5. *Columbus Dispatch*, Feb. 18, 2000, 2E.
6. *Columbus Dispatch*, Feb. 18, 2000, 2E.
7. Nick Hornby, *Fever Pitch*, p. 124.
8. *Columbus Dispatch*, May 5, 2000, p. E2.
9. *Columbus Dispatch*, July 9, 2000, p. E3.
10. Bob Hunter, *Columbus Dispatch*, May 13, 1998, 1G.
11. *Washington Post*, June 16, 1994, p. B7.
12. Minneapolis *Star-Tribune*, Feb. 28, 1994, p. 2C.
13. Minneapolis *Star-Tribune*, Feb. 28, 1994, p. 2C.
14. *Time*, September 14, 1998, p. 19.
15. *The New York Times Magazine*, March 2, 1986, p. 40.
16. *Newsweek*, June 13, 1988, p. 56.
17. Robert Eastaway, *Cricket Explained* (New York: St. Martin's Press, 1992), p. 18.
18. The entry for January 28, 1944.
19. Albert Camus, *The Stranger* (Vintage Books, 1946), chapter 2, pp. 27-8.

20. *Chronicle of Higher Education*, November 16, 2001, p. A44. The second sentence seems somewhat garbled and probably ought to read, "... and other sports on clubs..." rather than "... and other clubs...."
21. *The Wall Street Journal*, Aug. 4, 1995, p. B10.
22. All these facts and the quote come from Simon Kuper, *Football against the Enemy* (Orion, 1994), pp. 85-92.
23. Michael Stein, "Cult and Sport: The Case of Big Red," from Janet C. Harris and Roberta J. Park, ed., *Play, Games, and Sports in Cultural Contexts* (Human Kinetics Publishers, Inc., Champaign, Illinois, 1983), reprinted from *Mid-American Review of Sociology*, 1977, 2(2), 29-42: beginning of article quoted.
24. Cited in Martin Ralbovsky, *Lords of the Locker Room* (Wyden, 1974), pp. 54-55.
25. *Minneapolis Star and Tribune*, July 15, 1984, p. 20A.
26. *Kansas City Star*, Jan. 8, 1990, 6C.
27. *Kansas City Star*, October 3, 1989, p. 7A.
28. See William Schneider, "The In-Box President," *Atlantic,* Jan. 1990, p. 42.
29. *Columbus Dispatch*, May 20, 2000, p. H1.
30. March 12, 2003.
31. *The Wall Street Journal*, June 12, 1998, p. B1.
32. Allen Barra, *Village Voice*, July 9, 2002, p. 163.
33. David Cort, "Soccer: The Rabble Game," *The Nation,* August 30, 1965, p. 100.
34. *Time,* June 11, 2001, p. 34ff.
35. *National Geographic*, Oct. 1997, pp. 56-7 and 61.
36. *Economist*, Jan. 11, 1997, p. 53.
37. *The New Yorker*, Oct. 29, 1979, 146.
38. "Queeg," *Red Dwarf,* series 2, episode 5.
39. *Times of London*, 12/17/98, from the Internet.
40. *Times of London*, October, 24, 1999, from the Internet.
41. *Times of London*, Feb. 27, 2001, from the Internet.
42. *Economist*, May 22, 1999.
43. *Jerusalem Post*, International Edition, Dec. 14-20, 1980, p. 15.
44. Umberto Eco, *Foucault's Pendulum* (Harcourt, Brace, Jovanovich: 1988), p. 463.
45. Geoffrey Wheatcroft, "Who Needs the BBC?" *Atlantic Monthly*, March 2001, p. 53.
46. Hugh McIlvanney, *The Sunday Times*, February 2, 1997.

47. Stella Bingham, based on the BBC television serial by Keith Waterhouse, *Charters and Caldicott* (Penguin, 1985), p. 145.
48. *Minneapolis Tribune*, Aug. 24, 1980, p. 9C.
49. *The Washington Post*, Feb. 19, 1992, p. B4.
50. *Columbus Dispatch*, Sept. 30, 2000, p. H4.
51. *Columbus Dispatch*, Nov. 1, 1996, p. B1.
52. *The Guardian*, Jan. 14, 1992, Ego section, p. 12.
53. *The Washington Post*, Aug. 2, 1984, Sec. E, pp. 1 and 7.
54. From the Reading (U.K.) *Chronicle*, Jan. 9, 2009, via the Internet: "Wally Downes is warning that football matches could turn into boring four-hour affairs and become abused by advertisers if video technology is introduced. The Reading coach believes bringing in goalline technology will ruin the sport and make it more like American football where matches often take three hours to complete."
55. *Columbus Dispatch*, Aug. 17, 2001, p. A5.
56. James Michener, *Sports in America* (Random House: 1976), p. 375.
57. David Winner, *Brilliant Orange* (Bloomsbury, 2000), pp. 188-189.
58. Winner, *Brilliant Orange*, pp. 97 and 101.
59. *The New York Times*, May 24, 2002, sec. 4, p. 10.
60. Nick Hornby, *Fever Pitch*, p. 76: "Young working-class and lower-middle-class males bring with them a complicated and occasionally distressing set of problems."
61. Tom Humphries, *The Irish Times*, June 21, 1994, p. 14.
62. James A. Michener, *Iberia: Spanish Travels and Reflections* (New York: Random House, 1968), p. 626.
63. According to Simon Kuper, *Football Against the Enemy*, p. 175.
64. Colin Shindler, *Manchester United Ruined My Life* (Headline, 1998), p. 264.
65. The *Economist*, December 2, 2000, p. 56.
66. See David Winner, *Brilliant Orange*, pp. 97 and 101.
67. See also Simon Kuper, "The World's Game Is Not Just a Game," in *The New York Times Magazine*, May 26, 2002, p. 36ff., listing many more examples.
68. James A. Michener, *Caravans*, pp. 296-99.
69. *Economist*, June 14, 2000, p. 6.
70. Michael Novak, *The Joy of Sports* (Basic Books: 1976), p. 59.
71. Here I'm sure someone will bring up Cuba. Cuba tries to avoid hierarchies, it will be said, but it is also a baseball-loving country. But

Cuba is communist rather than socialist like Sweden, so it is very much afflicted with a hierarchy.
72. Janet Lever, *Soccer Madness* (Chicago and London: University of Chicago Press, 1983), pp. 5-6.
73. Cited in Thomas Kuhn, *The Structure of Scientific Revolutions*, 2nd edition (The University of Chicago, 1962), p. 151.

CHAPTER 7
The Historical Roots of Soccer Prejudice

George Washington played cricket. The father of our country, so revered by traditionalists, nevertheless played a foreign sport. The father of our country played a sport invented by his enemies. It is true that I'm going a little bit beyond the evidence in saying this, for the evidence shows only that he played a simplified form of cricket. But if he did even that much, it is startling, and so it's reasonable that he also played cricket itself.

The evidence comes from a letter written by one of his troops during the Revolutionary War, in which it is related that George Washington "did us the honor to play Wicket with us" (Wicket being a simplified form of cricket).[1] Apparently, then, there was no prejudice against foreign sports back then. So when did it arise? And how did soccer prejudice first arise? The answer is that it apparently arose because of the prejudice against foreign (that is, English) sports that already bedeviled cricket. What happened to cricket in America? The answer isn't at all what one might expect.

The average baseball fan believes that cricket never even existed in America. It is true that if you look at histories of baseball written by reputable historians, they will talk about cricket. But the average fan knows nothing about any of this. He or she believes that baseball was invented by Abner Doubleday in 1839 in Cooperstown, New York, that his invention has no connection with sports from other countries, especially England, and that prior to that time there were no team sports being played here. For such people, baseball is practically identical with America. Michael Novak, for example, says that "baseball is early America."[2] Or consider this quote:

> The one constant through all of the years ... has been baseball. America has rolled by like an army of steamrollers. It's been erased like a blackboard – rebuilt and erased again. But baseball has marked the time. This field – this game – it's a part of our past.... It reminds us of all that was once good, and what could be again.

That is a quote from the movie *Field of Dreams*,[3] and it is obvious that that quote resonates with many Americans.

Yet, the truth about the origins of baseball is quite different. One simple fact shatters this myth, which is that George Washington played cricket. Not only did our first president play a form of cricket, cricket has been called America's first modern team sport. Granted, in Washington's time there were probably nothing but casual games of the sort we find described in Chapter 7 of Charles Dickens's *The Pickwick Papers* (which was in recent years portrayed on the reverse side of the British ten-pound note). But eventually, more or less permanent teams were established, of which the first was the St. George Cricket Club of New York, founded in 1838. It was not until 1845 that the first baseball team was founded, the Knickerbocker Base Ball Club (again of New York). As a sport, cricket had a big advantage over baseball in that its rules were already formalized whereas the rules of baseball were still in a state of flux even after it had become our national pastime. Cricket thus attracted the big crowds first and so became our first modern team sport.

The big question is, If cricket was acceptable to the father of our country, why did it ever become unpopular, so unpopular that the average baseball fan doesn't even realize it had ever been here? When did this happen? Something happened to sports in America in the nineteenth century, something between baseball and cricket. That something that happened is still with us, for it meant that when soccer and rugby came along, Americans who saw those sports felt no particular reason to play them, or if they did play them, they did so only after they had tinkered with the rules. Whereas other people throughout Europe and Latin America never dreamed of modifying imported sports – they either accepted them or rejected them – we Americans had a different mindset. We took rounders and modified it, we took rugby and modified it, and we initially accepted soccer but quickly lost interest as we became bewitched with our own version of football. Why did we act so differently?

First of all, the general cultural climate of the newly born United States encouraged Americans of that era to think about themselves in highly flattering terms. The general viewpoint of Americans at that time, as indeed it still is today, was that America was the best country in the world, not because of noble bloodlines or splendid palaces or a rich past or a powerful army, but because of our new system of government. The Old World of Europe was thought of as hopelessly mired in past traditions that prevented it from trying a new system. We were superior. Our system of government was superior. It was only natural under these deliriously exciting circumstances for Americans to think that we had the edge not only in politics, but in all sorts of other ways as well. Cricket, then, having been invented by the English represented the old way of doing things, and because it was old it must be inferior, while baseball, invented by Americans, represented something new, so it must be superior.

The second attitude was that for a while in the nineteenth century, at a crucial moment, Americans generally felt stifled, even threatened, by the British. They impressed our sailors onto their ships. They burned our Capitol during the War of 1812. Even after that war, which because of the Battle of New Orleans we felt we had won, we thought of Britain as a threat, especially because of the close proximity of a British territory, Canada. This, after all, was the high point of British imperialism. They had trade practices that we disagreed with and felt were to our disadvantage. (This is rather ironic, given that those against globalization protest against our own trade practices today.) We were in debt to them until World War I, and they collectively owned a large amount of American land.[4] The result of this Anglophobia was that the Federalist Party, which in foreign affairs was pro-British, was dead by the 1820s, while the Know Nothing Party, which was anti-immigration, was able to emerge a couple decades later.

It was only natural in these circumstances that we began to feel differently about not just the British people but about British *culture.* Before that time, Americans took British culture for granted. No one seemed to have any particular distaste for British culture. But some time during the nineteenth century (and maybe even earlier), Americans began to feel frustrated and squashed by British culture. It was omnipresent. One couldn't get away from it. In 1849, this frustration resulted in a riot that left twenty-two dead in New York City. The cause of the riot seems absurd today, a competition between Shakespearean actors, one British, one American, but it obviously seemed important enough back then. According to one historian, "England still exerted on the American mind an influence so strong" that a writer of that period, William Gilmore Simms, called it "pernicious."[5] That was in the 1840s, and it was right about then that baseball and cricket began vying with each other to see which would be the national pastime.

Of course, there wasn't total Anglophobia. It was absurd, for example, that people would riot over Shakespeare, but what was even more absurd was that, in championing the American Shakespearean actor over the British one, they had any feelings at all about the matter. Why didn't they just reject Shakespeare as a British cultural relic that should be shunned? The fact is that they didn't. But that doesn't negate my thesis, for we can still find this sort of mixed up thinking today: most Americans today aren't Anglophobes and some are even Anglophiles, *except when it comes to sports, where Anglophobia is rampant.*[6]

Since it was during the period between the 1840s and the 1860s that baseball became our national pastime, and since cricket had been played prior to that, we need to examine what exactly happened to cricket. Did all of American society decide one day that they would play cricket no more? Or was it a gradual process in which everyone played both sports at the beginning of this period but in which people slowly began to prefer baseball? Or was it always the case that cricket was preferred by some groups and baseball by other groups? In any case, what were the reasons given by people for rejecting cricket? If there were different groups, were there debates between them and can they be reconstructed? Finally, were either of these groups prejudiced against the other group's sport?

To begin with, the very early history of sports in this country is difficult to reconstruct. Sporting attitudes from that era are shrouded in mystery because most games were played on a very informal basis, and furthermore there were no polls taken that would give us any firm information. We do know that both baseball and cricket had to contend with people who thought of sport as disreputable, as associated with gambling, drunkenness or rowdiness. Baseball and cricket also had to contend with feelings that these were sports for boys rather than grown men. However, both of them began gaining momentum in the 1840s and 1850s. Initially, cricket was the more successful of the two. A sports manual from 1858 devoted eighteen and a half pages to cricket, but only four and a half to baseball. It stated that cricket was "the leading game played out of doors ... the favorite game of the country village and the country town, as well as of the larger commercial cities."[7] But a year later, *Harper's* suggested that baseball was overtaking cricket.[8] It is true that there had been numerous statements made throughout the 1850s that baseball was the national game, but the evidence seems to be that that was not yet true until the very end of the decade, and that even then cricket was still very much alive. By the end of the Civil War, however, it was clear that baseball was the winner of the competition. Cricket was still played, and it even thrived, for it entered a golden era in the 1880s that continued until World War I.[9] Nevertheless, it never constituted a serious threat to baseball again.

As for the people who played cricket, the evidence seems to be that it tended to be the English expatriate community, the English who were living abroad in America. Yet, some Americans did play, mostly in Philadelphia, but also in other places. In Philadelphia, they tended to be from the upper classes, but that wasn't true elsewhere. Moreover, there was a great deal of excitement produced by some international competitions. In 1859, an All-England (cricket) Eleven arranged to play three games against American teams and two against Canadian teams. They won all five games handily. These games drew a large number of spectators (24,000 to one of them, some of whom were probably baseball fans) and in turn caused the formation of a number of cricket teams.

As for any debates that occurred before baseball began overtaking cricket, very little material seems to remain, which isn't surprising given that these debates would not have occurred in a highly public venue like Congress, but rather on playing fields, in the homes or workplaces, and in bars. We get occasional snippets of information from newspaper articles and books, but that is about all. However, *after* baseball began overtaking the competition, there were plenty of statements made about why cricket was losing. Those that referred to the actual game (as opposed to its national origins), said much the same sort of thing:

> Cricket is too solemn and deliberate a game for a Yankee, and Base Ball would seem too lively an exercise for Mr. Bull [that is, the English].[10]

> Americans do not care to dawdle over a sleep inspiring game all through the heat of a June or July day. What they do, they want to do in a hurry. Englishmen differ materially in this particular. The latter will spend half an hour over a glass of 'arf and 'arf and an hour of conning a column of the *Times*. An American dashes off a whiskey cocktail or smash and reads the *Herald* summary in about three minutes. Thus the reason of American antipathy to cricket can be readily understood. It is too slow and every man is not engaged.

> In baseball, all is lightening. Every action is swift as a seabird's flight and there is no one who has not something to do.[11]

Another baseball fan began by comparing English and American train conductors:

> In the case of the Englishman, the cry to the engineer is, "all right," while the American screams, "Go ahead!"[12]

What strikes the soccer fan of today about these quotes is how silly they are! Those of us Americans who love soccer know perfectly well that the English aren't too slow when they play soccer. In fact, *both* baseball and cricket are slow sports compared with soccer, and while baseball may be somewhat faster than cricket, the difference is infinitesimal compared with the difference between either sport and soccer. Nor would anyone think that everyone in baseball is engaged during the action because the team at bat is mostly on the bench, while for the team in the field the action usually involves just a couple of the players (the pitcher and catcher).

But the point is that *these explanations were accepted*. The idea that cricket is slower than baseball is probably still accepted. I once heard an American challenge a young Englishman about what he took to be the prissy sport of cricket, and the Englishman replied by talking about West Indian bowlers and how dangerous they were. Now I had a vague idea of what he was talking about (from having read the sports sections of British newspapers for many years), but the American making this challenge was completely at a loss and had nothing to say.

So the Americans who came to favor baseball were wrong when they insisted that the English were slow, but they passed this belief along to their children, who passed it along to their children, and so on.

Some of the sniping back and forth between the two sports emerged from the international series that I mentioned above. During the first of these, some baseball players challenged the English cricketers to a baseball game, after which one of them replied that they would do so if they were given a year to develop their skills. Whether this was accepted or not isn't clear, but in any case the Civil War intervened. Nearly a decade later, another All-England visit occurred, in 1868. As with the earlier series, many spectators went to the games, although not as many as before and not as many compared with the crowds that baseball was attracting at that time. Also, as with the earlier series, the English dominated, but this time they did consent to play baseball, playing seven games. They lost to American baseball players but won against those in America who were playing cricket. One baseball fan, criticizing the belief held by these cricketers that baseball was a childish game compared with cricket, insisted that they then should have improved dramatically by the seventh game.[13]

What is most important about this period, as far as soccer is concerned, are the many statements indicating that there was prejudice on both sides. At the first cricket convention in America in 1857, one of the subjects discussed was that most Americans didn't understand cricket; rather, "they knew only that it was an English game, and that was enough not to touch it."[14] In the same year, it was reported that cricket was "rapidly making its way into popular favor as one of our national games, despite some prejudice against Englishmen."[15] In 1861, it was reported that:

> Three years ago it was a difficult matter to find any one member of the American ball playing community ... that could regard the English game of cricket with any favor.... We must endeavor to remove the prejudices that exist against a game that emanates from a foreign country, and ... we must overcome the same prejudice that exists among the generality of cricketers against the American game of ball.[16]

What this last quote shows is that there were feelings described as prejudice on both sides of the debate. Baseball lovers were thought of as prejudiced against cricket, and cricket lovers were thought of as prejudiced against baseball. Oddly enough, the cricket teams that visited from England lacked this prejudice. As one observer noted, such visitors

> have shown our resident English cricketers an example of the absence of that prejudice against every game but their own, which it would be well for the interests of cricket in this country if they would follow.[17]

If cricketers from England weren't prejudiced against baseball, why were cricketers here? Perhaps the English living here felt besieged since they were living in a foreign country. Or perhaps they were just being snobby. In any case, they were thought of as prejudiced. But as the first quote shows, the baseball fans were thought of as prejudiced as well. The final word on the matter might be this quote in 1862 from a newspaper that commented that since cricket "is not an *American* game, but purely an English game, it will never be in much vogue with the Americans."[18]

Just as important as these remarks are the beliefs of a later generation. At first, it was believed that baseball was American only in the sense that we had taken the English game of rounders and had modified it. "By the end of the [nineteenth] century, however, the notion that the national pastime was even slightly tainted by foreign influence offended many."[19] This led to a big debate. On one side was Henry Chadwick, an American who had been born in England and had lived there as a child, but who had later moved to America and become a promoter of baseball. He insisted, on the basis of his experience with rounders, that baseball had developed from this English game. On the other side was Albert G. Spalding, an American-born baseball player who later became a sporting-goods magnate, who insisted that baseball was invented entirely in America and owed nothing to other countries. As one writer put it, "But Spalding, brushing aside such dissent as almost treasonous, argued that baseball, like America, must be 'free from the trammels of English traditions, custom, conventionalities.'"[20] The result of this debate was that a commission was formed to investigate the matter "for all time," and in one of the documents that Spalding himself deposited with this commission, we learn the reason perhaps for his vehemence on this topic. He had traveled overseas as a baseball "missionary" and had been "taunted" with the rounders theory "around the world, generally spoken in derision of our game."[21] So, it was wounded national pride, and perhaps the failure of his missionary efforts, that led Spalding to insist upon the opposing theory. The commission duly investigated and heard the story of how one Abner Doubleday had invented baseball in 1839; they further decided that baseball owed nothing to any English games. Spalding himself insisted that "the tea episode in Boston Harbor, and our later fracas with England in 1812, had not been sufficiently forgotten in 1840 for anyone to be deluded into the idea that our national prejudices would permit us to look with favor, much less adopt any sport or game of an English flavor."[22] A member of his commission responsible for investigating the matter reported that one of the early baseball players in New York said that "the reason they chose the game of Base Ball instead of – and in fact in opposition to – cricket was because they regarded Base Ball as a purely American game; and it appears that there was at that time some considerable prejudice against adopting any game of foreign invention."[23] According to these quotes, people at the beginning of the twentieth century remembered or believed that in the

Soccer, the Left, & the Farce of Multiculturalism

1830s and 1840s, no American would have deigned to play a sport of English origin, so the conclusion was reached that baseball must be of American origin.

Eventually, a Robert W. Henderson of the New York Public Library found information that strongly suggested that baseball was indeed invented from rounders. That, of course, hasn't dispelled the myth about Abner Doubleday. My purpose, however, is not to get involved in the debate over this issue because it doesn't matter. Either we got baseball by modifying rounders or by inventing it ourselves, and either way we didn't have an English sport. My purpose instead is merely to show that as early as 1857, people were commenting on the prejudices of ball players concerning the national origins of games and that such prejudices may have existed for many years prior to that date.

Most of what I have been saying so far is entirely uncontroversial. Nearly every historian who talks about the early days of baseball mentions cricket. And most of them talk about the feelings of nationalism or nativism that were rife during that era and how it influenced the competition between the two sports.[24] But I should acknowledge that one Jules Tygiel has suggested that there never was any competition between cricket and baseball because cricket, outside of Philadelphia, was really confined to the British community living in America. They developed separately, he maintains, "rather than in any true competition with each other."[25] I think that for various reasons he is wrong about this. First of all, as he himself acknowledges, Americans in Philadelphia did play cricket; it wasn't restricted to the British community there. And even if it had been so restricted, one reference from this period refers to "animated and disagreeable debates" between the two groups of fans.[26]

In addition, when a baseball convention was held in the late 1850s, their goal was to "give this association of the Base Ball Clubs of Manhattan Island a similar standing which the Marylebone Club of London exercises over the game of cricket throughout the British Islands."[27] Now if cricket was confined to the British community, how would any American have ever heard of the Marylebone Club of London? Today's baseball fans in America have virtually total separation from cricket fans, so how many of them have heard of this club? One in ten million? Finally, at any time someone could have knocked some sense into the baseball lovers by pointing out the obvious, by saying something like the following:

> Gentlemen, hadn't we better consider if we are taking rather a gamble in choosing baseball over cricket? We don't know at this time if baseball will ever become accepted elsewhere, while we already know that cricket is accepted in England and may yet spread to other lands. If we choose baseball while others choose cricket, we will have no international competition. Moreover, even if we didn't invent cricket, there is a great deal of satisfaction in beating the other guy at his own game.

Of course, given our physical isolation from the rest of the world at that time, and given the cultural isolationism that resulted from that physical isolation, it was apparently rather unlikely that anyone would say such a thing. Moreover, while the experience of other countries, such as Brazil, shows that the sports of an immigrant community can take over a country, that didn't happen here. The question is, Why? and the answer seems to be that we thought of ourselves as superior in every way to Europe.

Suppose, however, that Tygiel is basically right, that there never was any real competition between baseball and cricket. Does this defeat what I am saying? Not at all, for it just means that the prejudice against cricket had solidified even earlier than others have been suggesting. That prejudice must have developed at some point. If it didn't develop during the 1850s, then it must have developed earlier. It can't have always existed, for recall what I said about George Washington. If, then, there was no real competition between cricket and baseball, that was because there was already so much prejudice against cricket that there could be no real competition. Cricket prejudice had already destroyed cricket's chances before the competition could begin, before baseball had even been invented. At what point in time this prejudice began, I leave it to others to determine. The earliest definite proof I have of it is in the quote from 1857, but probably it had been around for quite some time, maybe even from the period right after the Revolutionary War, though I suspect the War of 1812 is a more likely beginning. But that it existed is certain.

To summarize, baseball and cricket, which were probably played informally for years, began developing clubs and organizations beginning in 1838 (when the St. George Cricket Club was formed). Initially, cricket had the edge, but eventually baseball overtook it. Why? At some point, whether during this period or earlier, the average American didn't want to have anything to do with cricket because of its English origins, and this hostile attitude was exhibited in the American belief that Americans were too active and energetic to play that slow English sport of cricket. By the end of the Civil War, cricket was done for.

Now it is my contention that this hostility to English sports and the belief in the superiority of anything invented by Americans eventually had an effect on soccer. The fact that baseball won out over cricket meant that there were a large number of people who felt that our own sport was superior, which meant in turn that we were going to turn our backs on what the rest of the world was doing. It is true that we sent out "missionaries" to teach baseball to the rest of the world, but when it didn't catch on (except in the northern half of Latin America and in Japan) we continued to ignore what was going on elsewhere. We had our own sport, and we didn't really need the rest of the world. Naturally, when soccer came along, it was lumped into the category of "English sport," and so was thought of as inferior.

That, at any rate, is my contention, but the evidence is admittedly much harder to find than in the case of baseball and cricket. Nevertheless, I think it is reasonable. Before I explain why it is reasonable, let me first recount the story of football in America. Colleges and universities had long been playing some versions of football-like and soccer-like games on an informal basis. In the 1870s after the rules of soccer had been formalized in England, several Ivy League colleges adopted soccer and even played what is sometimes considered the first intercollegiate football game but which was actually a soccer game. However, Harvard stood aloof, preferring its own version, a version that was more like rugby, and it managed to get all the other Ivy League colleges to go along with it, after which football spread throughout the land.

There are several points of interest missing from this account. Why did Harvard reject soccer? Why did the other Ivy League colleges reject soccer after they had taken up football? (They could have played both, after all.) Why did colleges in the Midwest and the South accept football? (This is particularly relevant for the South, for there is no obvious reason why they would have accepted a "damned Yankee" sport.) Why did the masses, who seldom went to college in those days, accept football rather than soccer?

Concerning the first, there seems to be no answer available. The situation here is different from that of baseball, where there were many people involved in various places. Because there were so many people, it is not surprising that some statements about their opinions have come down to us. With football, however, we are talking about why a small number of students at a particular time and place decided to play a certain game.

In this case, we just don't have much information. Nevertheless, we can take a guess. Soccer was rejected because it wasn't tough enough, for that is the reason that has come down to us. Even though there is no evidence for this, it is reasonable to believe because that is what we soccer fans keep hearing from the football crowd. And of course, the reason that having a tough sport was important was that it no doubt fit in with an image we had of ourselves as more rugged than the English.

The other questions I don't have answers to, either, at least not in terms of actual evidence. But it is nevertheless reasonable to believe that all these people accepted football rather than soccer for the simple reason that they thought of it as an American sport and soccer as an inferior foreign sport. Probably, most of them never even saw soccer being played until after they had seen football being played. That is, once the Ivy Leaguers took to football and had abandoned soccer, what other people were likely to see being played was football rather than soccer, since they were generally not in a position to travel overseas to see what was happening elsewhere. And if they did happen to see soccer, they were quickly told by everyone around them that it was an inferior, foreign sport. The result was that although there were many divisions in American society at this time, they all became united by the acceptance of football. Rich and poor, North and South, white and black, urban and rural, Protestant and Catholic, all of them accepted football rather than soccer. The only people who resisted were the new immigrants, and their children succumbed to football fever as readily as everyone else.

And I say that the only reasonable explanation of this phenomenon, whereby so many groups normally to some degree antagonistic to one another all agreed on football, is that they were taught to think of soccer as an inferior foreign sport, and they thought it inferior because it wasn't rugged. And they accepted this sort of teaching because they were already predisposed to think of foreign practices as inferior to anything American.

There is one last question to answer: Why did America reject rugby? The form of football that Harvard was playing resembled rugby enough so that the only competition they could find was in Canada, where rugby was played. Accordingly, in 1874 Harvard arranged for a series of games with McGill University, which was playing rugby. There were to be two games of rugby and two games using Harvard's own rules. This series left the Americans wholly enthusiastic about rugby, and so they abandoned their own game. Moreover, the other Ivy Leaguers, when they saw the new game that Harvard was playing, decided they liked it and abandoned soccer.

The crucial question here is, *Why are we not now playing rugby?* Given that Harvard managed to win over all the other Ivy Leaguers to its brand of football, why are we not now a rugby-playing nation? The answer is simple: we aren't playing rugby because we immediately began tinkering with rugby until we got something we liked. We did this because we thought that anything we did was superior, with the result that we turned our backs on the rest of the world, preferring domestic competition to international competition. As one person close in time to this process described it:

> Being bound by no traditions, and having seen no play, the American took the English rules for a starting-point, and almost immediately proceeded to add and subtract, according to what seemed his pressing needs.[28]

This author goes on to say that while a few Americans knew the rules, most were ignorant, but instead of getting them all to learn these rules, they just decided *it was easier to make up new ones*. And this simply exhibits the first factor mentioned above, that we were a new nation and that we thought that everything we did was better than what others were doing. So, we had no qualms in rejecting rugby for our own version of it.

From a soccer fan's point of view, there is very little reason to prefer either of football or rugby over the other (just as there is very little reason to prefer either of baseball or cricket over the other). What reason can now be given for preferring football over rugby? It is interesting that not much can be said. Most Americans can easily summon up a reason for rejecting soccer (too little scoring). And most can also quickly summon up a reason for rejecting cricket (too slow). But what is wrong with rugby? Here the American sports fan will probably flounder a bit before saying, "Well, it doesn't have the forward pass." There is a lot of passing in rugby, but it is all lateraling sideways and backwards. It is never thrown overhand forward. That is what football has that rugby doesn't. And why is this so important? (Does lacking a forward pass make rugby as bad as soccer?) Presumably, the forward pass represents a sort of American directness, a willingness to simply get things moving.

However, the forward pass wasn't present initially. In the source just cited, the reason given for rugby's inferiority was that rugby had a scrum from which the ball emerged at random, while football had a snap back to the quarterback, which was deliberate and didn't leave as much to chance, thus allowing skill to shine forth.[29] But no one would think of that today. What people would think of today is the forward pass.

Now let me put this idea of the superiority of the forward pass in context. First, rugby is a game in which many people get to pass and touch the ball, compared with football. Surely, that very democratic aspect of the game should count in any comparison, shouldn't it? So what if you have a game that features one quintessential part of America if that same game horribly violates the spirit of another quintessential part of America? Second, the directness of the forward pass as a way of getting things done and getting things moving is counteracted by football's huddle, in which a great deal of time is wasted in talking things over. In rugby, there are no huddles. The players simply do things right away. But third, that forward pass which is supposed to be so wonderful can effectively be done only once during a play. Once the ball passes the line of scrimmage, no more forward passes are allowed. In rugby, there can be many passes during what we would consider a play, and in soccer, there can be forward passes all the time.

We can see how prejudice against English sports reigned in these early days of American sports and how stupid it was. Baseball was considered superior to cricket because cricket supposedly reflected a English slowness. Yet, when soccer came along, emphasizing that the English weren't slow, the baseball players did not change their minds about the English. Meanwhile, those who liked football abandoned soccer, probably because it was too wimpy. If so, then the American football fan could chortle about how wimpy the English were. Of course, the fact that the English also played rugby, which is more rugged than football, was ignored. So, we see this rather pathetic need on the part of American sports fans and athletes to believe that they were better than the English, even if it meant being in denial about some obvious facts of life about English sports. Once the prejudice took hold, no one was going to go over to England to see what their sports were actually like.

Meanwhile, we tinkered with rugby until we got something we liked. Tinkering, incidentally, was done not only when football was first born; it has also continued to this day. One of the things I learned while researching this book was that the word "touchdown" refers in rugby to an actual act of touching the ball down to the ground in the end zone, while in American football one needs merely to get into the end zone with the ball. Nevertheless, we still refer to this as a "touchdown." This is a relic of the earlier rule which got lost along the way because rule changes are so frequent in football. Another such relic is of course the very word "football," which seems so inappropriate for our brand of football. "Crunchball" or something similar would be more descriptive.

But the point about tinkering brings us to a very important question: Suppose that Harvard had preferred soccer rather than rugby? Would we now have soccer today? No. If we don't have rugby today, even though we once had it, then there is no good reason to imagine that we would now have soccer today if all those Ivy Leaguers had preferred soccer. Rugby got changed by the people at Harvard, and there is no good reason to imagine that they wouldn't have tinkered with the rules of soccer as well. Even today the first reaction of the average American upon seeing a soccer game is to demand that the rules be changed. Never mind that even with changed rules, the American would probably still ignore it. And never mind that a few billion people in the world are quite satisfied with those rules; the rest of the world needs to bow down to our sporting preferences. So, if Harvard had played soccer, today we would have some version of soccer which would be as far from actual soccer as football is from rugby. Heaven only knows what it would look like. Maybe there would be no goalie. Maybe it would be more like Gaelic football, in which one can score in a variety of ways. Maybe one would be allowed to use the hands in certain situations. But of one thing we can be certain: if Harvard had preferred soccer, we would now be playing the American version of soccer and not what everyone else is playing.

Could all of this have happened differently? We know that in Brazil things did happen differently. In Brazil, no doubt there was among the many expatriate English groups a sense of English superiority and snobbery. This can be seen from the very beginning. In 1894 when the Englishman Charles Miller, who grew up in Brazil but was educated in England, returned to his home in Brazil with two soccer balls, the game was introduced to the other English expatriates. The upper classes of Brazilian society were also welcomed, but everyone else (especially blacks) was excluded. Yet, instead of turning their backs on the game of soccer and inventing some new Brazilian game, the ones who were excluded persisted in their efforts to get included, with the result that today, not only is everyone included, but also the inclusiveness led to the Brazilian style of play, which is the most admired in the world. Perhaps this persistence was due to the fact that Brazilians, unlike Americans, simply didn't feel themselves to be doing new and exciting things and so felt no need to run off and invent a new game. Or perhaps it was because the Brazilians had no other competing ball games or because they were already familiar to some extent with some version of soccer. Or perhaps it was just because they did feel that they wanted to beat the other guy at his own game, especially after having been excluded from it.

Most countries – not just Brazil – in the late nineteenth and early twentieth centuries had to come to terms with English sports. How should they react? They had no sports of their own, but meanwhile the resident English were playing some interesting and fun-looking games. Should they play these games as well, even though their feelings about the English were ambiguous at best? Or should they shun them? Most countries decided that they would play the games but at the same time would try to beat England. Instead of inventing new games or new rules for English games, they would play soccer in some new way. Scotland was the first to do this, changing soccer from being a purely dribbling game to a game that included passing. The change here wasn't a rule change, but a change in the way the game was played, a tactical change. Other countries changed the game basically by imprinting their own cultural stamp on the game, but they kept the rules intact. It was only here in the United States that people decided to reject the games entirely or to tinker with the rules, that it wasn't worthwhile even to beat the other guy at his own game or to change the tactics or to invent an American style of play. We wanted to change the rules entirely, with the result that we became isolated.

Another way of looking at the situation is to consider how we might have reacted if soccer had come from Spain or Italy rather than England. Some time after the Revolutionary War, we felt smothered and threatened by English culture (as I have already mentioned), and one response to this, odd as it may seem, was to glorify Christopher Columbus. The science historian Owen Gingerrich has related this strange turn of events as follows:

> The doctrine [that early Americans] were trying to forget was the standard British view that one of theirs, Sebastian Cabot, was the first to make landfall in North America – Columbus had merely found some small islands in the Indies. In the aftermath of the Revolution, Americans desperately needed some non-British heroes. Columbus filled the bill even though no one knew much about him.[30]

If at that time our anti-British feelings caused us to turn to an Italian hero sailing for Spain whom no one knew anything about, it is possible that if soccer had come to us from Italy or Spain we might have accepted it without any fuss. Certainly, our feelings toward Italy and Spain at that time were quite different from our feelings toward the English. On the other hand, though, we rejected the metric system when it was first proposed, even though it came from France rather than England, so it's an open question whether we would have accepted soccer if it had come from some country other than England.

Of course, there is another factor that kept soccer prejudice alive for so many years, and that is the physical isolation of America from much of the rest of the world. Most Americans lived (and still do live) quite far from a foreign country. Communications and transportation were not so advanced as to allow the average American to see what was going on in other countries. Those who could travel overseas to Europe and to see what was happening in sports over there probably had no interest in such sports anyway. Such people would have been wealthy and so were probably more interested in sports like polo or tennis rather than soccer. Our geographical isolation encouraged our cultural isolation. If our geographical situation had resembled that of Belgium, say, where the nearest neighbors are just a few dozen miles away, the situation would have been vastly different. It would have been difficult for us to ignore what our neighbors were doing and not to notice when they were doing something quite different from us. It would have been difficult to avoid assessing our own sports environment in contrast with other sports environments to see whose was best. But we lived in splendid isolation and ignorance, never quite realizing that other people were experiencing pleasures in sport that we weren't.

An amusing parallel to our feelings of being stifled by British culture in the nineteenth century is occurring today to a different country, for the French are currently going through what we Americans once went through. The French don't take kindly to the fact that their own culture is now being overwhelmed by another culture. After all, their own culture ruled the "civilized" world in centuries past. We can see this in Leo Tolstoy's *War and Peace*, which is about Russia during the Napoleonic Wars. The Russian upper classes had become so Frenchified that they could barely speak Russian anymore. They hardly knew their own native tongue.[31]

The situation is quite different today, however. The French now feel overwhelmed by English-speaking culture, specifically, primarily (but by no means wholly) by American culture. We Americans have watched their efforts with amusement. The French try to keep certain English words out of their vernacular, but it is impossible. Officials demand that radio stations play some percentage of music written or performed by French artists, but most people want to listen to something else. But any American who is inclined to be smug about this silliness on the part of the French should take a look at the sports pages of any American newspaper. The mere choice of sports in that newspaper, as contrasted with the choice made by foreign newspapers, shows that we once went through this same sort of thing *and that the effects are still with us.* Our newspapers focus on *our* sports and do not deign to pay attention to "foreign" sports.

Other Explanations

In the last chapter, I insisted that our hostility to soccer is worthy of being called prejudice, and in this chapter I traced the roots of that prejudice to our sense of superiority together with feelings of Anglophobia at a crucial period in the nineteenth century. I further observed that this prejudice has been maintained because of our geographical and consequent cultural isolation from the rest of the world. But are there other explanations for our hostility? People have suggested one thing and another to me down through the years, but it seems to me that my explanation is best. However, I do want to consider two other explanations, both given by academics. The first is given by Andrei S. Markovits and Steven L. Hellerman in their book *Offside: Soccer and American Exceptionalism.* Their theory begins with the claim that all the various ways in which America is exceptional – that is, different from the rest of the world – are the result of the same cause. That means that the reason why we haven't taken to socialism, for example, is the same as the reason why we haven't taken to soccer. In fact, they call socialism the "original" American exceptionalism.[32]

Initially, this seemed to me a strange thesis. The idea that we rejected soccer and socialism for the same reason or reasons wasn't one that struck me as at all plausible initially. After all, Americans who hate socialism have investigated it very carefully and know it through and through, while Americans who hate soccer really know nothing about it. Also, if soccer and socialism have been rejected for the same reasons, then one would expect that both of them would have been embraced by the same sorts of people. But that hasn't been true at all. I have known many American soccer fans, and I have known many American socialists. There is almost no overlap between the two groups. Most American soccer fans are apolitical, in the center or somewhat to the right of center. I know only a few soccer fans who are leftists. Likewise, most American leftists hate or are at best indifferent to soccer. Markovits himself is an exception to this pattern. And so am I. And so are one or two other people I know. But the fact is that the overlap between America's soccer fans and its socialists (or in my case, former socialist) is vanishingly small. And that suggests that America's rejection of both soccer and socialism has different causes.

Nevertheless, there is perhaps something to what they are saying. We may have rejected socialism because we thought that our system was superior and could do a better job of handling the problems that socialism was supposed to handle. And as I have been arguing, we rejected soccer because we thought our sports were superior to sports invented by foreigners. And almost certainly we have rejected the metric system because we saw our system as superior to or at any rate no worse than the metric system (though in this instance we inherited the English system from the English rather than inventing our own). In all three of these "exceptionalisms," there is the arrogant American attitude that we were doing things in a way superior to that of others and that those others, if they had any sense, should adopt our ways.

What is objectionable about Markovits and Hellerman's thesis is the way they present it, which includes a great deal of what I would call "excess baggage," conceptually speaking. That is, it includes all sorts of concepts that simply don't need to be there. To begin with, they offer no proof that all the different ways in which America is unique are related. They simply assume that to be the case. For example, on page 9 of their book they assert, "We argue that America's sports exceptionalism is deeply rooted in other exceptionalisms that constitute essential features of American life." Yet, they don't in fact argue for this. One of America's exceptionalisms is our rejection of the metric system, which nearly everyone else accepts. But the metric system is mentioned only once in their book, on page 291. And even there they merely quote someone else instead of talking about it themselves. How exactly, then, did they argue for their claim without talking about the metric system?

For that matter, the idea that our rejection of socialism is the "original" American exceptionalism can be questioned since we rejected the metric system long before we rejected socialism. After all, the metric system was introduced in the early nineteenth century, but the rejection of socialism *in the relevant sense* did not occur until much later. I emphasize the words "in the relevant sense" simply because it is no good saying that America rejected socialism when it first emerged in the early nineteenth century, because most other countries did so as well. How, then, would our rejection of it make us exceptional? Our exceptionalism with respect to socialism only became evident when other countries adopted it or developed strong socialist parties, but that wasn't until much later. Now it is true that not all other countries adopted the metric system when it was first invented. Britain was a notable standout, for example. But given that most other countries accepted it, that is enough to say that the first instance of our exceptionalism concerned the metric system.

Next, on pages 8 and 9 of their book they explain why socialism wasn't accepted here in America, and they give seven reasons, almost none of which have any bearing on our refusal to accept soccer. Reason number four is:

> The abundance of cheap land allowed individuals to seek their fortune apart from inhabited areas.

What this has to do with our rejection of soccer is never explained, and most of the other reasons are just as irrelevant. The closest they come to something that actually relates to soccer is in reason number seven. Here is the first part of what they say:

> Perhaps the most important common denominator of all exceptionalisms and the single most pervasive underlying variable for an understanding of American politics and society is the quintessentially bourgeois nature of America's objective development and subjective self-legitimation from its very inception to the present.

Perhaps the factor of our bourgeois nature does explain our rejection of soccer, but they do not argue for this. Plus, it is a stretch to say that this factor is "quintessential," that it represents the most "pervasive underlying variable" for understanding our society. During much of American history, many people lived in rural areas from which the clash of the bourgeoisie and the proletariat was far removed (as their own remark about abundant land in reason number four illustrates). Anyway, what does our bourgeois nature have to do with our rejection of soccer? Here is how they continue their reason number seven:

> In short, bourgeois America created a new *liberal* identity priding itself on being of European origin, yet also on transcending – and bettering – this origin's old aristocratic framework by a new republican virtue in a new world.

At last we get to something that seems relevant. I think it's true that our belief that we could "transcend" or better Europe's institutions had a great deal to do with our rejection of soccer. As I have been saying, we thought we could invent better things, not just in government but in other areas as well, and so when we adopted rugby, we tinkered with it and came up with football. But now comes the big question: *what does our belief that we could do better than Europe have to do with our bourgeois nature or a liberal identity?* This question is never answered. It is never even asked. Apparently, the authors take it for granted that our bourgeois nature will automatically lead to a belief that we could do better than Europe. But even if that is true, it needs proof. And anyway, the authors neglect the possibility that this belief arose independently of any bourgeois nature, for many cultures throughout history have thought of themselves as superior without having a bourgeois nature. Moreover, many early Americans lived in rural areas, yet it is likely that they would have developed these same feelings of superiority on their own.

Let me consider another thing said, by Markovits, in an interview with the *Chronicle of Higher Education*. The interviewer asked if soccer's failure here was the result of its foreign origin. Here is Markovits's reply:

> It's a vestige of the historical construct of "sports" that arose in the two most advanced industrial societies – Britain and the U.S. – between 1860 and 1920. America created its own industrial modernity, which doesn't have a large, mass-based socialist or social democratic labor party, and it created its own sports: baseball, football, and basketball. By the time soccer came here the American masses already had baseball.[33]

Here, Markovits talks about two developments in America – that of industrial modernity and that of sports – and automatically assumes that they are related. He might just as well have talked about the development of important inventions during this period (like the telegraph, telephone and radio), or race relations (for after all, this period included the Civil

War), or the rise of the suffragettes. Why is our rejection of soccer related to the rise of "industrial modernity" rather than these other developments? No reason is given. The only advantage to mentioning the development of industrial modernity is that our development didn't lead to socialism. But so what? I still don't see how this is related to our rejection of soccer.

It is true that the authors have explained something related to sports by appealing to the rise of the bourgeoisie and industrial modernity (and the corresponding failure of socialism). It's just not what they think they have explained. They haven't explained why we rejected soccer, but they have explained why sports were transformed from a casual, informal affair to the big business that it is today. For that one does need to talk about the rise of the bourgeoisie, industrial modernity, and mass society. But beyond that, I cannot see any reason to mention such concepts. Sports in America and the rest of the world might have remained at the casual level it was at in the year 1860, and we might still be playing baseball and rejecting soccer and cricket even for informal games.

If we focus just on the idea that we Americans thought of ourselves as superior and capable of inventing new traditions and institutions, then it is reasonable that we rejected both soccer and socialism for the same reason. But the factors of abundant land, our bourgeois nature, and industrial modernity, if they are relevant to our rejection of socialism, are also irrelevant to our rejection of soccer, and so are quite beside the point.

Markovits and Hellerman have expounded what I think is a theory that, to the extent that it is correct, is also a theory that places too much emphasis upon concepts that are utterly irrelevant. But at least they seem to touch upon what I regard as the correct theory. The same cannot be said of Sam Whitsitt, who wrote an article in 1994 on why Americans have rejected soccer. Markovits and Hellerman's theory is wrong to some extent, but Whitsitt's is just plain loony. According to Whitsitt, we rejected soccer in favor of football because football was a White, Anglo-Saxon, Protestant (WASP) game, while soccer wasn't. Football was developed in the WASP culture of our Ivy Leagues, while soccer hadn't been. Among other things, this means the following: "American football ... is finally antifoot, even opposed to the lower body – as is, correspondingly, WASP culture in general." He then adds, "Only a few short years ago it was still possible that audiences could be ecstatic about seeing, in the film *Lethal Weapon*, Mel Gibson's bare butt." In football, there is a "prejudice against the lower half of the body.... It is so embarrassingly obvious to all of us spectators that no one talks about it." He goes on to admit that there are kickers in football, but argues – and on this one point I agree – that they aren't really representative members of the team.³⁴

Anyone who undertakes to explain that group A is different from group B because of factor x had better make sure that factor x applies to only one of these groups. It is no good saying they are different because one is affected by factor x if in fact both of them are. In that case, nothing has been explained. But making this elementary mistake is exactly what Whitsitt has done. He argues that we like football and not soccer because of our original WASP culture. Yet, does this explain our *difference* from the rest of the world, particularly England? England is where WASP culture *originated*. It, too, was a WASP culture at the time that we invented football, and if so, and if WASP culture rejects soccer, then why did England relish soccer and reject our football?

In addition, the idea that football is prejudiced against the lower half of the body is utterly ridiculous. While reading Whitsitt's article, I was reminded of a time in my childhood when I felt mildly embarrassed about the position of the linemen when awaiting the snap of the ball, for their butts were so prominently displayed to the spectators. (Not naked, of course.) And one of the first things I was taught about making a tackle in football is that it is worthless to grab the upper half of the ball carrier's body. You have to grab the lower half to bring him down. No, football is not prejudiced against the lower half of the body. For that matter, many of us played kickball when we were young, kickball being the children's version of baseball in which the ball is kicked rather than batted. So, it is false that WASP culture in general is antifoot. Finally, so what if football developed in our WASP culture while soccer didn't? What does this explain? We would still want to know why something that developed in our WASP culture became so popular beyond that culture whereas something that was not developed there did not. Whitsitt's ideas are doomed.

Judging the Early Prejudices

I have to admit that the reaction of the early baseball players, even though prejudiced, was not wholly unreasonable. Or at any rate, I don't know that I would have reacted any differently. If someone urged me to play a sport that had been invented by Osama bin Laden, I would probably be more interested in slugging them than in playing such a sport. I know that this contradicts slightly what I said in the last chapter, that the true sports fan doesn't care who invented a sport, but as time presses on, such strong emotions will fade and one can think about things in a more objective light. What is striking is that this didn't happen with respect to soccer and other English sports. It should have been evident by the beginning of the twentieth century that England had something important to offer the rest of the world in the sport of soccer, for that is when the rest of Europe and South America took to soccer in large numbers, and by continuing with our prejudice against things English, we made a grievous error. After either World Wars I or II, during which we were *allied* with the British, Americans should have overcome this prejudice, because obviously our relations with the British had changed so drastically since the first half of the nineteenth century. Later, the supposedly tolerant and open-minded 1960s was perhaps the best time to have overcome this prejudice, for that was when many young Americans began questioning everything (or so they thought) about American society. Yet, it didn't happen that way. Finally, after September 11, the British became our staunchest ally. Isn't it time for us to drop our animosity towards British sports? Why are so many Americans still fighting the War of 1812? And especially, why are so many American leftists, who don't like wars and who don't like America very much, still fighting this war?

Endnotes

1. Bonnie S. Ledbetter, "Sports and Games of the American Revolution," *Journal of Sports History* 6 (1979), p. 30.
2. Michael Novak, *The Joy of Sports*, p. 59.
3. Cited in Charles Fruehling Springwood, *Cooperstown to Dyersville: A Geography of Nostalgia* (Westview, 1996), p. 1.
4. See John E. Moser, *Twisting the Lion's Tail: American Anglophobia between the World Wars* (New York: New York University Press, 1999), p. 2.
5. Benjamin Spencer, *The Quest for Nationality* (Syracuse University, 1957), p. 74.
6. It is nevertheless true that the occasional Anglophobia emerges in unexpected places. The American academic Cary Nelson has tried to persuade other Americans that the subject of cultural studies was invented in Britain. He describes one reaction to his efforts as follows: "My friend Vincent Leitch, who ought to know better, stood up in the audience, waving his arms as he scaled some Bunker Hill of the imagination, and declared that he 'thought we had thrown off the yoke

of the British two hundred years ago.'" [Cary Nelson, *Manifesto of a Tenured Radical* (New York University Press, 1997), p. 54]
7. Cited without attribution in Harold Seymour, *Baseball: The Early Years* (New York and Oxford: Oxford University Press, 1960), p. 14.
8. *Harper's*. Cited in David Quentin Voigt, *American Baseball: From Gentleman's Sport to the Commissioner System* vol. 1 (Pennsylvania State University, 1983), 7. No date listed (perhaps Oct. 22, 1859).
9. George B. Kirsch, *The Creation of American Team Sports: Baseball and Cricket, 1838-72* (University of Illinois, 1989), p. 213.
10. Kirsch, p. 94; from the *Jersey City Daily Courier and Advertiser*, July 2, 1859.
11. *Chadwick Scrapbooks*. Cited in William Ryczek, *When Johnny Comes Sliding Home: The Post-Civil War Baseball Boom, 1865-1870* (McFarland, 1998), p. 54.
12. *Funk and Wagnalls*, vol. 18, p. 243. Cited in Ryczek, pp. 54-5.
13. Cited in Kirsch, p. 219.
14. *Porter's Spirit of the Times* 2 (May 9, 1857), p. 19. Cited in George Kirsch, p. 30.
15. *Clipper* 5 (May 16, 1857), p. 26. Cited in Kirsch, p. 92.
16. Kirsch, 97. *Clipper* September 7, 1861, 164.
17. Cited in Kirsch, p. 219.
18. Seymour, *Baseball*, p. 31.
19. Dean A. Sullivan, *Early Innings* (University of Nebraska, 1995), p. 279.
20. Cited in David Quentin Voigt, *American Baseball: From Gentleman's Sport to the Commissioner System*, vol. 1, 7.
21. *Early Innings*, p. 282.
22. *Early Innings*, p. 290.
23. *Early Innings*, p. 292.
24. For example, Harold Seymour, *Baseball*, p. 31: "Besides, during a 'time of intense nativism, many Americans experienced an instinctive aversion for cricket just because it was English.'" The source for Seymour's quote is not given.
25. Jules Tygiel, *Past Time: Baseball as History* (Oxford University, 2000), pp. 7-8.
26. Kirsch, 97.
27. *Porter's Spirit* 4 (April 3, 1858), p. 68. Cited in Kirsch, 63.
28. Walter Camp, *American Football* (New York: Harper and Brothers, 1891), p. 8.

29. Walter Camp, *American Football*, pp. 9-10.
30. Owen Gingerich, "Astronomy in the Age of Columbus," *Scientific American* vol. 267 (Novmber, 1992), 101.
31. See especially Book X, Chapter XVII.
32. Andrei S. Markovits and Steven L. Hellerman, *Offside*, p. x.
33. *Chronicle of Higher Education*, June 14, 2002, p. A14.
34. Sam Whitsitt, "Soccer: The Game America Refuses to Play," *Raritan* 14 (Summer 1994), pp. 61, 63, and 64.

CHAPTER 8
The Persistence of Prejudice: American Cultural Isolationism

Prejudice against cricket, and later soccer, was the result of their foreign origins. Yet, why has this prejudice persisted? Why is it so strong that even leftists succumb to it? I say that it's because of our cultural isolationism. That isolationism was partly spurred by our geographical isolation from the rest of the world at a time when communications and transportation were much more difficult than they are today. But it is more than that. As I pointed out in the last chapter, we felt ourselves to be superior to the Old World of Europe, and so felt little need to know about or understand what was going on in other countries. The *cultural* isolation that I am talking about should be differentiated from the isolationism that America experienced before World War II and which occasionally emerges even today among a few politicians. That isolationism was a deliberate *political* policy of turning our backs on the politics of the rest of the world, on its alliances, on its diplomatic intrigues, on its wars. Still, probably the national impulse to be politically isolated was a result of our impulse to be culturally isolated.

In this chapter I want to recount the various ways that Americans are isolated from the rest of the world culturally. We are most isolated when it comes to sports, but there are also other areas in which we are isolated as well. Before proceeding, however, let me acknowledge that in certain areas Americans are not so isolated. Americans have long been acquainted with foreign authors like Shakespeare, Jane Austen, or even Fyodor Dostoyevsky. Lovers of classical music have always been entranced with European composers like Bach, Beethoven and Mozart. And the Beatles from England had a huge impact when I was young. With the development of planes like the Boeing 747, many Americans now travel to Europe and other places. British television shows regularly come to America, and cable companies often provide Spanish-language television channels. Americans have become much more open to and knowledgeable about religions like Buddhism that were once just names to us. We love foreign food. Yet, the dominant trend in American cultural life has been and continues to be our cultural isolation from the rest of the world. Let me recount the ways.

Sports: International Rules

I have already talked a lot about sports of course, but let me add one point. Prior to getting involved in soccer, I would occasionally hear about "international rules." I thought these rules were a compromise among all the nations playing a sport. Now I know that in fact everyone else plays by these international rules, while we insist on having our own rules. Then when we get into international competition, we must suddenly play by rules we aren't familiar with. This hurts us, naturally, and isn't very smart, but my main point here is that we are isolated in terms of the rules we accept, even when we play sports that everyone else plays.

The Metric System

Soccer is accepted almost everywhere else, but rejected by Americans. The metric system is similar. It is accepted almost everywhere else, but is rejected by Americans. I think the reasons are probably similar. In both cases, it is feelings of arrogance and cultural superiority. "Let them adapt to the way we do things" is the way that most Americans think on both subjects. Most Americans seeing soccer for the first time see no reason why we should adopt it and immediately begin to make suggestions on how it should be changed so as to be more acceptable to Americans (though they would be angered if foreigners said that about *our* sports). Likewise, most Americans see no reason why *we* should adopt the metric system when our own system works perfectly well for us. The only dissenters are scientists, who use the metric system regularly.

The irony here is that what we think of as our system actually came to us from England, the very same country that developed the rules for soccer. As I said in Chapter 6, this is typical of the contradictions that afflict the soccer haters of this country.

Foreign Languages

While we Americans have always spent some time learning foreign languages, the general belief of the American populace is that this is a waste of time. I had no strong feelings one way or the other on this topic when I was young, but getting involved in soccer put me firmly in the opposing camp. During the late 1970s, I was playing on an intramural soccer team at the University of Minnesota. Because so many of the teams were composed of foreign students, it quickly became evident how important it was to know foreign languages when one is dealing with foreigners. They could understand everything we said, whereas we couldn't understand anything they said. This didn't help us one bit on the playing field. Even before I observed this, soccer had forced me to learn a little bit of some foreign languages. I wanted to read as much as possible about soccer, but so little of it that was available was written in English that I just had to spend some time gaining at least a rudimentary reading knowledge of some foreign languages. My experiences not just reading about but also playing soccer simply reinforced this belief. We need to learn foreign languages because knowing them is so useful in international business, diplomacy, espionage, and war.

Eventually, in the 1980s, various educators began to agree with me, though their convictions hadn't been reinforced on the soccer field the way that mine had been. Still, their concern wasn't shared much by the general public, for when the terrorists struck on September 11, it was revealed that only a minuscule number of people in America had graduated the previous year with a major in Arabic.

There are many stories of howlers connected with our refusal to learn foreign languages, stories such as the Chevy Nova, which when marketed in Spanish-speaking markets was a flop because "no va" in Spanish means "it doesn't go." Here is one I noticed on my own. Some time during the 1970s or 1980s, the expression "mano a mano" became popular. It is Spanish for "hand to hand," but it's not clear that everyone understands this. Many people seem to think that it is just a hip way of saying "man to man."

There are also many horror stories of people speaking foreign languages being treated in some terrible way by one of our bureaucracies, because it was assumed they were English speakers. There are stories of people assumed to be mentally ill or put in prison for crimes they didn't commit, simply because they couldn't communicate with the people around them who were all English speakers.

Have things changed much since the 1980s? A little. There are now summer camps for foreign languages, and there are even Spanish-language immersion schools. Yet, there are still plenty of Americans who for the life of them just cannot see the importance of learning foreign languages. I've argued with these people in Internet discussions, but not even the shock of 9/11 changed their minds. There continues to be a vast swath of the public that sees no need to learn a foreign language, the reason being that so many other people speak English.

Knowledge of Geography

Once involved in soccer, I couldn't help but to learn more about the world. About the only facts I knew about Brazil when I first began my involvement in soccer were that it was in South America and that its inhabitants spoke Portuguese. Knowing the latter put me ahead of all the people who think they speak Spanish, which is true of most Americans. Most Americans, however, are ahead of the American I once met who assured me that Brazil was in Australia. But I began to read more and more about Brazil until I knew far more than the average American did. I also began learning about many other parts of the world. I hung a bunch of maps on the walls of my apartment just to remind me of all the countries I was now learning about.

Most Americans have little incentive to learn geography. (How many knew where Afghanistan was before 9/11?) When I was an undergraduate in college, the general view among my friends was that geography was a ridiculously easy subject and therefore could be ignored. (I shared this view myself, I'm embarrassed to admit.) Still, it always pays to know some geography, just as it pays to know arithmetic, and most Americans know little or nothing about geography. This ignorance was exhibited in various standardized tests beginning in the 1980s, and it always shocked people that some of our students couldn't even pick out the United States on a map.

But having some knowledge of geography can be helpful. It can pay if you meet someone from a foreign country and exhibit some knowledge of it, which often delights them. I was once taking a taxi from the Minneapolis-St. Paul airport, and the driver was a black man who obviously – obviously to me, anyway – was from Africa. I asked where he was from, and he said Minneapolis. I said I meant originally. Then I hazarded a guess. "Eritrea?" I asked, for he looked like some immigrants from Eritrea I had once seen playing soccer in a Minneapolis park. He was utterly astounded, and pleased as well. He said he was actually from nearby Ethiopia, the enemy of Eritrea, but because I guessed so close to his true country of origin he was willing to overlook this blunder. He also said that others had guessed he was from Europe.

I should add that when I was growing up I somehow learned that one shouldn't ask people where they're from, that it wasn't polite. When I got involved in soccer, I was meeting foreigners frequently, and I decided to dispense with this rule. I always asked people where they were from, and no one ever seemed bothered about answering this question, especially if I showed some knowledge of their country. The only time I ever received a negative reaction to this question was when I guessed about someone and guessed wrong. But even that didn't always work out badly, as the instance with the taxi driver showed.

General Knowledge of Other Cultures

Not only is our knowledge of foreign geography abysmal, our general knowledge of other cultures is hopeless. Many Americans, as I've already mentioned, imagine that Brazilians speak Spanish instead of Portuguese. Lots of Americans (including me before I got involved in soccer) don't know the difference between the terms "English" and "British." Many Americans imagine that Iran is an Arab country instead of a Persian country. Probably the worst mistake recently was the American who shot a Sikh after the 9/11 attack, thinking that he was a Muslim extremist and not understanding that Sikhs are of a different religion (one that has its own problems with Muslim extremists). Unfortunately, it usually isn't until a war comes along that Americans learn about some other culture.

Think of the contrast, however, with the countries of Europe. While for many Americans, the nearest foreign country is hundreds or thousands of miles away, for Europeans the nearest foreign country is just a stone's throw away. One can't help but knowing about other cultures when they are right on your doorstep, when they are so close that you can get their television and radio stations. We are both blessed and cursed by our geography, blessed because it is so difficult for invaders to get to us, but cursed because we have little incentive to learn about anyone else.

News from Other Cultures

Americans are generally ignorant of what is happening in other countries, until some disaster strikes. Accordingly, the impression that many Americans have of the rest of the world is quite distorted, to say the least.

This ignorance is the result of our major news sources – the local news on television, the local newspaper, and magazines like *Time* – preferring not to cover foreign news unless something terribly important or unusual has happened. By contrast, the *Economist* (which comes from Britain) gives coverage of various regions of the world even if nothing especially urgent is happening.

Of course, *The New York Times* has a great deal of news that the usual sources for Americans don't have. Many intellectuals I know read the *Times* and listen to National Public Radio (NPR), and so are much better informed about what is happening in the rest of the world than ordinary Americans are. But even these sources can't give one everything, as I quickly learned when I got totally involved in soccer. They weren't covering soccer, for example. But they were also ignoring many other things.

As a result of many years of relying on foreign as well as American sources for my news, I am convinced that one cannot be fully informed if one simply relies on the news sources in one's own country. Think of it this way. The world has many billions of people in it, and those people are doing lots of things. Some of what they are doing is not newsworthy, some of it will interest only their friends or perhaps their neighborhood or local region, some will be of interest only to the people in that country, but some will be of interest to others.

Since so much is happening, the media in each country take on the role of filters for the average person. They assume that they know what is best for you and that they know what you want to hear. Then they give it to you. The other news, the news that they think you don't want to hear or ought not to hear, they toss out. Every type of media uses this system. It can't be helped because there is so much news to report, and decisions have to be made. I once heard a friend rave about a new cable channel (I think he was talking about Cable News Network – that is, CNN – but it might have been something else) that he said covered *everything*. I almost laughed in his face. *No one can cover everything*. There is too much happening for that to be possible. So the media act as filters for you so you won't be overwhelmed.

However, the main trouble here is that the people in a given country's media will tend to think alike, and so they may all discard news that is interesting to you as an individual. They will all tend to have the same sorts of blind spots, which they absolutely refuse to recognize because these blind spots are so much a part of their thinking. I recognized early on that one of our media's blind spots is foreign sports. With my voracious appetite for soccer news, there was never enough in the American media to satisfy me, and so I turned to the foreign media. In addition to hearing the latest doings in the world of soccer, I also learned of the latest doings in the rest of the world about other things. Of course, the foreign media also have their own blind spots. But I believe that if you use both foreign and domestic media, you are much more likely to learn about important things that are happening than if you use just your own country's media (and I don't care if it's NPR and *The New York Times*). The British probably have blind spots in their coverage of the news; obviously, they don't pay much attention to our sports. And there are probably other things that they don't notice either. But it is unlikely that the British have *exactly* the same set of blind spots that we Americans do. The British media will notice things that the American media won't. Of course, the more countries you rely on to get news from, the better off you are when it comes to learning what the truth is. The British and the Americans may have some blind spots in common that aren't shared by others, so it is not enough just to rely on the British either. You need to rely on other countries as well.

In addition, using foreign media allows us to learn how they see us, for they see us in their own unique ways that may startle us when we learn about them. The quote by Hugh McIlvanney in Chapter 6, who said that insularity is our national sport, might surprise even the most sophisticated Americans, for the simple reason that his description includes them. Almost none of our pundits who write for *The New York Times* or any other such organ complain when Americans describe the Super Bowl as the greatest sporting event on earth. Many other examples like this could be given.

Now there is nothing particularly difficult or subtle about what I am saying. Most people who are college educated should be able to understand it. Yet, I know of almost no other Americans who rely on the foreign media for foreign news. As I said above, most Americans rely on their local sources (and CNN), while the more sophisticated ones rely on *The New York Times* and NPR. It's not enough. Here's an example of what I mean. Some years ago, Robert Mugabe, the leader of Zimbabwe, was in the news. What was surprising was the very different ways that the American and the British media treated him. In Britain, the big scandal connected with Mugabe was that he accused Tony Blair of having homosexuals working for him; in other words, Mugabe was homophobic. Yet here in America, this was rarely reported.

I know some people will say that they listen to the BBC on the radio or watch BBC America on cable TV. And that is admirable. Still, listening to the BBC on the radio means getting it from a feed, and that feed is controlled by our media. The real way to listen to the BBC is on shortwave, where no other Americans are controlling what you hear. As for BBC America, I was very disappointed with it when it first came along. I was expecting to see important soccer games televised, but they show none. In this case, even though the filters are foreign, they still block out what they think Americans don't want to see, and so one doesn't really get the news that people in Britain would get. Anyway, with the Internet, one can now easily read British newspapers like *The Times* (of London) and *The Guardian*, yet almost no one seems to do so. I am constantly hearing the sophisticated say, "I read an article in the *Times*," meaning *The New York Times*. Only once have I heard a person say, "I read an article in the *Guardian*," and she was younger and presumably less indoctrinated in the proper ways of doing things.

The rise of the Internet has changed things, for a number of us now tend to rely on the Internet for news, and we rely on bloggers from other countries who have interesting things to tell us that our own media won't. Here again, though, people who are sophisticated tend to rely on Google rather than Yahoo, which hampers them. The advantage of Yahoo over Google, in terms of news, is that Google simply has a list of news items, while Yahoo has Yahoo sites in a number of countries, each with its own selection of news. One of the first things I do in the morning is to look at the news on the various Yahoos. I start with America's Yahoo, then I look at Canada's, Britain's, India's and Singapore's. Occasionally, I will look at the Yahoo of a country speaking a foreign language to try to puzzle out what they are saying. Checking the news in this way gives one a much better idea of what is happening in foreign countries than relying on a list, as Google does.

Shortwave Radio

Shortwave radio, although it relates to my previous section, needs a special section all its own. Most Americans don't know anything about shortwave radio, which they confuse with ham radio. Shortwave radio consists of stations which broadcast on certain bands of the electromagnetic wave spectrum and which are generally (though not always) run by governments. For example, Britain's station is the BBC, while our own is the Voice of America. Ham radio consists of individuals talking to each other on roughly the same bands. So, shortwave is similar to the ordinary AM and FM bands, while ham radio is similar to CB radio (which with the advent of cell phones is something probably few young people know about these days).

Another misconception is that shortwave can only be listened to at night, though in fact I've listened to the BBC when it was daylight in both London and the U.S. A third misconception is that a station from, say, Spain will broadcast in nothing but Spanish. In fact, stations typically broadcast in a number of different languages in order to get their messages out.

Because AM and FM are so prevalent and so easy to receive, we Americans generally see no reason to try anything else. (The situation is different, I've been led to believe, in much of the Third World.) Shortwave reception is not as good, admittedly, but in the days before the Internet, it was the best way to get foreign news direct from foreigners. Yet, it is strange that so many Americans are ignorant of it. I once spent an evening with some graduate students in political science, and despite the fact that one was doing a Ph.D. thesis on government communications, none of them knew anything about shortwave. In frustration from this and the general lack of knowledge I noticed among most people, I once spent the last fifteen minutes of the last day of an introductory philosophy class informing the students about shortwave. I knew it was ridiculous to be talking about such a subject in a philosophy class, but obviously it wasn't being taught in any other department.

Not only are Americans ignorant of shortwave, they are resistant to using it as well. In a more orthodox leftist phase of my life, I regularly listened to the English-language broadcasts of Radio Havana, but my efforts to get other leftists to listen were a complete failure.

The Most Distant Sub-Culture on Earth

What is the most distant culture or subculture on earth from our own culture? I'm not asking about distance in terms of actual physical distance, but distance in terms of knowledge. Which subculture are we *least* familiar with? It would have to be the cricket subculture of south Asia. Others are going to argue with this, citing one or another culture in obscure parts of the world, but I have to disagree. Many obscure cultures are shown on our television shows, are featured in magazines like *National Geographic*, or are discussed in college classes. Moreover, simply because of their physical and cultural remoteness, they are a challenge to the adventurous among

American travelers, who will go there and come back telling us what such people were like. The result is that we now have at least a basic familiarity with formerly isolated tribes in the most remote places on earth. But the cricketing subculture of south Asia is never shown on our television shows, never featured in *National Geographic*, and never discussed in our college classes. Because we Americans are trained to ignore "foreign" sports like soccer and cricket, it never occurs to even our most adventurous travelers to go explore the world of cricket in south Asia. Very few Americans have any knowledge of cricket to begin with, much less cricket in that part of the world. Face it, the cricketing subculture of south Asia represents, in terms of our awareness and knowledge of it, the most culturally distant spot from the United States. So here is a challenge to leftists who are baseball fans. Why don't you spend the next year focusing on cricket in south Asia instead of baseball here in America? If you are truly the multiculturalists you say you are, this shouldn't cause you any distress.

An Irritating Comparison

Granted that we are culturally isolated from the rest of the world, why is this so? Why are we so culturally isolated? I have suggested that part of the reason for this was our geographical isolation, but that is only part of the answer. In the last chapter, I also talked about how we felt ourselves to have a political system that we felt was vastly superior to other political systems, and we naturally began to feel that in the other ways we did things we were superior as well. We became uninterested in what was going on elsewhere. Yet, we needn't have been uninterested. We still might have been interested in other cultures, even though we felt superior.

Oddly enough, we inherited our cultural isolationism, our lack of interest in other cultures from *England*. I've already talked about this, but it bears repeating. Although England and America have chosen different sports and so have followed vastly different trajectories in terms of sports, it is amusing to see how similar we are. When the World Cup was first invented, the English had no interest in entering. Despite having been the first to codify the rules for soccer, and despite having brought those rules to the rest of the world, the English had no interest in competing with all these other people who had become so entranced by their sport. They remained stubbornly aloof. It wasn't until 1950 that England finally entered the World Cup, the reason apparently being that the lack of soccer during the war years had made the English sporting public hungry for competition. When the European Cup was instituted in 1955, again the

English disdained to enter the competition. Their teams had their own games to play, and they were too busy to play Continental teams. We have inherited this lack of interest in the rest of the world.

The same sort of stubbornness about learning foreign languages and studying foreign cultures that is so common today in America was once true of England as well. In the nineteenth century, Friedrich Engels complained of the culturally isolated English, of their "insular narrowness and insular conceit." He added that "up to quite recently the average English manufacturer considered it derogatory for an Englishman to speak any language but his own."[1] These attitudes changed during his stay in England, he acknowledged:

> About the middle of this century what struck every cultivated foreigner who set up his residence in England was that he was then bound to consider the religious bigotry and stupidity of the English respectable middle class.... The exhibition of 1851 sounded the knell of English insular exclusiveness. England became gradually internationalized, in diet, in manners, in ideas.[2]

Likewise, we too are gradually becoming internationalized, in diet, in ideas, and, most slowly of all, in sports. But what is ironic here is to contemplate the attitudes of the soccer haters of America. They may have escaped from English sports, but they haven't escaped from English insularity.

Let me conclude my discussion of our prejudice against soccer by saying that it was the result of three factors: our belief in our own superiority, our feeling culturally threatened by the British at a critical time in the development of our sports, and our lack of interest in other cultures. All these guaranteed that we would be prejudiced against soccer and other foreign sports for a long time.

Endnotes

1. Friedrich Engels, "On Historical Materialism," in Lewis S. Feuer, ed., *Marx and Engels: Basic Writings on Politics and Philosophy* (Anchor, 1959), p. 63, n. 3.
2. Engels, "On Historical Materialism," p. 50.

Chapter 9
The Ugly American Leftist

I had a friend in high school and college who always seemed to be the first one to embrace a new liberation movement. Naturally, he protested against the war in Vietnam. He had also grown a beard in high school at a time when that was absolutely forbidden and when no one else dared. He was the first person to introduce me to feminism. He was, despite being white, into black rights and Indian rights. He also was avid about using marijuana (something that I always shied away from). If there was a new movement brewing, he would be among its first supporters.

After a couple years of college, he traveled throughout Europe and settled in Amsterdam. Because of the spirit of toleration there, he could no doubt smoke marijuana to his heart's content. Now this was in the early 1970s, and anyone who knows anything about the history of soccer knows that at that time Holland was playing some of the best and most exciting soccer in the world. A whole generation of talented Dutch players – including Johan Cruyff, Johan Neeskins, Ruud Krol, Johnny Rep, and Arie Haan – were beginning to achieve acclaim for Dutch soccer, which had formerly been filled with nobodies. In 1970, Feyenoord won the European Cup, and for the next three years it was won by Ajax, located in Amsterdam. My friend, in other words, was living in Amsterdam right at a time when Dutch soccer was gaining global pre-eminence. Did he go to any soccer games while in Holland? No, not a one. It never seemed to occur to him that going to a soccer game while abroad might be an experience worth having. To put it bluntly, someone who talked a great deal about being open-minded, who was all in favor of every liberation movement, who was in favor of eliminating all prejudices, just couldn't overcome his own prejudice against soccer. At a time when Holland was playing the best, the most exciting, and the most interesting soccer in the world, he never went to a single game. I've lost track of this friend, but the last time I talked to him, he was living in a black neighborhood and playing, of course, basketball.

For me, this story epitomizes Sixties culture in America. Like it or not, my fellow leftists from the Sixties just couldn't handle the idea that Sixties toleration and open-mindedness should be extended to the sport of soccer. My friend is a perfect example of what I now call the Ugly American Leftist. The concept of the Ugly American Leftist comes from the concept of the Ugly American, which in turn is a concept that refers to the legions of Americans from earlier generations who viewed foreigners as hopelessly inferior, as primitive, as savage, as offering nothing at all in the way of new ideas to live by. My generation learned that we should not be Ugly Americans. We baby boomers learned that we should avoid that kind of thinking and the behavior that went along with it. Except in sports. Somehow, my generation, even those who were leftists, just couldn't manage to treat soccer and other foreign sports as legitimate parts of foreign cultures. Somehow, we just couldn't avoid thinking that all those soccer-playing foreigners would be much better off playing our sports and that it was a sign of inferiority on their part that they continued playing their own sports. The members of my generation who went off to foreign cultures to immerse themselves in those cultures somehow never came to respect their sports. When it came to sports, somehow my generation just never got the message.

Now one might say that the American left is no different from the rest of America in this respect. The rest of America feels the same way about sports in the rest of the world, so why pick on the left? But first of all, the left prides itself on its ability to overcome prejudices that others cannot and on its awareness of cultural differences that it takes the rest of society another generation or two to become aware of. Secondly, it also has set a standard that others are supposed to live up to. One of the most frequent complaints of leftists is the awful way that mainstream society treats certain people, how reluctant it is to acknowledge their problems, how even more reluctant it is to push for any changes. So, it is only fitting to hold the left to standards it has set for others. Finally, the excuse that the rest of America feels the way it does about sports just isn't true. While there are many non-leftists whose feelings about foreign sports are barbaric, the people I saw at the Minnesota Kicks games included (as I've already mentioned) many people, such as those in R.O.T.C. and in fraternities and sororities, whom one would not expect to be open-minded about other cultures. The same can be said about many other non-leftists. Tom Peters, the management guru, has stated that when doing business abroad, one shouldn't talk about American sports because even if the listener is familiar with them, he or she will think it is boorish. He said:

> I'm careful ... never to resort to baseball, football or other U.S. metaphors. It's not just that other people won't understand; often they do. But talk of a "full-court press" telegraphs cultural insensitivity.[1]

I've never heard an American leftist say anything like that! That it would be said instead by a capitalist!

What are leftists saying? I've encountered many horrible gaffes made by leftists down through the years, and for those who don't believe me, most of the examples I'm going to give can be checked because they are in the public record.

Let me start with an example that shows how seldom leftists follow Tom Peters' advice. This comes from a letter to the editor submitted to the *Times Literary Supplement* by Gore Vidal. This magazine comes from Britain and is read in many different countries, not just the United States. Wouldn't you think, then, that an American leftist writing a letter to such a magazine would take care to avoid using expressions from baseball that might not be understood by foreigners? After all, if someone like Tom Peters has figured this out, why not Vidal? Vidal, however, couldn't manage to perform this elementary task in international etiquette. He just couldn't help using the baseball metaphor "zingers from right field."[2]

Let me give an example of a typical leftist and what his interests are. Political theorist Michael Walzer wrote a column telling about his daily newspaper-reading habits. First, he said, he reads the obituaries, then he checks on what has happened in the Middle East.

> Next I enjoy the sports pages, spending as much time as possible with the baseball box scores. After that, I work my way through the foreign news, country by country.[3]

Wouldn't you think that someone with that much interest in foreign news would also have some interest in foreign *sports*? Apparently not.

Yet another example comes from an article in *Harpers* which was about saving languages spoken by just a few people. It is soaked with leftist sensitivity. What are we to make, then, of the following passage?

> Increasingly, our own language, English, dominates the world. It is the lingua franca of science, the Internet, the movies, rock and roll, and even sports. The word for home run in Spanish is *jonrón*.[4]

I'm sure that people in Rio, Naples, Cairo, Teheran, and Beijing (to take just a few cities whose inhabitants speak foreign languages) would agree that English dominates the world. They might even agree that English dominates the world of sports. But they might wonder, or even bristle, at the example used. "Baseball?" they might ask, with astonishment or even puzzlement (for some might not even know what it is). "Why not soccer, which is more of an international sport than baseball is?" The use of baseball rather than soccer would probably be seen as typical American arrogance, which was exactly the opposite of what the writer was trying to convey in his article.

Another example comes from a cartoon in the *New Yorker*.[5] It shows a number of businessmen gathered around a table. From their dress and from the scenery outside that is visible through a window, it is clear that they are Arabs, or at any rate from the Middle East. One of them says, "Oil, oil, oil! Doesn't anyone ever talk about baseball anymore?" This was thought to be so cute that it was included opposite the title page of Lawrence Frank's baseball book *Playing Hardball*. Now I'm not Arab or from the Middle East, so I can't be sure exactly how this would be taken by such people. But I do know how the American left would take it if, instead of baseball, the man had referred to *Baywatch* or McDonald's or anything else that they regard as a typical monstrosity of mainstream America: they would have been exceedingly angry. They would have written many letters denouncing this, saying they were canceling their subscriptions, that they had thought the *New Yorker* was more culturally sensitive than that, and so on. But in this case, there wasn't a whisper.

Another example is Lawrence W. Levine's book *The Opening of the American Mind*. The whole premise of Levine's book is how awful Americans once were about other cultures, but how they were beginning to become more enlightened and tolerant. (The title was chosen in conscious opposition to Allan Bloom's *The Closing of the American Mind*.) Yet nowhere in his book does Levine talk about being enlightened and tolerant of other cultures' *sports*. Nowhere does he himself exhibit these traits in connection with sports. He is quite happy to give examples of what he regards as unenlightened behavior, but it never seems to occur to him that the numerous rants of Americans against soccer can be classified in the same way. Here, for example, is a quote from a diary by a nineteenth-century American about new Irish immigrants, whom the diarist judges very harshly: "Our Celtic fellow citizens are almost as remote from us in temperament and constitution as the Chinese."[6] Levine uses this quote as an example of how culturally backwards and intolerant mainstream Americans can be, but what is the difference between that complaint and the many complaints I have heard about soccer from other leftists (and non-leftists)? If there is a difference, Levine never tells us what it is. Nor does he champion soccer, either. He simply ignores sports altogether. Isn't it fair to say that his mind isn't very open about foreign sports?

During the 1970s, one could always blame the bad media coverage of soccer on the older generation, which didn't "get it." But now it is my generation that is running things, and the coverage is still bad. Take, for instance, the African Cup of Nations. This event receives hardly any coverage in *The New York Times*, which is to the left of center, compared with the much greater coverage that it receives in *The Times of London*, which is to the right of center. Why is a newspaper that is progressive giving such poor coverage to a major African sporting event? Other American newspapers give even less coverage than *The New York Times*. The Minneapolis *Star-Tribune*, for example, gives vanishingly small coverage, if any, even though it considers itself progressive.

For that matter, *The New York Times* often considers itself the world's newspaper. Accordingly, they ought to be giving a huge amount of coverage to the world's favorite sport. But they don't. The lion's share of their coverage still goes to our sports, to baseball, football, and basketball. Another example along these lines is the *Chronicle of Higher Education*. This weekly is an important organ of academia, and the reason I bring it up is that its back pages are reserved for members of its readership to write about something deemed interesting and important. I have been reading the *Chronicle* since 1985, and not once have I seen an account on the back pages of someone talking about their experiences with foreign sports. Prior to the 1960s, this wouldn't have meant anything, but remember that today many educators talk about the importance of multiculturalism and learning about other cultures, so wouldn't one think that learning about foreign sports would count as something interesting and important?

Another example occurred in connection with a cricket World Cup match between India and Pakistan on March 1, 2003. This was a huge match. Both countries shut down. Movie theaters stopped showing their movies and showed the game instead, so that those without a television could watch. A billion people were affected. So, how was this covered in our media? It was almost completely ignored. It was ignored by, for example, *The New York Times*. Yet, the silence wasn't total. The *Wall Street Journal* had a preview of the game. Keep in mind that *The New York Times* leans left, while the *Wall Street Journal* leans right. Also keep in mind that the *Wall Street Journal* is basically a business newspaper that at that time didn't have a sports section. For me this was just one more example of the left making utter fools of themselves. It was just more evidence that leftists just could not manage to get over a traditional American prejudice, while conservatives were somewhat better able to.

The mainstream media has in general been either indifferent or hostile to soccer, but that wouldn't have mattered so much if there had existed legions of readers of these newspapers who wanted soccer news and who decided to get their sports news elsewhere, namely from publications further to the left. But that wasn't the case. The further to the left one went, the less soccer news one found (which is still true). Let me begin by discussing the coverage by the leftist media of the 1999 Women's World Cup. How much coverage did the leftist magazines give to the 1999 Women's World Cup? The *Nation* paid no attention to it. *The Progressive* paid no attention to it. *In These Times* paid no attention to it. It is not that these magazines pay no attention to sports, for they occasionally do have some articles on sports. No, it was just pure prejudice against the sport of soccer that led them to ignore the accomplishment of these women. (And if it wasn't prejudice against soccer, then it was prejudice against women, which is sexism.) After all, even our news weeklies managed to cover this event.

This lack of coverage of soccer is true of these magazines generally. Certainly, *The Nation* gives no coverage whatsoever to soccer. In fact, I have yet to see a kind word about soccer in that magazine. Once *The Nation* went so far as to call João Havelange, the former head of FIFA, a fascist.[7] The man has his faults, but in fact he was elected to be the head of FIFA because he promised the people of Africa and Asia that he would get them more slots for the World Cup. A fascist who promises to help the Third World isn't much of a fascist, one would think, but *The Nation* thought otherwise. As for other leftist publications, such as *In These Times* and

The Progressive, they too treat soccer shabbily. Likewise, NPR was always a huge disappointment for me as a soccer fan. I very early on figured out that the program "All Things Considered" was a misnomer and gave up listening to them.

In the mid-1980s, there was a soccer riot in Europe, and I read in the local paper that a British group called the National Front was involved. When I mentioned this to a British friend, he groaned and said they were neo-Nazis. Horrified, I anxiously awaited the next issue of *In These Times* (which during those years I foolishly subscribed to) because I assumed they would have much more information on the National Front than the local paper had. But to my surprise and disgust, they hardly mentioned the National Front. Instead, the writer talked about how the problem was that soccer fans were too macho.[8] This was absolutely outrageous! We soccer fans couldn't win. Here in the U.S., we were being denounced by the average American because soccer was a wimp sport, and now the left was denouncing us because our sport was too macho. Never had I seen *In These Times* denounce American football as a macho sport. Only soccer.

In October of 1999, *Ebony* magazine produced a list of the twentieth century's 100 best black athletes. Everyone on this list was American or else involved in American sports. There were no soccer-playing foreigners on the list. Not even Pelé made this list! Many people in the rest of the world would be inclined to say that Pelé was not only the best *black* athlete of the century, but quite simply the best *athlete* of the century. But that wasn't good enough for the writers and editors at *Ebony*. Not having Pelé on this list, or anyone from Africa or Europe, simply showed the prejudice that *Ebony's* writers had against soccer and other foreign sports. Notice that the list they produced would have been perfectly appropriate *if* they had been listing the century's 100 best *African-American* athletes. But they didn't use the term "African-American." They used the term "black." In doing so, they ought to have considered the sporting achievements of every black in the world, but they very xenophobically focused on no one but Americans or those playing American sports.

These examples are those that are in the public record and so can be checked. But I want to give a couple other examples that cannot be checked, but which I and others experienced. A few years ago I attended a reading at the Ohio State University by Nick Hornby. It was a strange event, since in attendance were a number of groups with little in common. The woman who introduced him (and who never introduced herself, by the way) went on and on in a vaguely leftist way about Hornby, but then finally got to the topic of soccer, which, as she put it, "the English mistakenly call football." Never mind that as I mentioned near the end of Chapter 3 this idea is already ludicrously stupid. My point here is how culturally insensitive it was for a liberal or leftist to say such a thing. Consider an analogy: A Christian college invites the Dalai Lama to give a talk, but introduces him by saying, "However, in spite of all this, he hasn't accepted Christ into his heart." How would liberals and leftists react? Wouldn't they be outraged? So why weren't they similarly outraged by this incident?

Here is my last example. In the 1970s and again in the 1990s, I happened to support teams that had black South Africans on them. When I lived in Minnesota, the Minnesota Kicks had Ace Ntsoelengoe. I now live in Ohio, and the Columbus Crew had Doctor Khumalo. I don't know much about Ace's status back in South Africa, but I know more about Doctor Khumalo. He was said to be "our favorite sportsman," and I have it on good authority that he was a personal friend of Nelson Mandela.[9] So, he was very famous among South African blacks. I suspect the same was true of Ace Ntsoelengoe. Yet, the leftists of Minnesota and the leftists of central Ohio paid no attention. If these two men had been visiting authors or musicians, it is hard to imagine such indifference. But since they were soccer players, the fact that they were widely admired by blacks in South Africa meant nothing. The only thing that mattered was that they played soccer, which was enough for leftists to shun them.

This completes my list. There are many other examples I could have used, except that they aren't in the public record. Incidentally, anyone inclined to doubt my claims about the left and soccer should listen to another leftist, in this case, Katha Pollitt, who writes for *The Nation*. She says, "I don't like baseball. I have long known that this makes me unable to talk to most men (and even some women) of my own professional-chattering-intellectual-espresso-drinking class, for whom baseball is the divine pastime."[10] She then continues by naming and describing some of these people, which includes, "for some reason, virtually every red-diaper baby and social historian over the age of 40." Of course, since this was written in 1997, these people would now be over 50. What Pollitt's statement shows is that most older leftists she knows are sports fans, but that the sport they follow is baseball. She goes on to mention soccer, but she says nothing about these baseball fans also being soccer fans.

Foreign sports are to my generation of leftists what homosexuality was to my parents' generation. My parents' generation simply fails to understand the point of being open-minded and tolerant of homosexuals. They will go to their graves not understanding this. But my generation, including its leftists, simply fails to understand the point of being open-minded and tolerant of foreign sports. They will also go to their graves not understanding this. They will ignore the hate speech directed against us soccer fans. They will fail to realize that their attitudes toward foreign sports mirror those of other Americans toward foreign cultures in general. It is a sad and pathetic record.

It is true that on rare occasions I have heard individual leftists talk about soccer and do so without prejudice. At the beginning of his book *Freedom Rising* about South Africa during the period of apartheid, James North wrote a very informative and colorful passage relating that South Africans' choice of sports depended upon their ethnicity. (It turns out that Afrikaners like rugby, English-speaking whites like cricket, and blacks like soccer.) This wonderful passage is what I was hoping many American leftists would provide for me, that is, information about foreign sporting cultures, instead of which most of them regarded such cultures as vastly inferior to American sporting culture and so not worth commenting on. Another example is from Camille Paglia, who had this to say about the 1998 World Cup:

> The star of the tournament for me was the Paraguay team's goalie, José Luis Chilavert, an extraordinary athlete built like a mesomorphic Roman gladiator. What speed and power! I haven't seen such raging, testosterone-fueled dominance on the field since the heyday of linebacker Lawrence Taylor, defensive genius of the New York Giants. Chilavert's saturnine, burning maleness practically blew out my TV set.[11]

And Janet Lever has written a fine book about soccer in Brazil. There are also occasional instances of the liberal media being helpful. The *Village Voice* has the occasional article on soccer. And Public Broadcasting Service (PBS) during the 1970s and early 1980s broadcasted *Soccer Made in Germany*, which was better than what the networks were broadcasting at that time.

But all of these examples were the tiny exceptions to what was otherwise the vast phenomenon of leftist hatred of or indifference to soccer. And while I can't explain exactly the occurrence of the two media instances just mentioned, I think I can explain the others. Janet Lever is a woman, and when she first began exploring Brazilian soccer (at the 1966 World Cup), women were still in the throes of traditional roles. It made sense that a woman of that period would be much more open to foreign sports than leftist males of that period. As for Camille Paglia, it is not so clear that she is a leftist. At any rate, her opinions on other issues do not line up exactly with what other leftists believe. (She defended Sarah Palin during the last election.) Even if she is a leftist, she is a very unorthodox one, so it is not surprising that she would be unorthodox on sports, too. And James North is somewhat younger than the leftists of my generation. He is just the other side of that generational fault-line that exists between my generation of leftists, who came of age in the Sixties, and the next generation, who came of age in the Seventies and who thus were more likely to take soccer for granted.

In general, if leftists are interested in soccer, it is because (as I have already pointed out) they are *younger* leftists. Such leftists are much more likely to be open-minded and tolerant of foreign sports than their elders are. But several points need to be kept in mind about them. First of all, they haven't politicized this issue. That is to say, they haven't offered a critique of sports here in America (which I will offer in the next chapter). Secondly, they seem blissfully unaware that their elders are intolerant, or to the extent that they are aware, they do not condemn. Thirdly, they aren't any more tolerant than *others of their generation*. Fourthly, some of them are just as prejudiced as their elders. (Recall the young postmodernist professor I mentioned in Chapter 1.) Fifthly, while they like soccer, they are just as prejudiced about cricket as most Americans are.

It is sad but true. The leftists of my generation just don't get it. They never will. Encountering their prejudice is jarring. It is as jarring as it is to read older fiction and encounter the "N" word used for blacks in an author you had previously thought of as enlightened. But just imagine, being outdone in open-mindedness and cultural sensitivity by capitalists, by people in fraternities and sororities, and by people in R.O.T.C.! It's not a very good legacy or record.

Endnotes
1. Minneapolis *Star-Tribune*, Dec. 1, 1992, p. 2D.
2. *Times Literary Supplement*, Dec. 15, 2000, p. 15.
3. Michael Walzer, *The New Republic*, Sept. 28, 1998, p. 10.

4. Earl Shorris, "Last Word: Can the World's Small Languages Be Saved?" *Harper's*, August 2000, p. 36.
5. *The New Yorker*, Aug. 21, 1978, p. 34.
6. Lawrence W. Levine, *The Opening of the American Mind*, p. 125.
7. *The Nation*, July 29/Aug. 5, 1996, p. 15.
8. *In These Times*, June 12-25, 1985, p. 11.
9. My authority was a Columbus Crew official, but see also Simon Kuper, *Football Against the Enemy*, p. 140.
10. Katha Pollitt, *The Nation*, Dec. 8, 1997, p. 11.
11. Camille Paglia, *Salon*, 7/21/98, from the Internet.

Chapter 10
A Leftist Critique of American Sports

As I have already mentioned, we simply didn't question our sports environment back in the Sixties. That was the time when we supposedly questioned everything, but in fact, we didn't. We never questioned why we hated soccer and cricket, we never questioned our devotion to school sports, we never questioned why we were so ignorant of sports elsewhere. But most of all, we never questioned our own sports. We never looked at them critically. America's sports are sacred cows, even for leftists, and questioning them is simply not done. I say that resistance to these attitudes is long overdue.

From a leftist point of view, the most important questions are, What specifically can we say about American team sports in terms of fairness? That is, what can we say about the sports of baseball, football, and basketball as far as fairness goes? As everyone knows, these three team sports are dominant in America today. Do they deserve this dominance? Are they sports worthy of being supported by the American people? Are they democratic? Are they worthy of being supported by the left? Are they egalitarian in any way, or do they privilege certain people at the expense of others? If they privilege people, in what ways do they do this? A close examination of these questions reveals many unexpected features, features that (as I will argue in the next chapter) many American leftists don't want to look at. Let me begin with baseball.

Baseball

Some early fans of baseball in the nineteenth century felt that baseball was to be preferred to cricket because baseball could be played on any old field whereas cricket required fields that had been carefully groomed. That certainly was an egalitarian point in baseball's favor (for it means that the poor will have a greater chance of participating). However, that observation ignores other factors. To begin with, baseball contains a definite hierarchy in terms of the amount of action received when the players are in the field. The pitcher and catcher get an enormous amount of action, the infielders get somewhat less action, while the outfielders get the least amount of action. Of the outfielders, the right fielder gets the least amount of action of anyone on the field.

There is nothing subtle about this observation. You don't need to be an Einstein to see this. Everyone who knows the least little bit about baseball is aware of it, yet there are seldom complaints about it. It is true that these facts should be modified to some extent because while the person playing right field probably plays in every game, the person who is pitching doesn't. In fact, that person can be relieved during the game, which is less likely for the players at the other positions. Nevertheless, we can still say that the right fielder gets significantly less action than the infielders and catcher. I heard one right-fielder for a college team state that he often didn't have anything to do during an entire game. Even when the rotation of pitchers is taken into account, it is still probably true that the right fielder, over the course of five or so games (or however many it takes to rotate the pitchers), gets less action than someone who pitches in one game.

Does any of this change when the players are at bat? That is, are the outfielders compensated for their lack of action in the field with more at bats? No. When the players are at bat, baseball suddenly abandons its rigid hierarchy and goes egalitarian. Each batter gets a turn at bat before anyone gets a second turn. That is highly commendable, of course. It is just that the egalitarian batting arrangement cannot make up for the anti-egalitarian fielding arrangement.

We have to acknowledge that baseball, from the standpoint of radical leftism, isn't America's pastime. It is America's caste-time. It is a caste-time because of its hierarchy, which is rigid. Rigid hierarchies are seldom defended by leftists, so it is a mystery why so many American leftists love baseball. Conservatives, it is true, defend some hierarchies, if they allow for upward mobility. However, I cannot see that there is any upward mobility here. During the time I followed baseball, I cannot remember a single right-fielder ending up at pitcher. But even if this had happened, it still would be a hierarchy, and according to leftist doctrine, hierarchies are bad.

This hierarchy in baseball also leads to other problems. Who is most likely to end up in the outfield? It turns out that two groups are most likely to end up in the outfield: blacks and left-handers. For blacks, being stuck in the outfield rather than being allowed to pitch is just another symptom of racism in America. It of course doesn't mean that blacks are unsuited for pitching, catching or playing in the infield. It just means that, the social climate being what it is, if a black baseball player comes along, he is likely to find himself shunted into the outfield. This was pointed out by the black journalist Brent Staples in *The New York Times Magazine*.[1] Strangely enough, although this article came out over twenty years ago, and although it was printed in a magazine widely read by leftists, I never hear other leftists make this criticism of baseball. I have on occasion mentioned this fact to white leftists, and when I do, it always produces a shock. I don't know if they are shocked that someone they view as perhaps to the right of them has noticed racism where they haven't, or if they are shocked to learn that their beloved baseball isn't quite the innocent pastime that they think it is. What happens next is interesting: they get defensive on behalf of baseball rather than angry on behalf of blacks.

As for left-handers, the fact that left-handers tend to be in the outfield is the result of the very structure of the game. Those who are naive might think of baseball as a very symmetrical game. If you stand at home plate and look out over the field, the playing area seems perfectly symmetrical. There is one base off to your left and another in a corresponding position off to your right. The only asymmetry would be the different distances that generally exist from home plate to the left and to the right field fences.

Yet, baseball is not quite symmetrical, and the reason for that is that the players run around the bases in just one direction. That dynamic factor is enough to introduce asymmetry. The players are supposed to run counterclockwise, and that makes all the difference in the world, if you are left-handed. As a left-hander myself, I remember being told that we left-handers had an advantage when we were at bat because we were a little bit closer to first base. Of course, what they *didn't* tell us is that we have our backs to first base, so that we must turn around before we get going. But even worse is that I always felt that I was running around the bases in the wrong direction. I would vastly prefer to run clockwise than counterclockwise. The reason for this is that as a left-footed person, my left foot is probably slightly longer than my right one. That means that when I lean to the left, my shorter right foot is off the ground, but when I lean to the right, both feet are solidly on the ground (more so than when I am standing upright). So when I run counterclockwise, and I lean to the left to make a turn, it feels slightly awkward. It's like walking upright with two legs of different lengths. But running clockwise – that is, running to third, second and first in that order – feels so much better.

Another consequence of the dictated counterclockwise direction for running is that if I hit the ball to the infield, it is likely to go to either the first baseman or the second baseman, both of whom are fairly close to where I am running (namely, first base).

But the most important consequence is that we lefties are excluded from some positions. Catcher, third base, shortstop and second base are positions that we are excluded from because of the direction of running. Throwing to first base is more important than throwing to any of the other bases because it is at first base that most runners are thrown out. So people must be able to throw to first base easily, and it turns out that it is a little easier to throw to first base from the other infield positions if one is right-handed. For either right-handers or left-handers, there will be times when one has to turn one's body after catching the ball in order to make the throw to first. But for left-handers, one must turn a little more than one does if one is right-handed. That extra amount of turning for the lefty means everything to the baseball-minded. It means that lefties are wholly unsuitable for those infield positions.

It is true that lefties are preferred for first base. A left-handed player at first can more easily throw to second for a double play than a right-handed player can. But while right-handers are not *preferred* for first base, they are not *excluded* from first base the way that left-handed people are excluded from those other positions.

I grant that every pitching rotation needs left-handed pitchers, and that for baseball lovers, this means that things even out, for if you happen to be a left-handed pitcher, you have a great advantage over many other people, both right and left-handed. But if you happen *not* to be a left-handed pitcher, if you are a leftie who isn't a pitcher, then you basically have just four positions to choose from whereas a right-handed person who isn't a pitcher has double that number, eight.

On balance, baseball is not especially kind to left-handed people.

So far I have been talking about problems that baseball has in connection with its hierarchy of positions. But there is something else to be said in connection with the size of people who play baseball. While baseball tends to be for people of more or less average size – and that is quite commendable – there was an ugly incident involving a short person a

Soccer, the Left, & the Farce of Multiculturalism

number of years ago. This happened on August 19, 1951, when Bill Veeck, manager of the St. Louis Browns, used Eddie Gaedel as a pinch-hitter. Gaedel was a mere three feet, seven inches tall, and the manager of the opposing team, the Detroit Tigers, protested to the umpire that Gaedel wasn't officially on the team. Unfortunately for that manager, Veeck had signed Gaedel fair and square. As Veeck expected, Gaedel drew a walk. But the next day, the league banned Gaedel from baseball because it "was not in the best interest of the game."[2]

I'm sure that baseball's defenders will agree with this decision, that allowing such a person on the field would have ruined the game. But that is doubtful. A very short person wasn't likely to be very good at many of the field positions, compared with people who were taller. So, short people weren't likely to appear very often in a game, except when pinch-hitting. What's so bad about having such people in the game? The baseball lover will say that a very short person is much more likely to draw a walk than a person of ordinary size and that to get a walk on the basis of size rather than skill is a bad thing. My reply is: So what?

Let me compare this situation to that of ice hockey. In the early 1970s, the Philadelphia Flyers acquired a goon. I believe that they were in fact the first hockey team to acquire a goon. A goon is a big player whose skills at skating and stick-handling were minimal, but whose large size could be used to intimidate and hassle opposing players. Once Philadelphia acquired a goon, pretty soon every team decided that they needed their own goon in order to even things up. It says something about the difference in status between large men and small men in our society that goons were allowed to play in ice hockey but that short people were not allowed to play in baseball, even though their usefulness was about the same. A goon wasn't likely to do much, except obstruct the opposing players from playing. Goons weren't likely to score themselves, and in fact, it would have been pointless to allow more than one of them on the ice at once. Two goons on the ice for your team meant a severe handicap in terms of moving the puck forward. One, goon, however, could be a blessing. Likewise, two very short people would not be necessary for a baseball team, but one could be a blessing. Nevertheless, the powers that be in baseball decreed that short people couldn't play anymore.

These, then, constitute the sorts of things that any leftist might say about the game of baseball. I am ignoring things that leftists could say about how the American fans of baseball prefer it for jingoistic and xenophobic reasons. I am interested in the structure of baseball only.

Several of these problems could be avoided if the rules of baseball were changed. The inequality between pitchers on the one hand and right fielders on the other could be made to vanish in the following way. There are nine field positions in baseball, and by chance there are also nine innings of play. Instead of having fixed field positions, why not have a rotation system such as exists in volleyball? During the course of the game, a player could start at pitcher for the first inning, move to catcher for the second, then through the infield and finally through the outfield for the remaining innings. It is true that many people are not especially suited to be pitchers and when they happened to be pitching, the other team would get a huge break. But then the other team would no doubt have its weak pitchers, too, so these things would even out.

As for the left-handed imbalance, this could be solved very easily with the following rule: any time a batter hits the ball, he or she is allowed to run to either first base or third base, so long as no one else is on any of the bases. Introducing this rule would reduce the importance of throwing to first base, because some of the time the infielders would have to throw to third base instead. Throwing to third-base would mean that left-handed infielders would be preferred, just as right-handed ones are when the throw is to first base. Since the throw might be to either base, depending on where the batter went, there would no longer be any reason to exclude left-handed infielders.

With respect to short people, the simple thing is to allow them to play.

With respect to blacks, blacks would benefit from the field rotation suggested above, for then they couldn't be relegated to the outfield most of the time. They would get to take their turn at pitcher just like everyone else. Still, given the existence of racism, the fact that they have been relegated to the outfield means that probably some other way of hurting them would be found. No doubt racist teams would require much higher standards for black players, but dealing with that is a general problem of society and not baseball in itself.

So far, I have been talking about problems related to the structure of baseball. But let me point out that at the time that I developed this critique, there were no Asians playing professional baseball in America. That has changed a little in recent years. I have already mentioned that blacks tend to get stuck in the outfield, but Asians didn't even get that lowly status. They were simply not part of the game at all. I can't give any reasons for this practice (other than racism), for it seems incomprehensible. We all knew that baseball was played in parts of Asia, such as Japan and Taiwan. In fact, we knew that Taiwan was so good at producing young ballplayers that the Taiwanese regularly won the Little League World Series. Yet, none of these players ever made their way over to America. And none of the Asians in America ever made it to the pros. So, American baseball hasn't been kind to Asians, which is just one more reason to think it just isn't the innocent sport that people think it is.

It is instructive to compare baseball to cricket in terms of the amount of action with the ball that the players receive. I have to admit that I am not so conversant with cricket that I know exactly how much action the players typically get. I know that there are undesirable positions in cricket. But I also know that no one gets to dominate in cricket the way that the pitcher gets to dominate in baseball. The bowler must trade off with another bowler after every six throws of the ball. And if the bowler becomes less than effective, he must be replaced, and he must be replaced not with someone from the bullpen, but *with someone else on the field*. The advantage of such a system over the system used by baseball is that it equalizes to some extent the action among the players on the field. Admittedly, those who are second-stringers don't get the action that they would in baseball. But for the people on the field, the action is spread around more equitably.

Batting in cricket is also arranged in a different way. There is a batting order in cricket, just as there is in baseball. Occasionally, it is true, those at the bottom of this batting order don't get to bat (if a team feels it has enough runs and wants to end an innings – note the plural! – so as to ensure that the game gets concluded on time). But theoretically, everyone has a chance to bat. What's more, those who are gifted at batting are rewarded for their skills in a way that gifted baseball batters aren't. Any batsman who isn't put out gets to stay at bat. In baseball, a person who hits a home-run obviously isn't out. Nevertheless, *his time at bat is over* until the entire rotation has been gone through again. A person who hits the equivalent of a home run in cricket (called hitting over the boundary) gets to stay at bat.

The point is this. Baseball rewards those who are highly skilled at throwing the ball with extra action, because they get to be pitcher. Pitchers get lots of action, while those who aren't very good with the ball get stuck in the outfield. But baseball *doesn't* reward those who are good at batting. In cricket, by contrast, those who are stuck in the undesirable positions who nevertheless happen to be good hitters can make up for the small amount of action they received in the field by getting to have a great deal of action at bat. You can stay at bat forever in cricket, if you are highly skilled at batting.

I have already hinted that baseball is inconsistent in that it is anti-egalitarian – a meritocracy, if you wish (though I think it's a rigid caste system) – during the time when the team is in the field and egalitarian when it is at bat. Baseball could be made consistent by either making it totally egalitarian or totally anti-egalitarian. Egalitarian baseball would involve introducing the rotation of field positions which I suggested earlier, for that would mean that both fielding and batting were run along egalitarian lines. For anti-egalitarian or meritocratic baseball, we could try this: allow those who are the best batters to lead off the batting *in every inning*. The best batters would always lead off the inning, and if they batted successfully, the batters lower down on the ranking would then get to bat.

Now I am suggesting this meritocratic baseball just because some who aren't leftists, and perhaps even some who are leftists, are going to try to justify the huge inequalities of baseball by saying that pitchers deserve more action because they are more skilled. To such people, I say, "All right. Just be consistent about it. Let those who are the best batters get more batting. Don't switch over to an egalitarian scheme when it comes to batting." It is impossible to justify baseball as it currently stands, no matter whether one is a leftist *or* a believer in meritocracy.

Would I follow baseball if any of these modifications were adopted? No. But then lots of baseball fans have suggested modifications for soccer, without having the slightest inclination to follow soccer were any of them to be adopted. However, in my case the reason I wouldn't follow modified baseball is not because I thought it inferior to soccer, but merely as a matter of temperament. Temperamentally, I like a faster game than baseball, whether modified or not, though I'd be more likely to follow it with such modifications than otherwise.

Basketball

Next, let me consider basketball. Basketball doesn't have the problem of distributive justice that baseball has. By that I mean that whereas there are huge disparities between the amount of action that the pitcher and catcher get compared with the amount of action that the right fielder gets, in basketball the ball is passed around so frequently and each player gets the ball so frequently that basketball can claim to be a sport of equality in this respect. The only situation in which there is inequality is when one player is significantly worse than the others. In that case, the others may not pass the ball to him. However, such a person can console himself knowing that he will get plenty of opportunities for action on *defense*, for his opponents will notice that he isn't as good as his teammates and so will try to exploit the weakness that he represents by dribbling in his area as often as possible.

The point is that even when basketball seems to be unequal in terms of the amount of action received, it is still equal.

Likewise, basketball doesn't favor either right-handers or left-handers.

Blacks have as good a chance of becoming professionals in the NBA as whites do. In fact, they may have a better chance. Nor are they relegated to the worst positions, because there is nothing corresponding to right field in basketball. At best, perhaps the forwards have more chances for glory than the guards do, while the guards perhaps take more flack than the forwards do. But the differences here are I think minimal.

However, there is a feature of basketball that should give every leftist pause, and that is that it privileges those who are tall. (And since it privileges those who are tall, it generally excludes those people who are members of ethnic groups not noted for tallness.) The problem here is a matter of context, and in some contexts this won't be a problem, and in other contexts it will. I'm going to leave this problem till later on in this chapter.

Football

Now we come to football. Football, like baseball, has a hierarchy. To begin with, football has some positions that see very little action. I am thinking of the field goal kickers and the punters. However, the main problem of distribution in football isn't so much that some of the players on the team get less *action* as that they get less *action with the ball*. Many of the players on the offensive team are in fact *excluded from carrying the ball*. They are nothing but peons, nothing but support personnel for those who *do* get to carry the ball. Just as in baseball the pitcher gets to control much of the action, so in football the quarterback gets to control much of the action. In fact, the quarterback gets to give orders to the rest of his teammates. There is, as far as I know, nothing like this in the rest of sports (except in rowing).

It is true that for the defense, the players are equal to each other. They aren't under the thumb of the quarterback, so none of them gets any more action than any other, except when the other team's offense decides to focus on what they regard as a weak spot in the defense. And since it isn't their job to play offense, the point about not getting to carry the ball doesn't matter so much. Moreover, any defensive player can pick up a fumble and run with it.

Nevertheless, a comparison with rugby is instructive. In rugby no one is the quarterback, or alternately, everyone is. Many people make passes, and many people receive those passes. In addition, everyone plays both offense and defense. The point is that rugby is like football, except that it is more egalitarian in terms of action with the ball. Rugby is the democratic or socialist version of football, and therefore ought to be preferred by those leftists who like goal-line sports.

As for the treatment of blacks in football, just as blacks tend to get shunted away from pitching, so blacks tend to get shunted away from the position of quarterback. At least, this has been true in the past. Football and baseball have similar problems, and I've always been amazed that other leftists haven't been willing to see these problems.

There is also another feature of football that needs to be noted, namely that it privileges big people. Just as basketball privileges the tall, so football privileges the big. That isn't necessarily a problem. It depends on the context. Shortly, I will look at that context, but first I want to look at soccer.

Soccer

Now let me compare these sports to soccer. A problem shared by baseball and football is their anti-egalitarian structure. By contrast, in soccer the ball gets passed around frequently, just as it does in basketball. No player gets significantly more action than any other player, and certainly no player *automatically* gets more action, merely as the result of playing a given position (such as pitcher or quarterback). Everyone gets to be quarterback in soccer. I concede that a very good player will get more action than the others, but that is because the others will realize that they can pass to that player and know that he or she will score, or at least not lose the ball. I also concede that the goalie gets somewhat less action than the other players. (It is interesting that those unused to soccer imagine that the goalie gets more action than the other players and not less.) Yet, soccer is such a fluid game in terms of the roles of the players that one cannot speak categorically on this point. The Colombian goalie, René Higuita, played what ought to be called a goalie/sweeper position, for he roamed far outside of what was traditionally thought of as the goalie's domain. José Luis Chilavert of

Paraguay came upfield to take free kicks and even scored some goals. But even ignoring these examples, if soccer is a little bit less egalitarian than basketball, it is still a far cry from the inequalities of baseball. The goalie typically gets much more action than the right-fielder in baseball and is more important besides.

A feature shared by football and basketball is that they exclude people of average size. Football is for the big, basketball the tall. However, soccer is for average-sized people. In fact, people who are undersized can thrive in it. For those Americans who don't believe me – and one young woman I talked to seemed surprised that soccer had this feature – consider the following list of those who have done well in soccer, despite their size: Pele (5' 9" and 130 pounds in his first World Cup), Garrincha (5' 7"), Diego Maradona (5' 5"), DaMarcus Beasley (5' 7" and 125 pounds), Bertie Vogts, Nobbie Styles, Thomas Hässler, Ryan Giggs, Bebeto, Romario, and Guiseppe Signori. Each of these players was undersized, either in height or weight or both. These are the ones whose exact size I happen to know about. Probably, there are others (such as Johan Cruyff, who certainly looks thin in photos). And every one of these men is famous throughout much of the world, except DaMarcus Beasley, whom I mention because he's an American. The same thing is true among women soccer players. Tiffany Milbrett was in her day the most dangerous forward in the world, but she was smaller than the average woman.

Soccer, then, approaches a democratic, progressive ideal. Unlike football and basketball, it doesn't exclude people of average size. And unlike baseball and football, the players are treated as equals. I admit it isn't perfect. There is the matter mentioned earlier about the lesser amount of action that the goalie gets. Those who are extremely tall or extremely small probably aren't going to succeed, either. But I don't know of any other sport that does better in terms of both including people and being egalitarian in terms of spreading the action around, both values that leftists claim to aim at. Rugby tends to be for bigger people. Cricket is hierarchical, even if not as hierarchical as baseball is. Sports like lacrosse, ice hockey, and field hockey have goalies and so have the same problem as soccer does in terms of the lesser amount of action of the goalie. Moreover, field hockey has the additional problem that it must be played right-handed.

Soccer, then, approaches a democratic ideal as well as or better than any other team sport, which just may be why it has become the world's most popular sport.

School Sports

Now I said earlier that while football privileges the big and basketball the tall, these needn't be problems since what is important in judging here is the context. After all, these sports are just two of many sports, and while they privilege the big and the tall, and while soccer privileges people of average size, other sports privilege in their own way. Horse racing privileges those who are very light, wrestling privileges those who are very strong, women's gymnastics privileges women who are slight, and so on. However, the problem with the privileging that goes on in football and basketball is that it is done in a certain context, the context of the public school.

Those two sports are the two main sports in our public schools, and here I am thinking of not just high schools, but public colleges and universities as well. Since public schools are funded and run by the government, that means that *our government privileges the big and the tall*. Not only that, but some ethnic groups are almost entirely excluded from these sports, since they are too small and too short to participate in them. Neither college football nor college basketball has much participation by Asians, so a policy of sizism ends up being a policy of racism, also.

Now, many people in recent years have protested against many other sorts of privileging in our public schools. They have protested against the privileging of whites over blacks, of men over women, of heterosexuals over homosexuals, and so on. In fact, such people seem to be against any sort of privileging. It stands to reason, then, that if privileging is wrong, then privileging the big and the tall over those of us who are other sizes is wrong and shouldn't be done. Exactly how to rectify this situation could lead to a number of different proposals. But first I want to point out that so far those who say they are against all and any sort of privileging in our schools have been completely silent about this sort of privileging. I have pointed this out to people on various occasions and have chastised them for their silence. They have either not bothered to respond or else have told me that it is unimportant. But since it is a sort of privileging, and since they are saying there shouldn't be any privileging in our schools, then logic demands that they be against this sort of privileging as well. And their silence is all the more reprehensible since what deserves to be called institutional sizism is so *visible*. Institutional racism or sexism is usually hidden away in the depths of an institution's bureaucracy, but institutional sizism is visible to anyone who looks at the media or goes to any of the games. There just is no excuse for the silence from leftists on this issue.

Let me suggest some ways to counter institutional sizism, and I'll begin with my own preferred way.

To begin with, I think all public schools – and I include public universities in this proposal – should be abolished and replaced by a voucher system. The fact is that public schools are inherently oppressive. With respect to sports, if football and basketball are the two main sports in our schools, then I (and perhaps others) will feel oppressed. If soccer is the main sport and those two are lesser sports, then others will feel oppressed. Either way, people will feel oppressed. If this were true of just sports, then probably no one would care too much. But oppression runs through the public schools on many different issues. Should we teach evolution or not? Should we have sex education or not? Should we teach reading by means of phonics or not? Should we have busing or not? Should we teach foreign languages or not, and if we do, which ones? Should we teach primarily European culture or Third-World culture? Should we have harsh discipline or should we try to make learning fun? Should the school year run throughout most of the summer, as it does in other countries, or should there be a long summer break, as we now have?

Every one of these issues has caused controversy, and no matter which decision has been made people have felt oppressed. If evolution is taught, then religious fundamentalists feel oppressed, but if it isn't taught, then those who are secular and who champion science will feel oppressed. The same can be said for all the other decisions that have to be made. The sensible thing to do is to eliminate the public schools and replace them with a system of vouchers. That way parents can choose which sort of school to send their children to. If they don't like any of the choices, they can band together with other like-minded parents and set up their own school. With respect to sports, some of the schools in such a system will retain football and basketball as the main sports, others may shift to soccer or some other sports, while still others may drop sports altogether. Many alternatives are possible.

Suppose we retain the public schools, however. What then? The best thing to do is to drop sports altogether and let sports be promoted by private clubs, as they are in Europe. Why, after all, should we privilege the athletic over the unathletic in a public school? A mother writing to Ann Landers has touched on this issue:

> I recently asked [school administrators] if there would be a spelling bee and was told such activities were discouraged because they

weren't fair to the children who weren't good spellers.... When I asked if sports were going to be eliminated because our child isn't good at any of them, the school administrators didn't think it was funny.[3]

The point is that if we are going to eliminate spelling bees, then we ought to eliminate sports as well. Moreover, there is no obvious way to avoid privileging one type of athlete over another. Make football and basketball the two main sports, and the big and tall will be privileged. Make soccer the main sport, and average-sized people will be privileged. Each sport will privilege some type of athlete. This is just unavoidable. How, then, do we make it fair for everyone? Even the policy of emphasizing all sports equally still is problematic. Do we include cricket or not? After all, there may be someone who is incredibly gifted at cricket who isn't gifted at any other sport. (The best cricket batsman in the world a few years back – India's Sachin Tendulkar – was, by one account, only five feet tall, which is too short for many other sports.) And some sports cost a lot of money. Since football is so much more expensive than other sports, to include football means spending a lot more on the big than on other athletes. Is that fair? Probably not. The best way to deal with the situation, then, is to eliminate all sports in our public schools and let private clubs take up the slack.

And let me point out that private clubs aren't completely unknown in America. Suppose you want to become a boxer. Since our schools do not have boxing as a school sport, would-be boxers must develop their skills through private clubs. Ditto for the various forms of Asian martial arts. Ditto for bowling. My suggestion here would simply put every sport into the same boat.

But supposing we do insist upon having sports. What should we do then? We should obviously choose soccer as the main sport. The reason is simply because, of all team sports, soccer seems to include the biggest percentage of the population (as well as being egalitarian in terms of action). Not many are tall enough for basketball, nor big enough for football. But a hefty chunk of the population is the right size for soccer. Soccer, then, should be the main sport in our public schools, if we insist upon having sports at all. It is true that there would still be privileging, but the privileging will include a higher percentage of the student body than any other sort of privileging.

Finally, for those who want the minimum amount of change, there is the system used in South Africa. An article in the *Chronicle of Higher*

Education pointed out that in South Africa, there are teams associated with universities that do not require the athletes to be students and which basically just use the brand name of the school in question.[4] Why not use that system? Why must teams be so intimately tied to schools? Why deprive those who won't make the NFL or the NBA of a chance at making a salary? And if the teams are basically separate entities, then my objections about privileging will not matter (at least, they won't matter very much).

These are my preferences. Other leftists may opt for other possibilities. While I suspect that many leftists today won't want any change at all (despite generally wanting change), some in the future may opt for even more stringent changes. For example, whereas I don't have any problem with *private* schools emphasizing football or basketball, other leftists might conceivably have a problem with this. Some leftists have objected to the Boy Scouts, which is a private organization, privileging heterosexuals over homosexuals, so they might conceivably object to private schools that emphasize football and basketball (assuming they were ever to develop leftist objections to such sports; today, they'd be more likely to object to a school that *didn't* have them). My only objection to such schools would be if they were the only schools in an entire region. Otherwise, I don't see a problem.

Other Contexts

So far I've argued that football and basketball exclude many people, but that this needn't be a problem. It depends on the context, and in the context of a public school, this becomes a problem (though not in the context of a private school). The government, which runs public schools, has no business privileging the big and the tall. Likewise, it would seem that the government has no business helping professional teams for these sports, either. Or if it does so, then the help would come after it has helped more inclusive sports. Accordingly, local governments ought not to be providing stadiums for professional football and basketball teams. Let them provide their own stadiums.

It ought to be a source of displeasure for leftists that our country reveres exclusive sports so much. And while the personal preferences of the average citizen cannot be helped, leftists ought to protest vigorously against local governments *favoring* such sports. Let the fans of those sports pay for them. The government shouldn't have to.

Exploitation in the Schools

Now let me take up a new topic in connection with school sports, namely their exploitative nature. At least, they are exploitative at the college level for football and basketball. This has been pointed out before by others, but I don't think they realize the full extent of how damaging the situation is for many of those involved. Because our college athletes are supposed to be amateurs, the money that should be heading their way goes elsewhere. This wouldn't be a problem (or much of a problem) so long as most of those playing went on to play professionally. But as I've already indicated, neither football nor basketball has minor leagues (to speak of), so any athlete who can't quite make the NFL or the NBA and whose college eligibility has run out has to leave the game (or else go abroad). In other words, athletes who could be making a decent salary cannot do so. This doesn't happen in baseball, which has minor leagues, nor in ice hockey nor in soccer. In fact, the whole situation is unheard of in soccer-playing countries, where such people would have been playing for professional teams at one level or another. But for people in football and basketball, there are only college teams below the level of the NFL and NBA, and those have limited years of eligibility.

The people in America hit the hardest by this situation are obviously blacks from the inner city. Blacks from the inner city spend an inordinate amount of time perfecting their basketball skills, but if they can't make the NBA, what happens to them? There are few teams for them to play on after they leave college. It is a tragedy, but one that is seldom mentioned, even by those who are the most concerned about inner-city blacks.

Objections

Those who favor American sports have probably been itching to get in a word edgewise, so let me consider some objections to what I have been saying.

(1) "You complain about the dominance of football and basketball in our schools, and even how the players get exploited by the system. But the fact is that the money raised by these sports allows players in other sports to compete. Other college sports are funded by the revenues from football and basketball. Sports such as wrestling or gymnastics, sports which don't draw huge crowds, can be funded by the excess revenue generated by football and basketball."

This is a common myth. Whether it is the *reality* is a different matter. Some studies have suggested that the myth is wrong. However, I leave it to those who are competent to delve into these matters to investigate that topic. My response is just this. Although basketball is an inexpensive sport, football is quite expensive. Since football is expensive, a regrettably high percentage of the revenues of football *are plowed right back into football*. Suppose that instead of football, soccer had all along been the most important sport in our colleges. Suppose also that there was this same structure in which excess money was given to the other college sports. And suppose that there was no American prejudice against soccer, that people would show up at college soccer games in the same numbers that they now show up for college football games. That would mean a greater amount of money for those who participate in those other sports (such as wrestling, gymnastics, and so on).

Of course, it goes almost without saying that, despite what enlightened self-interest tells them, the people in these other sports have made no effort to promote soccer over football in our schools.

(2) "On the one hand, you complain that our schools privilege the big and the tall, while on the other hand, you complain that our schools exploit these same people. Don't these cancel each other out?"

Only in a superficial way. The point of a leftist critique is to exhibit problems in a society that are the result of inequalities. The fact that there are two opposed problems in this instance shouldn't be a bit surprising, for it frequently happens. White females are privileged by race but not gender over black males, who are privileged by gender but not race over white females. Since each has a privilege, does that mean they are equal to each other? Maybe. But does it also mean that we can ignore these two problems? Not at all. Likewise, the problems of institutional sizism *and* exploitation of student athletes should both be resolved.

(3) "The pitcher gets more action because he deserves it. He is more skilled than the other players. Ditto for the quarterback."

But what about the best batters in baseball? Why don't they get more opportunities than they do? And what about basketball? Why shouldn't the most skilled basketball player on the team have a special position in order to get most of the action, then? One can't justify both the inequalities of baseball and football *and* the equality of basketball.

(4) "Our sports tend to favor those who are big or tall because they are better athletes than people of other sizes."

This has the same sort of problem that the preceding objection has. One can't both justify the exclusion of people of average size in football and basketball *and* their inclusion in baseball. If football and basketball are superior because they use the allegedly superior athletic skills of the big and the tall, then baseball is an inferior sport.

Anyway, it is sheer prejudice to say that those who are big or tall are better athletes than those who aren't. People like Pelé demonstrated that ages ago.

(5) "You say that football privileges the big and basketball the tall. This just isn't true. Both those sports include people of other sizes."

The average weight in football and height in basketball is way above that of the average male in our society. That should be enough to show privileging. Look at it this way. Suppose we invent two new sports, which we will call smallball and shortball. Let's say that smallball has mostly small people on the teams, but with a few people who are about average. And let's say that shortball has mostly short people on the teams, but again with a few who are about average. Would this mean that big people and tall people are well served by these sports? Hardly.

One problem here is that sportswriters who focus on these sports tend to talk about those football and basketball players who are smaller or shorter than their teammates as small or short, even though in terms of the general population they are above average.

No, both football and basketball privilege the oversized, and those who don't think so are out of touch with reality.

(6) "OK, football privileges the big and basketball the tall. But how many people actually complain about this privileging? Why should this be part of a leftist critique if in fact no one actually complains about it?"

That no one – or in reality, few – complain about a situation doesn't mean that leftists are off the hook in terms of pointing out its unfairness. The left's usual explanation for people's failure to complain about something unfair that affects them is that the people are in a state of mind called "false consciousness." Often, people don't think about what their society is like compared with other societies or what their society could be like if things had been done differently generations ago.

It is true that almost no one in our society who is the wrong size for football and basketball complains that they have been excluded. It is also true that almost no one among those who are the right size for those sports complains about the way they are exploited by our schools and how the ones who can't make it into the NFL or the NBA are cheated out of the chance to play in lower-level professional leagues.

But for the leftist, the important thing is to point out types of unfairness, whether those who are treated unfairly notice them or not.

(7) "You don't have to be big to support football, and you don't have to be tall to support basketball."

That is true enough, but why would I want to? One doesn't have to be rich to support polo, but I don't know of anyone who isn't rich who supports it.

(8) "You probably wouldn't have made your school's soccer team, even if they had had one. So what difference does it make whether football and basketball are the two main sports, or whether soccer is?"

Let me answer this with an analogy. Suppose our most important school sport was polo. Polo is a sport for the rich, and the result would be that many good athletes from poor families wouldn't get to play. If someone were to say, "Let's get rid of polo and replace it with basketball and football, because those will be more likely to include athletes from poor backgrounds," would it matter if the person saying that would not be able to make it onto a team in those sports? Isn't what matters here is including more people? Likewise, what matters, or ought to matter to any leftist, in school sports is emphasizing sports that are as inclusive as possible.

(9) "What if we had size classifications in football and height classifications in basketball, just as we have weight classifications in boxing and wrestling? Wouldn't this solve the problem of institutional sizism?"

Perhaps. From a practical point of view, instituting size classifications in football is not going to happen, simply because football is already too expensive. Having several different football teams competing in a school just ratchets up the costs enormously. Basketball is in a better position to institute such a change than football is because it is so cheap in comparison.

Ignoring the costs, I would worry about how those in a lower size or height classification would be viewed. My suspicion is that the general public pays more attention to boxers in the highest classification than those lower down, and I suspect that the same would be true here. After all, the thinking will be that they are the ones who are the best, while the ones lower down are like golfers who are good after a handicap has been applied. They aren't good in absolute terms.

(10) "Isn't it racist to want to eliminate basketball from our schools? After all, basketball is strongly supported by many blacks."

One can just as well say it's racist to want to keep them in our schools. Keeping them in our schools is likely to mean that minor-league basketball will be sickly in comparison to college basketball, and that in turn means that the second-raters will have very little chance of making a decent living. The response that college basketball means that young players will get a chance to go to college doesn't mean much to me, because it should be their choice. Isn't it racist not to tell young blacks how all this could be different?

Moreover, one could say that it is sizist to want to keep basketball in our schools. Shouldn't black America be paying attention to those blacks who have been excluded from this sport simply because they were the wrong size? One of the ironies of black America is that American blacks have been justifiably angry about being excluded from jobs and housing because of a factor that they can't help, namely the color of their skin, and have then chosen to emphasize a sport that excludes people because of a factor that they can't help, namely their height.

Finally, while basketball is strongly supported by many blacks in America, especially in our inner cities, it is not strongly supported by blacks in other countries. In Africa, for example, soccer is king. Ditto for most of the rest of the world. You might just as well say that our schools are being racist by not making soccer our number one sport because the number one sport for African blacks is soccer.

(11) "You seem to be willing to destroy sports that give enjoyment to many people."

No, I just want them privatized. Let private clubs or private schools promote such sports. I don't see why governments should get involved at all.

Moreover, my idea is that after people read my book, they will realize that they are missing out on a lot by clinging to our sports and our sports environment and so will want to work for change. But for those who want to continue clinging, let me remind them of the social costs of, say, football.

(i) We train young men to play football, but we give them almost no opportunity to make money at it. There are currently no minor leagues to speak of, and the number of semi-pro teams is small, especially when compared with the number of semi-pro soccer teams in England.

(ii) It is very hard to play real football on a casual basis.

(iii) For those who agree with the idea of gender equality, football in our schools presents a big problem because there is no comparable female sport that would balance it. Often, male athletes who participate in some sport other than football (wrestling, for example) have to suffer because their sport gets dumped.

(iv) Football excludes people and in fact it excludes entire ethnic groups. I have pointed out that this is a problem in a certain context, namely a school context, and I have also discussed it as part of a leftist critique. But one could just as well discuss it as part of a broader critique, a critique about the democratic ideal. The democratic ideal is that opportunities should be open to all, or at least to as many as possible. By emphasizing sports for the big and the tall, we severely limit who may be considered an important school athlete. This is very hard to reconcile with our democratic ideal. Fans of football (and our other sports) are always talking about how it is American while soccer is foreign. What is interesting is not so much what they say as what they don't say, and what they don't say is that football is a very democratic sport. The reason they don't say this, of course, is that it is *not* a very democratic sport. Something that is American in origin, but not democratic, has severe problems.

(v) For college football, the necessity that the players be students who are not paid to play results in ridiculous "scandals."

(vi) The demand in our schools that players be students results in difficulties for those students when they need to practice or play. This interferes with their schoolwork and may lead to other problems. One such problem is that of professors being put under pressure to accommodate the athletes while other students are not accommodated. James Thurber wrote about this problem back in 1933 in *My Life and Hard Times*, but it is still a problem. Some athletes just aren't going to be good enough to do college work, yet we demand that they do. Why? Another is the demand that the athletes have to do schoolwork when they should be concentrating on their sports. After all, athletes generally have just a limited period in their lives in which to ply their trades while academic pursuits can be done at any time of life.

(vii) Football fans miss out on the enjoyment of international competition by following football, and football players miss out on the chance to represent their country. And our passion for the Olympics shows that we crave international competition, yet we voluntarily deprive ourselves of this by choosing a sport that has none.

(viii) We Americans are very ignorant of international affairs, and focusing on a sport that we invented and which we alone play doesn't help. When football was invented back in the nineteenth century, this didn't matter so much. The rest of the world was far away, and it didn't matter if we knew nothing about what was going on in Yemen, or even Germany. Today, as the attack of 9/11 showed, things are different. I'm not going to say that getting involved in soccer allowed me to predict 9/11. But I wasn't too surprised by it. As a result of soccer, I spent a great deal of time hanging around with foreigners, and ultimately reading about foreign affairs in our newspapers and even reading foreign newspapers. I knew after the fatwa against Salman Rushdie that we would some day be involved in a big struggle of some sort against Islam. My biggest surprise was the timing, because I didn't expect it to happen until about 2020 or 2030.

Even ignoring all this, I learned an immense amount about the world from immersing myself in soccer. As I said above, I don't like the idea of school sports, but if we are going to have them, of what use is it, as far as education goes, to have as our main sport one that does nothing to teach Americans about the rest of the world?

These, then, are football's social costs, costs which are seldom acknowledged. I think they are so high that football should be dumped from our schools, though I suspect this won't happen in my lifetime. Let me add, though, that change will probably come to college sports sooner or later. I'm not the only one pointing out the ridiculousness of our system with its utter lack of minor leagues in football and basketball. And while right now I seem to be the only one angry about institutional sizism, this is going to be noticed sooner or later, and when it is, there will be massive pressure for change.

(12) "The obvious reason for insisting that football and basketball players play on school teams is to make sure they get a college degree."

This won't work. Why not then get rid of baseball's minor league teams if it's so important to make athletes get a college degree, or make boxing a college sport so that would-be boxers can go to college? And why not apply this to other realms as well? Why not make all members of rock bands go through college, or all aspiring Hollywood actors? College isn't for everyone. Moreover, quite a few young men these days are opting not to go to college, so why make male athletes go? In addition, one's youth is the time to develop one's athletic skills, if one is so gifted. Why waste it in school? One can go to school later or in the off-season. (An example of this is Brian West, formerly of the Columbus Crew, who got a degree from The Ohio State University in the off-season.) But mostly, whether to go to college or not should be up to the athlete in question. Insisting that they go is too paternalistic, as though they can't make their own decisions.

(13) "If you are going to demand so many changes along leftist lines, why not make the ultimate leftist change, eliminating professional sports?"

Some leftists have wanted to eliminate professional sports, but not all have. Let me consider the reasons for such a change to see if it's truly leftist. As far as I can see, there were only ever four reasons why leftists thought that professional sports ought to be eliminated. The first was that which emerged in the Soviet Union and other eastern European countries. They wanted to use sports as a way to show the world how superior they were, and they could do this by using the Olympics. Since the Olympics demand that the participants be amateurs, those countries pretended that their athletes were really in the armed forces and that they trained only during their spare time. Of course, not many were fooled by this nonsense, and it is an open question whether it would have been used if the Olympics hadn't been so dead set against professionals.

The second reason was the reason used in places like Sweden. According to one informant, in Sweden soccer was regarded as an important and healthy pastime for the working classes, and they were expected to play as well as watch. Its purpose wasn't making money but uniting society. Players didn't start getting paid until 1968, and the top league remained amateur until the 1990s.[5] Now a big problem here is that the best athletes entertain us, yet while the athletes don't get paid, other entertainers do. The movie director Ingmar Bergman and the rock group Abba got paid, so why shouldn't athletes? It's a bit strange that leftists, who are so concerned with the exploitation of the workers, would be reluctant to pay athletes, given that the very idea of exploitation is that people get less than they deserve.

Thirdly, there is the reason that could emerge from the self-esteem movement and which I alluded to earlier. The problem with refusing to pay athletes because it could hurt someone else's self-esteem is a problem that, if applied consistently, would run throughout all of society. No one would get paid for doing anything. We couldn't pay scientists, for example, since some people aren't good at science, so it would hurt their self-esteem to see scientists getting paid. Exactly what sort of society would emerge if this were applied everywhere is quite unclear, and probably unworkable.

Fourthly, there is simply the idea that if there is professionalism, then some people will have huge amounts of money, and that is bad. But that will be true for all forms of entertainment, as we all know, and anyway this can be dealt with by instituting a progressive income tax.

Let me observe that the very idea of an egalitarian society is a somewhat mysterious one. For many decades of the twentieth century, egalitarians thought of the communist countries as egalitarian, yet it is perfectly obvious that they weren't egalitarian in terms of power. Similarly, many men who might have counted themselves as egalitarians in, say, 1965 would have been utterly surprised by the lengths that feminists would go in talking about gender equality. Moreover, most "egalitarians" I know have never thought about the inequalities in terms of size in our school sports programs (what I have been calling institutional sizism). So what exactly an egalitarian society would look like isn't so clear. The situation is quite different for the libertarians. For them, the ideal society is a society of minimal government interference, and that has been the ideal for at least a century and a half, if not longer.

In these circumstances, what can the egalitarian do? The egalitarian can show that a certain society is more egalitarian than another similar to it. For example, if our society weren't afflicted with institutional sizism but were otherwise the same, then it would be more egalitarian than it is now. Would our society be more egalitarian if we eliminated professionalism in sports and left everything else the same? There would be, it is true, more equality of income, but it would come at a big price, for athletes could legitimately consider themselves as exploited in comparison with other entertainers. It is as though we were to decide that while carpenters, electricians, roofers and so on, all deserved to be paid, plumbers did not. It doesn't seem very consistent.

Let me approach the issue from another direction: who is hurt by professionalism and who is helped? If there are people who can legitimately claim to be hurt by professionalism in sports, it would be those who struggled hard to become a professional and couldn't make it. But that sort of person exists in every profession. There are would-be teachers who just can't make the grade, would-be police officers who just cannot measure up, and so on. And while the high salaries of professional athletes cause income inequality, so do the high salaries of other entertainers. The solution is a highly progressive tax, not the elimination of their pay altogether. Moreover, athletes have the excuse that they have short careers, which singers and actors cannot use, so their high salaries are justified.

As for who is helped, we all know that sports help poor people escape from poverty. But there is more. Those of us who participate in a sport at a low level generally enjoy watching those who are the best. It would be silly to deprive us of those pleasures for the sake of a dubious equality. This is especially true if it were only done in sports, but not in other realms of entertainment. For a century now, people have gotten used to the idea that they can easily hear the best musicians and see the best actors. If we were to eliminate professionalism in these realms, then most entertainment would be reduced to what it was like before recordings preserved them. People prior to the twentieth century generally made their own music. Until about a century ago when recording became possible, most music was done in an informal, amateurish fashion. There might be special concerts at times, and of course the upper classes might have their own musicians, but for the bulk of the population music was something they created on their own. Children were encouraged to learn to play the piano or to sing, and then they would be expected to entertain friends and family. Sometimes the results were not especially pleasant, as in Jane Austen's *Pride and Prejudice* when Mary Bennet insists upon singing a song that is just a little too advanced for her. I don't know of any leftists who would voluntarily give up the chances that each of us has every day to hear the best singers and performers just by turning on the radio, the TV, or a CD player. Consistency demands that such people allow us sports fans to see the best, and that means getting to watch people who spend their time perfecting their skills rather than doing other things, and such people are the professionals.

Let me conclude this topic with a couple observations. First, in the movie *Bend It Like Beckham* the main character and her friend think of the women's professional soccer league here in the U.S. as something amazing and wonderful. To what extent they are leftists is unclear, but they are obviously very committed to the idea of women having equality in sports. (It's too bad that that league died, though a new women's league has recently been established.) Second, soccer as it is played in England seems to be the closest one can get to the ideal of equality while at the same time having professionalism. The professionals receive huge amounts of money and fame, of course, but those who aren't at the top have their chance to play the top professionals via the FA Cup. They get to have their time in the limelight.

What I have just provided is a critique of our sports, a critique that ought to have been given back in the 1960s, but which wasn't. It is true that I haven't covered all topics that such a critique ought to cover, but I'm ignoring things that leftists have already covered (such as the status of women). My two big points are that baseball and football are not egalitarian, in the way that soccer and basketball and other goal sports are, and that school sports, with their emphasis on football and basketball, privilege the big and the tall. To put this in other words, leftists ought to eschew sports with rigid and severe hierarchies like baseball and football. And they ought to be against the emphasis on football and basketball in our public schools since these sports exclude a high percentage of the student population on the basis of something they can't help: their size. There are plenty of alternatives to what we have today, alternatives that are more progressive, and it does progressives no credit to be supportive of a structure that is much less progressive than the alternatives. And these alternatives actually exist, to some extent, in other countries, so it's not as though anyone can claim that they are impossible to achieve. It just requires the will to make the changes that are necessary.

Endnotes

1. Brent Staples, "Where Are the Black Fans?" *The New York Times Magazine*, May 17, 1987, p. 29.
2. Minneapolis *Star-Tribune* 1/3/86, p. 2D. See also *The New York Times*, 1/3/86, II,4:1.
3. Ann Landers column, Jan. 17, 1994.
4. "A Clever Approach to College Sports," Chronicle of Higher Education, Dec. 12, 2003, A32-A34.
5. Eric Schlosser, "Sweden," in Matt Weiland and Sean Wilsey, *The Thinking Man's Guide to the World Cup* (Harper, 2006), 293-4.

Chapter 11
The American Left and the People's Game

Throughout most of the rest of the world, leftists regard soccer as a perfectly acceptable sport. It is known as the people's game. Leftists in other countries may talk about racism or labor problems in soccer, but they don't regard soccer itself as a problem, or if they do, they don't believe that eliminating soccer and accepting American sports would be any improvement. Anyone who doesn't believe this should spend a year reading the sports section of Britain's left-of-center newspaper *The Guardian*. Meanwhile, here are remarks made by two foreign leftists:

> Germaine Greer: "Football [i.e., soccer] is an art more central to our culture than anything the Arts Council deigns to recognize."[1]

> Harold Wilson (former Labour Prime Minister of Britain): "I know more about soccer than about politics."[2]

In addition, Nelson Mandela is very much a soccer fan, as should be clear from anyone who has read Simon Kuper's *Football Against the Enemy*. Likewise, soccer in Holland, as David Winner makes clear in his book *Brilliant Orange*, is shot through with leftist thinking. Foreign leftists who denounce soccer are few and far between. It is taken for granted that it is a sport of the people. Nor do foreign leftists in soccer-playing countries seem inclined to pay any attention to our sports.

By contrast, the American left acts as though soccer is the moral equivalent of, or even worse than, bullfighting. Or else they ignore it completely. Is the failure of the American left to embrace soccer, the sport of the working classes of Europe and the sport of much of the Third

World, due to some classic work in the past in which soccer was thoroughly denounced? If there was such a work, I never found it or heard reference to it. Nor did European leftists seem aware of it. I have to conclude, then, that soccer hatred or soccer indifference among America's leftists is simply the result of the usual American prejudice against soccer, a prejudice that leftists have somehow overlooked.

In the rest of this chapter, I want to enumerate all the different reasons why American leftists ought to have embraced soccer (or if not that, then to have become less enchanted with our own sports). These reasons relate to ideas that leftists themselves promote. Today's leftists promote the same ideas again and again, and many of them intersect with soccer. Even when those ideas don't point toward soccer, they certainly point away from our sports. Of course, the most important one is eliminating prejudices, but there are many others that can be enumerated.

Politicization

If anything can be said of leftists of today, it is that they want to politicize everything. Back in the Sixties when I was a student, conservatives would complain bitterly about this sort of thing. Even some of the older leftists seemed uneasy at the way that those of us in the New Left would politicize things. Feminists, for example, wanted to politicize relations between men and women, which had never been much of a part of politics. This led feminists to produce the slogan, "The personal is the political." More generally, the New Left's response to conservative griping was always the same: things are politicized *already*. Everything is political in some way or other already. It's just that those who favor the status quo don't want to acknowledge this.

It is strange, then, that the left – and keep in mind I'm talking about the American left here – doesn't want to politicize sports, except in the most minimal of ways. Leftists will occasionally note the labor problems of the players or the fact that blacks cannot easily become managers in professional sports. Recently, they have been pushing hard for gender equality in sports in our schools. Other than those few items, however, they refuse to politicize. Anyone who doesn't like politicization can ask leftists why they should be so reluctant to politicize sports. After all, the various problems I noted in my critique in the last chapter are generally the left's bread and butter. That sort of critique is what pays their rent. Why, then, should they be so reluctant to politicize in this instance?

I have occasionally met leftists involved in soccer, but it is because they have failed to politicize it that I think they still have some residual prejudice against soccer, or if not against soccer, then in favor of American sports. Otherwise, they would be attacking those sports as harshly as I have.

Being Critical

Being critical is one of the most important functions of today's leftist. The point of being critical is to reveal inequalities and instances of unfairness that otherwise would remain hidden.

But this general tendency to be critical vanishes when it comes to sports. The American left simply has no interest in being critical about this aspect of our culture. No American leftist has presented the leftist critique which I presented in the last chapter. Most leftists, in fact, would find it disturbing. I base that conclusion on the many statements I have heard leftists make and on the behavior they have so far exhibited. American leftists simply cannot bring themselves to give a leftist critique of our sports. They cannot bring themselves to attack baseball, football, and basketball. Occasionally, some feminists will make some faint bleatings against football, although they are outdone in their scorn by George Will, who is on the right. Will has long condemned football as exhibiting the two worst features of American society: violence and committee meetings. The black journalist Brent Staples attacked baseball, but his attack was accepted by few (by few *white* leftists, anyway). No one that I know of has attacked basketball.

The American left simply cannot bring itself to attack our sports, to look at them critically, to wonder whether all people are being served by them, especially by our school sports. Needless to say, this is hypocrisy. The point of being critical is to locate problems that might otherwise remain hidden, and as I pointed out in the last chapter, there are plenty of problems. There are plenty of instances in which some people are privileged over others, simply because of some unimportant feature about themselves. Yet, the American left remains silent. Face it, American sports are sacred cows, not just for Americans generally, but also for the American left.

Tradition and the Status Quo

Leftists have never been very fond of tradition, unless, of course, it is a tradition that they themselves started. Leftists usually challenge the status quo because the status quo turns out to be rife with social injustice inherited from a previous age when eliminating social injustice wasn't very important. Yet, leftists don't always do this. Baseball, football, and basketball are traditional sports in America and have been throughout the twentieth century and into the twenty-first. There is nothing in the history of these sports that suggests that they were chosen because some leftist looked at them in depth and decided that they were egalitarian. Occasionally, one can find something to the effect that baseball was more egalitarian than cricket because cricket needed carefully groomed fields, which were beyond the means of ordinary people. But that is only one feature of the sport; there are many other features of baseball that are not egalitarian. Nevertheless, today's leftists seem quite happy with these traditional sports and quite happy with this status quo.

Yet, if being a leftist means taking a hard look at traditions, then why haven't today's leftists been willing to do this?

Questioning Everything

One of the most hallowed beliefs about the Sixties, perhaps the most hallowed of all, is the idea that we questioned everything back then. We questioned the Vietnam War. We questioned the very existence of the military. We questioned the roles of men and women. We questioned the low status of blacks and why nothing had been done about this. We questioned the supposedly good life of the suburbs. We questioned the school curriculum, wondering why we weren't taking classes that were more relevant. We questioned the hair fashions that our parents imposed on us. We questioned their bland music and invented our own. We questioned democracy and wondered why we shouldn't have socialism or communism. We believed that we questioned everything.

But did we question everything? No. Since I lived through and came of age in that decade, I can state with absolutely authority that we didn't question everything. On the contrary, there seemed to be certain rigid limits regarding what would be questioned and what wouldn't. We simply never got around to questioning sports, or if we did, we did it in such a weak fashion that it hardly counts as questioning at all. At best, we questioned what relevance sports had to more important things like the Vietnam War or black liberation. But that is as far as we went. We never went further.

Here are some of the things we never questioned. We never questioned America's devotion to American sports. We never questioned America's fear and loathing of foreign sports. We never questioned the hierarchical nature of baseball. We never questioned the absence of Asians on our baseball teams. We never questioned the fact that blacks were rarely allowed to be pitchers. We never questioned the dominance of *American* sports in our public educational institutions. We never questioned the privileging of the big and the tall in our public educational institutions.

When I got involved in soccer in the Seventies, I started asking these questions, but no other leftists did. Even today, no leftists are raising these questions, forty years after the Sixties ended. They just cannot bring themselves to ask these questions. When I pushed other leftists to do it, they generally resisted or engaged in such questioning only grudgingly. Eventually, I gave up pushing them because it was so obvious that their hearts just weren't in it.

The first thing that can be said, then, about this business of questioning is that leftists are simply blind about the extent to which they questioned things when they say that we questioned everything back in the Sixties. But what is more important is that anything you are *unwilling* to question, even when shown that you ought to, represents one of your deepest values. When I urged leftists to question, when I pointed out to them the various types of social injustice in our sports environment, they simply plugged their ears.

The conclusion is this: American leftists value baseball, football, and basketball just as much as they value leftist principles. Any leftist who is offended by that conclusion can do the obvious thing, namely begin to question the sanctification of these sports by other Americans. But I very much doubt that today's leftists are capable of doing this, or if they are, it will turn out that they came of age long after the Sixties. Leftists of my generation will go to their graves worshiping these sports and hating soccer.

Questioning Authority

Along with the idea that people ought to question society's values, the left promotes the idea of questioning authority. This idea perhaps had its heyday during the Vietnam War, when the left felt it was important to question authority, particularly what we called the Establishment, in order to stop that conflict. The idea of the Establishment was the idea that certain people, whose voices were dominant, had a great deal of power in society and that they were misusing that power. They insisted that young men go off to serve their country in some dubious fashion, generally by killing harmless Third-World peasants. They insisted that young people get educated in an authoritarian setting, and then settle down in a respectable lifestyle, complete with a spouse, a home in the (white) suburbs with a mortgage, a 9-to-5 job, and membership in a church. When we were young, we New Leftists attacked these ideas, and we attacked the Establishment for trying to run our lives.

But the fact is that the New Left never got around to questioning everything, as I already pointed out. Like it or not, the New Left is associated with privileging the big and the tall, with white pitchers and blacks in the outfield, and with prejudice against foreign sports. The New Left never bothered to attack America's Sports Establishment. When I first got involved in soccer in the Seventies, it was plain that there was a Sports Establishment that hated soccer and was determined to run it out of town. This Establishment consisted of the football and basketball coaches in our schools (and often the other coaches as well), the professional coaches in all three of our sports, and the sportswriters and sportscasters in our media. All of them hated soccer, and they were supported in their xenophobia by most of the population.

Never have I heard a leftist complain about this Sports Establishment. Not once. Apparently, questioning the sports authorities doesn't count as questioning authority. Apparently, one must respect the sports authorities. In particular, one must respect the National Collegiate Athletic Association (NCAA), which has never really liked soccer and which has refused to allow for a spring soccer season. This puts American soccer players who come up through the college ranks at a disadvantage because everyone else in the soccer world is playing so much more at that age than they are. But that doesn't matter because one must never question the authority of the NCAA, for the left has never wanted us to question the authorities in sports.

"Rebels"

I cannot help putting this word in quotes when I use it to refer to the young rebels of today. I'm talking about the people who wear outlandish hairstyles and who pierce themselves and get tattoos, simply to rebel against society. Back in the Sixties, we truly did have something to rebel against because our parents were horribly intolerant of new fashions and new music. But the situation is changed today. Most adults my age went through it themselves, and so they are quite tolerant of outlandish fashions. So, the "rebel" is really rebelling against only the small minority who are too stuffy to tolerate it or those who have decided it has gone too far.

More to the point is that these "rebels" are ignoring the same things that the leftists are ignoring. Just as the leftists of my generation refused to rebel against our sporting traditions, so the young "rebels" of today refuse to do so as well. Like it or not, they have limits that they aren't aware of. Perhaps they will say that in rejecting soccer, they are rebelling against the rest of the world. But that still doesn't explain why they don't rebel against institutional sizism. Or perhaps they will say that sports are too unimportant to rebel against, but if so, let me remind them that sports occupy an entire section of the newspaper. Or perhaps they will say that they hate sports and so have no interest in trying to get new sports in, but let me point out that such people have never rebelled against the very existence of sports in our schools, in spite of any hatred they might have of sports.

Not even the most rebellious of "rebels" has wanted to rebel against our sports. Today's "rebels" have lines that they won't step over, but they don't even realize that those lines exist. If they did, they would either cross those lines or else stop calling themselves rebels. For example, it is impossible to imagine the son of a baseball-loving father rebelling by opting for cricket. It is not that playing cricket is too "edgy," for there is nothing obscene or inherently offensive in playing cricket (though it is less prissy than Americans think it is). No, it is rather that playing cricket instead of baseball is part of a prejudice that is so deeply ingrained in our culture that even those who imagine they aren't prejudiced do not see it. And this blindness gets passed on to today's rebels, who just would never think of rebelling in such a way.

Tolerance and Open-mindedness

Being tolerant and open-minded is, of course, one of the most important themes of Sixties leftists, but the tolerance and open-mindedness ends when foreign sports are in question. Somehow, they don't count. But why not? Anyone who demands that people be tolerant of and open-minded about, say, homosexuals can themselves be asked to be tolerant of and open-minded about foreign sports like soccer.

I know that some leftists will say that they already are tolerant and open-minded about soccer, but I have to wonder what this is supposed to mean. Surely they have noticed how many other Americans are *not* tolerant and open-minded about soccer. Why doesn't this knowledge galvanize them into action? Why don't they denounce such people? Leftists never do, and that is so uncharacteristic of leftists that I have to assume that in general they are *not* as tolerant and open-minded as they imagine. What, then, do they mean when they say they are tolerant of soccer? Can they explain what being tolerant of cricket is for them? How can one be tolerant and open-minded about these sports if one is ignorant of them and hates them? What is the difference between the traditionalist who is ignorant of these sports and hates them, and the open-minded leftist who treats them the same way? And is it any better if one "tolerates" Americans playing them but absolutely refuses to have them covered in the media?

Stereotypes

One of the left's biggest gripes concerns stereotypes. Stereotypes are generalized notions that we have about large groups of people. According to the left, stereotypes are always bad. They are bad because often they are negative ("Blacks aren't as intelligent as whites") and even when they aren't negative, they limit individuals with respect to their goals in life ("Girls are more nurturing"). If you use a stereotype concerning blacks, women, homosexuals and other groups that leftists have taken under their wing, you can bet that the left will rise up in righteous anger.

But when America's soccer haters use stereotypes against soccer, the left says nothing. As I argued back in Chapter 6, our media loves to talk about the violence in soccer. Yet, that violence is much less frequent than the soccer haters imagine it is, and anyway it is mostly associated with the English only. Furthermore, the biggest problem in soccer is not violence, but money. However, it is impossible to get through to our media on this topic. They continue to link soccer with riots. And leftists, who supposedly hate stereotypes, have never said a word about this.

Not only have they not said a word about the stereotypes hurled against us, they have even invented their own. I've heard leftists say that soccer (here in America) is a white sport. Never mind that it was Pelé who had introduced the sport to many Americans. Never mind that when I got involved, the sport was an immigrant sport. Never mind that it is still a Latino sport. Never mind that inner-city blacks have had good reasons for ignoring soccer – soccer still doesn't have a secure enough hold in American society that an inner-city black can count on it to escape poverty. Never mind that soccer is *the* sport of black Africa. Never mind that soccer does a wonderful job of achieving gender equality (especially in comparison with football). And never mind that soccer treats those of us who were the wrong size for college sports decently. The only thing that matters to these leftists is that it is most often played by suburbanites, who are usually white.

Even worse, they are saying that we are *racists*.[3] Now I'm sure that in any sufficiently large group of whites, you will find a few racists. The question is whether soccer fans here in America are racist as a group, and I've seen no evidence for that. Or to put it differently, I've seen no evidence that American soccer fans are any more racist than baseball fans are.

Social Injustice

Social injustice is one of the most important themes of the left, and it refers to the unfair ways that people are advantaged or disadvantaged in society, generally based on characteristics that are irrelevant to those advantages and disadvantages. Often, though not always, these are characteristics that one cannot help. For example, when hiring someone for a job, all that should matter is whether they can do the job. The color of their skin or their gender shouldn't matter, and neither one's skin color nor one's gender is something that one can help. If one is white, one will always be white. If one is black, one will always be black. If one is male, one will always be male (excluding certain expensive and time-consuming medical treatments). If one is female, one will always be female. Everyone understands this, and we all know that people have a tendency to denigrate those who are different in ways they cannot help, leading to extreme evils such as slavery.

But there are many other features we have besides the ones just mentioned that are also impossible or at least very difficult to change. Our size is, within limits, virtually impossible to change. As we reach adulthood, there is a certain height that we will reach and a certain weight. To some extent, these can be changed, depending on our eating habits. But there are limits. Some people, no matter how good or bad their eating habits, simply are always going to be big or tall, while others are always going to be short or small. Our size isn't going to change drastically.

I discovered this in high school when I was trying to gain weight in order to play football. I was 5' 9" tall and weighed 125 pounds. I simply couldn't gain any weight, no matter how much I ate. I was the reverse of the average woman, who wants to lose weight and is always on a diet. I was thin and hated it. I wanted to gain and couldn't do it. It wasn't until I learned that Pelé had been exactly the same size at the same age when he played in his first World Cup that I realized there was nothing wrong with my size. (That was a very liberating moment.) Instead, *there had been something wrong with the sports our schools had chosen to emphasize.* Back then, the two most important sports in our schools were football and basketball. I was too small for one and too short for the other. Today, the two most important sports at our schools are *still* football and basketball. The only differences between then and now are that soccer has been introduced in many schools and that women's sports have become much more important than they were back then. Nevertheless, soccer has nowhere near the importance in our schools that football and basketball do, and the most important sport for women at our schools is typically basketball.

It should be pretty obvious that this situation represents social injustice for those of us who aren't the right size for these sports. Why emphasize sports that favor the big and the tall rather than sports for people of other sizes? And why isn't this generally considered as social injustice? It was social injustice not to hire blacks on our professional baseball teams, but it is not considered social injustice to emphasize sports in which people who are neither big nor tall get to participate. Blacks were prevented from playing on the most prominent baseball teams, due to the color of their skin, while those of us who are undersized are prevented from participating in the most prominent school sports, due to our size. It is no answer to say that we can participate in other sports, just as it was no answer to say that those blacks could participate in the black baseball leagues. Nevertheless, the left is resistant to the idea that this situation, which I call institutional sizism, counts as social injustice.

Privileging

Privileging is what the left calls the practice of giving privileges to people who do not really deserve them. Whites were privileged as a result of racism, men were privileged as a result of sexism, the wealthy are often privileged because of their wealth, and so on.

Now everyone knows that football and basketball are the two most important sports in our (public) schools. And everyone knows that football privileges big people and basketball privileges tall people. Every leftist in America knows these facts. Yet, somehow leftists cannot bring themselves to draw the obvious conclusion. They somehow cannot quite realize that this institutional sizism, this privileging of the big and the tall isn't justified, any more than privileging whites or privileging males is justified. The logic is quite simple, however. Leftists say that it is wrong to privilege those who cannot help something about themselves. Size is something that people cannot help about themselves. Therefore, to privilege the big and the tall is wrong. But don't hold your breath waiting for the left to acknowledge this obvious point.

And with this in mind, let me also point out one of the more mind-boggling statements I've run across from someone who is left of center. This statement was made by Carl Bernstein, one of the Watergate reporters whose work inspired a generation of leftist reporters. At a college commencement at Nazareth College of Rochester, Bernstein said, "At the heart of the American condition today is a story that we have ignored for a generation in the media – race." This was reported in the *Chronicle of Higher Education* for May 30, 1997 (p. B9), and so it was said in the spring of that year. It is hard to know what to say to this except to shake one's head in disbelief. Our media have *ignored* race? Anyone who has lived through the past forty years knows perfectly well that our media have *not* ignored race. They are bringing up race all the time. It is hard to know of a topic that they focus on more than race, unless it is gender or the environment. Institutional sizism, however, is another matter. I've never once heard that referred to, whether by that name or by any description. I doubt that I will ever hear the media in my lifetime mention it. If any topic has been ignored, it is not race but institutional sizism.

Racism

In the last chapter I pointed out how racism makes its way into our sports. Blacks are typically excluded from certain positions in baseball. Asians were excluded from baseball altogether when I first began looking at sports critically. Asians are also for the most part excluded from football and basketball because they generally aren't the right size for those sports.

Nevertheless, few leftists have wanted to point out these facts. White leftists in particular, who are often baseball fans, get quite uncomfortable when I point out that blacks are much more likely to end up in the outfield than at pitcher. Instead of exhibiting the righteous rage that they usually exhibit, they get defensive. Now, getting defensive about race is something that rarely happens to these whites, for what usually happens is that they are pointing out to other whites some embarrassing statistic about blacks and whites. The fact that in this instance, at least, it is the white leftists who are getting defensive, rather than being on the offensive, suggests that baseball is simply too emotional a subject for white leftists to deal with. The article that I have already mentioned a few times by Brent Staples, which appeared in *The New York Times Magazine*,[4] would I thought turn the tide. I thought that this article in a magazine that many white leftists read would be enough to get white leftists to be critical about baseball. But it wasn't. The article, beyond an initial flurry of letters (mostly from non-leftists, as far as I could tell), simply vanished into nothingness in the public consciousness.

Here it is important to understand that I am talking about the status of blacks on the field. I am *not* talking about the status of blacks in the front office. I know that white leftists have complained often about the lack of black managers in baseball. But that is not the problem I am talking about. The problem I am talking about is the lack of black *pitchers* and the left's failure to notice this problem.

As for racism in sports, many white leftists go into spasms of rapture when they talk about the old Brooklyn Dodgers. (Most foreign leftists, not being baseball fans, have little interest.) The Brooklyn Dodgers have a mythical status among leftist baseball fans because they were the first major league baseball team to hire a black (namely Jackie Robinson). But let us put this event into context. In fact, let us put this event into a *multicultural* context. Specifically, what was happening in other countries at this time? Were we ahead of them or behind them with respect to integrating blacks onto our professional sports teams? No American leftist that I know of has ever bothered to think about the situation in this way.

But here are the facts. Jackie Robinson was first allowed to play in 1948. Yet in Brazil, blacks were officially allowed onto soccer teams as early as the 1920s! And they had been allowed unofficially at an even earlier date (sometimes by the use of disguises). Moreover, it's not even certain that excluding blacks was something that the Brazilians would have done on their own. It may have been something they inherited from the British, who introduced the sport to them in 1894.

Accordingly, the big question for any American leftist is, *Why were blacks integrated onto Brazilian soccer teams before they were integrated onto American baseball teams?* This question is especially potent given that blacks were freed from slavery in Brazil *after* they were freed from slavery here in America. One might have expected, then, that blacks would have been integrated into the major leagues of American baseball long before they were accepted in Brazilian soccer. But the exact opposite was the case. I know of no American leftist who has answered this question, for the simple reason that no American leftist appears to know anything about Brazilian soccer (aside from Janet Lever, who wrote a fine book on the subject). Yet, once a person *does* learn about this remarkable fact, we see in what sort of context the Brooklyn Dodgers' story needs to be placed. The major league baseball teams here in America were like Southern universities that took much longer than their northern counterparts to admit blacks. The Dodgers happened to be the first team to integrate. Now imagine a hypothetical person who admires whatever Southern university it was that first admitted blacks, except that they think it was the first *university* to admit blacks. Obviously, such a person is woefully ignorant of what had gone on in the North. Likewise, those leftists who admire the Brooklyn Dodgers are like this person in that they are woefully ignorant of what has happened elsewhere.

As for the treatment of Asians, I only once ventured to discuss this with a white leftist. I pointed to the absence of Asians in baseball, and the woman I was talking to immediately erupted in righteous rage, saying, "Yes, there are very few gays in baseball." I didn't bother to correct her. The fact that she had misheard what I said, the fact that she heard what she wanted to hear, the fact that she automatically heard the word "gay" instead of the word "Asian," indicated that there were well-traveled pathways in her mind and that she wasn't going to be thrilled to have me force her onto other, never-used pathways.

But the exclusion of Asians from baseball is dwarfed by their near total exclusion from football and basketball. Face it, the vast majority of Asians aren't the right size for these sports, yet the left is silent about this exclusion.

There is one last topic to discuss in connection with racism and our sports, and that is the topic of Islamophobia. The meaning of this word should be obvious: hatred of Muslims. By itself, this doesn't seem to connect with racism, but many leftists talk of Islamophobia as if it were a type of racism. As such, one can ask, Why is it racist to hate the dominant religion of the Middle East, which is Islam, but not the dominant sport of the Middle East, which is soccer?

Exclusion and Inclusion

Exclusion refers to the fact that some people have been denied certain opportunities simply because of some unimportant feature about themselves, such as the color of their skin or their gender. They have been denied jobs, homes in certain neighborhoods, and access to the best society. One of the left's themes is that no one should be excluded for any irrelevant reasons. All should be included, unless there is some good reason why they should be excluded.

Many of the points I have been making can be summed up by talking about exclusion. People who are short or small are excluded from the most important sports in our public schools, namely football and basketball. In fact, people who are of average height and weight are often excluded from those sports. Asians have been excluded from those sports, and in the past were excluded from baseball. Blacks are excluded from the position of pitcher in baseball and are often relegated to the outfield. Left-handers are excluded from certain positions in baseball; they, too, are often relegated to the outfield.

Yet, in spite of these multiple instances of exclusion, today's leftists have been almost completely silent.

Marginalization

Marginalization refers to the fact that some people have been on the fringes of society, often because of some feature about themselves that they couldn't help. It is related to racism and other forms of prejudice, of course. Those who are marginalized, or rather those whom the left regards as having been marginalized, are the minorities, women, and homosexuals. It goes almost without saying that leftists of today don't regard *me* as having been marginalized, even though I was too small for football and too short for basketball and therefore was on the fringe of sports in the American school. Such marginalization is unimportant to them. It also goes almost without saying that getting involved in some foreign sport such as soccer or cricket, despite the fact that this entails almost instant marginalization and despite the fact that most people in this country are prejudiced against these sports, doesn't count as real marginalization, either.

Self-Esteem

Some people in our society have their self-esteem squashed, simply because of who they are. Women and blacks, for example, are expected to do poorly in math, and the left has been trying to counter that expectation by raising the self-esteem of women and blacks when it comes to doing math. And that is admirable.

Where it becomes less admirable is their policy of ignoring *other* people who might need a boost in self-esteem. Why not think about the self-esteem of men like me who were too small for football and too short for basketball? Those sports are dominant in our schools, and the media fawns over those athletes who shine in them as well. The result was that I came to think of myself as "too small for sports." And I know that I am not the only person who thought this way. Of course, I wasn't too small for baseball, but within a school context one often forgets about baseball.

Nevertheless, *my* self-esteem and the self-esteem of other men my size are never considered. Nor is the self-esteem of the many blacks in this country who are too small to play basketball. There must be an enormous problem here, yet I have never seen a single word written about it. But the problem includes whites, too, and in fact it includes entire ethnic groups. (When I was living in Minneapolis, I occasionally played in pick-up soccer games with Hmong immigrants. They were all shorter than me, but could kick the ball twice as far as I could.) Somehow, though, the left never sees this problem. Somehow, the lack of self-esteem in those of us who were too small for football and too short for basketball never reaches the consciousness of the American leftist.

Role Models

Closely connected with the topic of self-esteem is the idea of a role model. The left thinks that role models are extremely important for certain groups (such as women and blacks) to have so as to show members of these groups that it is possible for them to attain to prominent positions. Then why isn't it important for those of us who were the "wrong" size for our schools' favorite sports to have role models, too?

False Consciousness

False consciousness occurs when people act unknowingly against their own self-interest or fail to notice that they are oppressed. Throughout America, one can go to a park or playground or gym and see young men playing basketball. Most of them are not tall enough for the professional game, though they are tall enough for soccer. Yet, they prefer playing basketball to playing pick-up soccer, and they support basketball over soccer. Isn't this nothing other than false consciousness? And if not, why not? Assuming it is, then shouldn't it be attacked? And if not, why not? What is the point of a concept like false consciousness if you aren't going to use it in every instance? For that matter, where is the concern among leftists for those blacks who are not tall enough for basketball? I have never seen any concern for such people. I have never noticed any criticism by leftists for the American black's love affair with basketball. What I see instead is the American black man walking down the street bouncing his basketball, even if he is too short for the sport. No one tells him about institutional sizism and how, if he is the wrong size, he will be hurt by it. To sum up, throughout America there are many men who spit on a sport that supports them, while supporting sports that spit on them. Yet, the left is silent about these instances of false consciousness.

Hostile Environments

According to current leftist thought, those who have been marginalized often find themselves in a hostile environment, either in school or in the workplace. Such people find themselves denigrated, simply because of who they are. Leftist policy, of course, is to change that hostile environment to a more accepting environment.

What kind of environment have those of us who are soccer fans found ourselves in, whether in the workplace or in school? An irremediably hostile one. This is due to the ridiculous prejudice of one's fellow students or co-workers. Admittedly, this isn't exactly the same as the hostile environments that others who are marginalized put up with because in this case the hostility comes not from who one is but from what sports one has chosen to support. But since marginalization also applies to religious groups (especially Muslims), who are marginalized because of a choice they've made rather than because of something they can't change, then marginalization should also apply to the sports that one has chosen to support.

A hostile environment of the sort that leftists want to change does exist on school campuses where football and basketball are the dominant sports. Such an environment exists for those of us who were the wrong size for those sports. To begin with, there is the fact that the mainstream media fawn all over the athletes in these sports, while paying little attention to athletes in other sports. The student newspaper does the same thing. So do one's fellow students. *But worst of all is that the very leftists who complain about hostile environments themselves are part of this hostile environment.* They themselves help create this hostile environment by saying and doing nothing against institutional sizism and by sneering at soccer. When I mention institutional sizism to such people, they just dismiss it as unimportant.

Sensitivity Training

Sensitivity training consists of sessions in school or in the workplace in which people are trained to be more sensitive to those who have experienced social injustice. The idea is that everyone else is racist, sexist, homophobic, and so on, so that they need training to get them to overcome their natural feelings of disgust at such people.

It goes without saying that sensitivity training never concerns itself with countering the feelings of disgust that Americans have about soccer and other foreign sports and those of us who play such sports. Nor is it ever about overcoming the feelings that I once had, that being the wrong size for football and basketball meant that I was too small for sports. No, that sort of feeling is never dealt with. Institutional sizism is not something that those who sponsor sensitivity training sessions are at all concerned with, which means that they could use some sensitivity training themselves.

Affirmative Action

Affirmative action is a type of compensatory justice in which minorities and women, who were discriminated against in the past when looking for jobs or when trying to get into the best schools, are now favored for those jobs or schools. Obviously, though, compensation can be applied for many types of social injustice. For example, we could have affirmative action for school sports. For the last century or so, the two most dominant sports in our schools have been football and basketball, and as I have been pointing out, this privileged those who were above average in height and weight. Why not advocate affirmative action for those of us who were the wrong size? I'm not thinking of choosing the smaller of two otherwise equally qualified football players, or the shorter of two otherwise equally qualified basketball players. I am thinking rather that, to compensate, schools should de-emphasize those sports and introduce soccer and other sports for those who are the wrong size for football and basketball. We've had a century now of sports for the big and tall. How about having sports for the next century be for people of other sizes?

How many leftists of today would support this type of affirmative action? I know of none.

American Studies and Area "Experts"

Within academia, there is a discipline called American Studies. This discipline studies exactly what it claims to study, America. Originally, the scholars in this discipline seemed to have no particular political bent, but now they all seem to be leftists. But during neither its initial apolitical phase nor its current leftist phase have these scholars talked much about sports.

Two of the points I have been trying to emphasize are the uniqueness of our sport environment (because of our rejection of British sports and our insistence on school sports) and our almost total *ignorance* of our uniqueness. Imagine a discipline called Chinese Studies that refused to examine foot-binding, and you will see what American Studies is like. Foot-binding was something that only the Chinese did. No one else could make any sense of it. It is therefore appropriate to study it in a Chinese Studies class. Likewise, our rejection of British sports and our insistence on the importance of sports in our schools is something that only we do. No one else can make any sense of it. Since these are features of America that make us unique, then they ought to be studied, yet they never are.

Another curiosity of academia is the area "expert." These are Americans (today generally leftists) who study another culture and then teach about it in our colleges and universities. Often, such people are completely ignorant of the sports of the cultures in which they are supposed to be expert. I talked to one such "expert" on France in the spring of 1998 who was totally unaware that the French would soon be hosting the World Cup. Another "expert" on India failed to identify the Indian cricket player on the page of the *Economist* I mentioned back in Chapter 6. (Recall that in an *Economist* survey of India and Pakistan, the first page of that survey showed a cricket player from each country.) When I showed this page to a young woman from India, she regaled me with information on the two players. Other such experts have more knowledge, but it is not as though they see such knowledge as terribly important, as something that needs to be communicated either to their students or their colleagues. Let us hope that a new generation of experts will truly deserve to be called experts.

Dead White Males

Leftists in recent years have been demanding that our schools teach something other than the works of what they call dead white males. People like Shakespeare, Plato, Rembrandt, Beethoven, and many others who form the basis of Western culture are now eschewed by our educators because they represent only a small segment of the cultures in which they lived. Women were excluded from using their talents as writers, philosophers, artists and so on simply because they were women. So were people who were slaves or otherwise marginalized. Accordingly, leftists have demanded that we stop teaching about dead white males and that we start teaching, insofar as this is possible, about everyone else.

By now the reader should be able to anticipate what I am going to say. These same leftists who demand that dead white males be de-emphasized in the classroom say nothing against sports in our schools that were invented by dead white males. Like it or not, our three main sports – baseball, football and basketball – were invented by dead white males. In fact, we can go further and say that they were invented by dead, white, nineteenth-century American males. If the problem with the culture of dead white males is that they are not representative of the past, then the culture of dead, white, nineteenth-century American males is even less representative of the past. After all, the culture produced by dead white males which used to be taught unthinkingly has the distinction of coming from a number of centuries and geographical regions: Mesopotamia, Egypt, Israel, Athens, Rome, England, Spain, France, Germany, and America. Such a list spans quite a variety of times and places. By contrast, dead, white, nineteenth-century American males represent only one century and only one region: nineteenth-century America.[5] Accordingly, the sports produced by such people ought to be condemned even more than is the culture produced by dead white males. Yet they are never condemned. The American left seems quite happy with the sports bequeathed to us by dead, white, nineteenth-century American males, nor does it ever demand that they be eliminated from our schools.

Let me look at a particular aspect of this problem. One of the few sports issues for leftists today is the matter of names of sports teams and their logos. Now that I am living in Ohio, I often see the image of the Chief Wahoo logo of the Cleveland Indians. Occasionally, some leftist will complain about this. The Chief Wahoo logo is deemed offensive and furthermore can lower the self-esteem of American Indians. Leftists say it ought to be replaced by something else. Perhaps even the name of the Cleveland Indians ought to be changed.

Yet, anyone should be able to see that this is a rather weak response by the left, no matter how progressive it sounds. Anyone who castigates the culture of dead white males would know what to do: reject the sports invented by dead white males and *accept an American Indian sport*. Why are these people supporting baseball at all? Why aren't they turning their attention to *lacrosse*, a sport invented by Indians? But the fact is that they aren't doing this. It is true that lacrosse has some support in this country, but that support generally is purely regional. People play it on the east coast, but not elsewhere. In my hometown of Minneapolis, for example, it has been all but unknown (though gaining in popularity in recent years), despite the fact that Minneapolis considers itself highly progressive and despite the fact that it has a large Indian population. (I know this because I lived in an Indian neighborhood at one point.) American leftists, especially white leftists, would rather support baseball, a sport invented by dead, white, nineteenth-century American males, than lacrosse, a sport invented by Indians.

Diversity

Diversity, one of the buzz words of today's leftists, is the idea that schools or workplaces should contain a variety of types of people. Of course, having a variety of people and even a variety of cultures represented in our schools and the workplace doesn't mean that a variety of *sports* will be allowed. There will be no diversity in sports. We will continue to have the same Americentric sports environment that we have always had. Demanding that soccer be promoted because it is favored by some among that variety of people is not part of the concept of diversity. Latinos are part of this wonderful diversity, but the fact that Latinos love soccer doesn't mean that soccer will get any special treatment from those loving diversity. And although people from cricket-playing countries are also part of diversity, their favorite sport will not be part of our schools at all, either as a sport or as something that is taught.

Diversity is valued because having a variety of types of people is thought to be more educational for our schools and to help increase productivity in the workplace. I'm not going to say anything about the workplace, but there is a lot to say about schools. The reason it is supposed to be more educational is that by forcing mainstream Americans to mix with people of other backgrounds, they become more familiar with them and their values. It is part of a liberal education. Here, then, is what one young woman from Sri Lanka said about America when she came to study here: "Sports [in America] are lame. Where is the cricket?"[6] Unfortunately, this is just one statement by one person, and few such statements make it into our media. But I think that learning that the rest of the world finds our sports lame is something that mainstream Americans ought to learn. It is just that I have no evidence that the people promoting diversity are actually interested in having our students learn such a thing. If they were, then they would be demanding that cricket be made into a college sport, which of course they aren't doing. No, what they want them to learn is the *other* things that such people can teach them, such as their literature, music, and religion (and how awful America is in ways other than our sports). But when it comes to teaching mainstream Americans about the sports of foreigners, that isn't part of the agenda.

Multiculturalism

For some years now, beginning in the 1980s and continuing to the present, there has been a cultural war between the right and the left. The nature of this war can be stated rather simply. The right prefers the traditional culture of Europe and insists that the basis of American democracy and our various institutions are the result of European culture. The left insists that this is nothing but Eurocentrism, and that this Eurocentric bias is wrong (because of various evils that Europeans engaged in, such as the slave trade and imperialism), so we ought to pay more attention and give more respect to the cultures of the Third World.

It is a battle between the Eurocentrists and the multiculturalists. Which cultures should we pay more attention to? Which cultures should we respect more? Which should we teach about in our schools? This has been the battle for many years. What is striking from a soccer point of view is that neither group describes itself accurately. The Eurocentrists prefer European culture, *except* when it comes to sports. Likewise, the multiculturalists prefer the culture of the Third World, *except* when it comes to sports. Both Eurocentrists and multiculturalists are content to retain our sports and exclude foreign sports from our schools. When it comes to sports, both groups are Americentrists.

One Eurocentrist wrote a book talking about how, in various aspects of our lives, our culture was derived from British culture. At one point, he quoted a poem written in Britain to show what he meant:

> We are the modern masters of the world,
> The arbiters, the heirs
> Of Egypt, Greece and Italy
> (We have no time for art
> But we know what we like!)
> We are the fulfilment of Man's promise
> The Cup-tie Final and the paper cap;
> We are the Soul of the Cash Register,
> The Secret of the Hire-Purchase System,
> The Vacuum, and the Vacuum-Cleaner.

This is from the Chorus of Sir Osbert Sitwell's poem *Demos the Emperor*. Notice the reference to soccer, the reference to the "Cup-tie Final." What is striking is that the author of the book, Russell Kirk, appears not to notice this reference. He never mentioned sports in his book.[7]

But if people on the right have been stupid, people on the left have been even stupider. Anyone who is a multiculturalist should have asked himself or herself the following question: In what way have Americans been *least* multicultural? In what way have they been most antagonistic to other cultures, whether European culture or the cultures of the Third World? The answer, simply, is in sports. Americans have been – and many continue to be – most antagonistic to other cultures' sports, no matter what part of the world those other cultures are located in. Americans have always been receptive to the music of Europe, whether classical or popular. We are beginning to be receptive to the music of the Third World. The same can be said for literature and the arts. In fact, in the visual arts Americans and Europeans have long been very receptive to other cultures. Again, when it comes to food, we are highly receptive to other cultures. But when it comes to sports, just to mention some sports to the average American can evoke an extremely negative reaction, even among Americans who espouse multicultural principles.

Now if it is in sports that Americans are least multicultural, then it stands to reason that sports should be the main focus of the multiculturalists. You would think that they would be chanting not only:

Hey, hey, ho, ho,
Western civ has got to go.

But also:

Hey, hey, ho, ho,
American sports have got to go.

Instead, they have ignored sports completely. They have been quite content to retain the status quo for school sports, despite the fact that the dominant sports of our schools were not invented in either Europe or the Third World. They have been willing to allow American sports to continue to dominate.

To be blunt, the policies of the multiculturalists are like the policies of a law-and-order politician who wants to rein in crime, but who focuses on the pickpockets rather than the murderers and rapists. Multiculturalism is nothing but a farce, perhaps the biggest farce in the history of American education. In fact, the left is so clueless about multiculturalism that it has demanded that we use the term "African-American" for all blacks. The problem here is that so many blacks in the world are not American. At the time this nonsense was started, most of the blacks I knew were foreign students who intended to return to their countries when they graduated. Was I really supposed to call them African-Americans when they weren't even American citizens? Surely not. Yet, how can one distinguish an African-American from a foreign black who is here for only a short time? No help is given by our leftists. It is true that from hanging around with many foreign blacks, I came to be able to distinguish them from American blacks. But these judgments weren't foolproof. Every time I watch Thierry Henry, I am struck by how much he looks like an American black, even though I know he is French. Surely one ought not to call someone who is French an American of any sort. Right? Yet to say this is to be accused of racism. And my response that the term "African-American" is nothing but American chauvinism, a pure instance of cluelessness about the rest of the world (and so, if anything, *anti*-multicultural) since it assumes that every black in the world is American, doesn't make a dent. What about blacks who have never been here or are citizens of other countries? Suffice it to say that no one who has any sense would ever call Nelson Mandela an African-American, since he is not an American. Notice that I'm not saying that the term "African-American" has no uses. I'm simply saying that it is factually wrong to use it to refer to all blacks in the world, since many aren't Americans, and that since it is difficult to tell which blacks one encounters here in America are American citizens and which are simply visitors, then it is wrong to demand that the term *must always* be used even for all American blacks.

As I said, multiculturalism in this country is nothing but a farce, and it will remain a farce until the multiculturalists become open-minded about foreign sports.

Lack of Curiosity

Every now and then a leftist will complain about how incurious former President George W. Bush was about other cultures. This complaint is one of a number of complaints made about Bush (or conservatives generally), and while it is by no means the most common, it is made often enough that it deserves to be included here. The brutal fact of the matter is that those leveling this charge almost certainly have no curiosity about foreign sports. Among the leftists I have known down through the years, I can remember only one who exhibited any sort of curiosity about cricket, and her curiosity was so mild that it is hardly worth mentioning. As for soccer, again the level of curiosity I have seen (among older leftists, anyway) has been so low as to be insignificant. It just doesn't exist. For an American leftist to call any other American incurious about other cultures is just utter blindness.

Otherness, Sub-alterity, Etc.

This odd set of terms can be summed up as follows:

> What appear to be cultural units ... are maintained in their apparent unity only through an active process of exclusion, opposition, and hierarchization. Other phenomena or units must be represented as foreign or "other" through representing a hierarchical dualism in which the unit is "privileged" or favored, and the other is devalued in some way.[8]

What this means can be illustrated in racial terms. The cultural units are those of us who are white, while blacks are the "Other." Whites were (and mostly still are) at the top of the hierarchy, while blacks were at the bottom. Whites took the best jobs and moved in the best society, while blacks had the grunt jobs and moved in lower society. White society and culture (in the past, anyway) was privileged, while black society and culture was devalued. But most important was that black society and culture were devalued *simply* because they were black.

The same thing can be said about women. Men constitute the cultural units, while women are the Other; men are at the top, women at the bottom; and so on. Again, women's contributions to society were devalued *simply* because they were done by women. The same thing can be said about the United States in relation to the Third World.

Now what leaps out when reading this passage is the word "foreign," a word that has been applied so often to soccer by America's soccer haters. Indeed, this whole passage describes very well the attitudes of such people, who see soccer as a threat and so have an us-versus-them mentality. They have constructed a hierarchy of sports with American sports at the top and foreign sports at the bottom. They privilege those who play and follow American sports while devaluing those who play and follow foreign sports, and they typically exclude those who play foreign sports in one way or another (for example, by refusing to consider them as athletes, by refusing to list them among the greatest of athletes, and in many other ways). Such thinking affects even those who don't consciously hate soccer, because their choices of fun activities are governed by the idea that soccer is worthless. People who throw around frisbees, for example, would probably be kicking around a soccer ball if they lived elsewhere in the world. In fact, it even affects the way people use language, since such people will unconsciously use sports metaphors from American sports rather than those from soccer or other foreign sports.

Most important, the soccer haters devalue soccer *simply* because it is foreign. As I argued in Chapter 6, the idea that soccer is bad because of the low scoring is just an excuse. The real reason is that it is foreign. Since it is foreign, a reason had to be found to sneer at it, and soon enough the soccer haters latched onto soccer's low scoring. Keep in mind that when I first got involved in soccer, most Americans didn't even know whether it had high amounts of scoring or low amounts. All they knew was that they were supposed to hate it.

Despite the fact that this idea of "Otherness" is perfectly exemplified by the thinking of the soccer haters, leftists have never noticed this. Indeed, when I pointed it out to one leftist, he immediately made a totally irrelevant and utterly mistaken remark. He claimed that soccer couldn't claim the status of the "Other" because it was played by Europeans, who hardly counted as those who are Other. But first of all, soccer in Europe is typically a lower-class sport; why shouldn't it, then, claim the status of those who are Other? Secondly, soccer is also the sport of the Third World, which should allow it to participate in Otherness. Finally, this person totally missed the point of my reasoning. My point had to do not with soccer as it exists in the rest of the world, but as it exists in *America*. My point was that the typical American treats soccer in ways that were described in the quotation above. My point was that *anything* that fits that description deserves the status of Otherness, no matter how much leftists may squawk about it. To say that soccer as it exists in America doesn't deserve this status because soccer is played by Europeans, who are of the First World, is like saying that the Third World doesn't deserve the status of the Other because half of the Third World is male. Face it, soccer is the sport of the Other.

Now we come to the important point: *how did the American left react when faced with genuine Otherness in the form of soccer and other foreign sports?* Why, they went scurrying back to the safety and familiarity of American sports. So much for their ability to respect the Other.

Let me get back to the quote at the beginning of this section. The sort of thinking this quote illustrates is associated with people like Jacques

Derrida, the French philosopher who invented a type of literary and philosophical analysis called "deconstruction." I'm not going to explain what deconstruction is, but I do want to say something about Derrida. One day I was looking at an issue of the *Times of London*, which happened to have an article about him. The reporter said the following:

> Derrida – the joker who appeared in *Paris Match* in a leather jacket, played professional football and was once arrested in Prague for alleged drug-peddling – threatens the very foundations of academic life.[9]

Derrida had played professional football? Since this was in a British newspaper, "football" here meant soccer. This was quite astonishing. Derrida had actually played soccer professionally?! No one had ever told me this before. I dashed a letter off to some friends I had at that time, one of whom had actually met Derrida, and asked them why they hadn't told me this before. They responded that they hadn't known about it. Of course, the reason they hadn't known about it was simply that, as American leftists, they had never thought anything of soccer and so had never bothered to look at newspapers like the *Times of London*. Later, I tried to verify this information, and while I was able to find that he had played soccer when he had been a young man, the information that he played *professionally* I wasn't able either to prove or disprove. I leave it to others to investigate. I have to admit that I am not much of a fan of Derrida's philosophy, which led one of my friends to quip, "John prefers the early Derrida."

To return to the main point, there is so far nothing in American leftism that indicates that they are capable of fully respecting the Other.

Postmodernism

The topic of postmodernism is related to the previous topic, as the following quote shows:

> "Postmodern" thinking ... means ... a relentless attentiveness and sensitivity to the "other." Postmodernism stands for a kind of hyper-sensitivity to many "others": the other person, other species, "man's" other, the other of the West, of Europe, of Being, of the "classic," of philosophy, of reason, etc.[10]

This quote proves what I was saying in the last section, that we cannot limit the idea of the Other. It's going to emerge in many different areas, and so it is best to rely on a general idea of what it means rather than to restrict it in advance. And that means that we have to count European soccer players, no matter what class they are from, as the Other, when considered from the standpoint of prejudiced American sports fans, who have devalued such athletes just as much as they have devalued those of the Third World. When sports are under consideration, then, we Americans need to think of the "Other" as opposed not to the West or to Europe, but only to America, which means that the "Other" in this instance refers to the entire rest of the world. Postmodernist thinking demands that we do this, even if American postmodernists would like to reject it.

Similarly, those of us who were the wrong size for our sports ought to count as the "Other." We were devalued as athletes because we weren't the right size. It goes without saying that no leftist today would allow such thinking.

Immigration

Many leftists say that they support immigration into our country. Most also go further and say that they support allowing those immigrants to keep their own culture (a position which can be called anti-assimilationism). It goes almost without saying that to keep one's culture entails keeping one's sports as well. Yet, I have never heard a leftist draw this conclusion explicitly. Nor do I have any evidence that they draw it implicitly, for that would mean (for example) demanding that soccer get more visibility here in the U.S. for the sake of Latino immigrants. But they haven't demanded this, and they seem to assume that all Latinos will abandon soccer for baseball.

Saying that you support immigration *and* that you are anti-assimilationist has sharp consequences. Look at it this way. Suppose a large number of people – say, twenty million – migrated from south Asia to this country. Since south Asians follow cricket, we would expect these people to eventually start a professional cricket league and to demand that cricket be instituted in our schools. How many American leftists would join them in supporting such ventures? I know of none.

Often, leftists will write articles telling white Americans that California is becoming less and less white. The tone of these articles is not alarmist, as they might have been had they been written by racists. Instead, the tone is rather smug and superior. The writers are in effect saying, "You racist whites had better get used to the fact that California is going to be dominated by non-whites in the coming years." What these articles *don't* say is that California is likely to be a state that pays more and more attention to soccer. As more and more Latinos enter California, to say nothing of the Iranians and other foreigners who are already there, soccer will become more and more visible as a sport in that state. Even now, Los Angeles has among the highest attendances in the MLS, something which wasn't true for their NASL team back in the 1970s. But the reason that these smug writers don't mention the looming importance of soccer in California is just that they themselves don't like the idea. Although their articles condescendingly talk about how hard it is going to be for white Americans to handle the California of the future, these writers will have their own problems handling the California of the future.

Cultural Imperialism

Leftists often rail against cultural imperialism. With the war in Iraq, leftists don't talk about this as often as they used to, since now they can rail against genuine imperialism, but particularly in the 1990s, they railed against cultural imperialism. Typically, the things they have railed against are the spread of our fast food restaurants and some of the more objectionable (to leftists, anyway) of our television shows, like *Baywatch*. What they ignore are other parts of our culture which are highly exportable as well, such as sports.

Reuben Abati is a Nigerian journalist who has this to say about cultural imperialism: "Every waking day, every human being on the surface of this planet" has to hear about American culture. So far he sounds exactly like the typical American leftist who complains about our cultural imperialism. It isn't until you look at his list of complaints that you see the difference between him and his American counterparts, for the first item on his list is basketball.[11] I have never heard any American leftist complain about the spread of basketball. The reason for that is simple: the American left loves basketball. Because of that love, such cultural imperialism doesn't bother them a bit, even though it bothers the cultures on whom it is being imposed and whom they are otherwise trying to help.

In Minneapolis once, there were some young girls from Somalia who were taught softball by some of the locals. This was written up with an accompanying photograph in the Minneapolis *Star-Tribune*.[12] No one seemed to think that this counted as cultural imperialism or as forcing immigrants to abandon their culture. On the contrary, a few days later a reader said that this was "a beautiful and poignant juxtaposition of America's national pastime and the world's future."[13] This is typical of the left's hypocrisy. It is true that I have no idea if the letter writer was a leftist, but even if he wasn't, where was the outcry from those who were leftists? Generally, leftists in Minneapolis are not shy about writing. If they can't get published in the very-progressive Minneapolis *Star-Tribune*, they will give vent to their opinions in the alternative press. (Today, of course, they could use the Internet.) But I heard nothing from them on this subject.

It is true that, if looked at from a narrow perspective, the letter writer can be seen as enlightened. He was happy that these refugees weren't being totally ignored. He was happy that some mainstream Americans took the time to teach them something that would help them become more integrated into American life. But the question is, Would the people doing this, as well as the letter writer, have been willing to have these Somalis teach them about soccer or about indigenous sports in Somalia? Not on your life. Their attitude would be that, since baseball is the best sport in the world, then there would be no point for them to learn about such things. To learn about their sports would be like learning how to count from those cultures that say one, two, many. But such thinking is the usual thinking of the imperialist. The imperialists force their culture on those they rule while refusing to learn anything in return.

Cultural Relativism

Many leftists today espouse cultural relativism, which is the idea that each culture's morals and values are right for them. What a culture has deemed to be moral is moral for that culture, and what a culture has deemed to be valuable is valuable for that culture. There are no international standards that could settle any disputes that might arise between two different cultures concerning what is moral and valuable. There are no absolutes in morals or values.

Of course, it is one thing to say this and another to accept it wholeheartedly. My question is, Are the leftists who accept cultural relativism willing to accept it for sports, or do they make an exception for sports? As far as I can see, such leftists make an exception for sports (and so are being hypocritical). It is true that such people never admit this explicitly. But such people *act* as though they admitted it. Recall the statement above (in connection with the Somalian girls) about baseball being the world's future. As I said, I don't know if a leftist made that statement, but what is important is that *no leftist rejected it*. And many similar statements have been made, concerning which leftists have never offered the slightest objection. Instead, such leftists have a problem with the fact that most of the rest of the world rejects baseball and our other sports. They would prefer them to play our sports, even if this means accepting baseball as some sort of moral absolute.

The Poor

The left has made poverty one of the more important problems that it wants to solve. It promotes welfare or socialism, it accuses the right of waging a war against the poor, and so on.

Nevertheless, the left has done nothing to help the poor when it comes to sports. In my travels to other countries, I observed that it was much easier for the poor in those countries to purchase a ticket to a sporting event than it was here. In America, the prices of tickets to sporting events are basically quite high, sometimes exorbitantly so. The result is that the fans at the stadium are generally well-to-do or at least solidly middle class. The poor are excluded. In other countries, the ticket prices are held down because part of the stadium is designed for standing. When I was in Rio, for example, I noticed that there was a section down front specifically designed for standing, which cost a mere thirty-five cents to get into. (That was back in 1981, of course, so the price has probably changed.) American leftists have never noticed such things because they hate foreign sports, and so they've never gone to games abroad. Accordingly, they have not thought about how the poor are excluded from sports in this country. Nor have they thought much about how our sports would work in the Third World. Football is quite expensive and could never really work there. Even baseball would be difficult for the poorest of countries, the reason being that its stadia are not much good for other sports (unlike soccer, whose stadia can often double as track-and-field stadia) and that a large number of baseballs must be given away when foul balls are hit. Basketball, too, needs a flat, smooth surface for bouncing a ball with a basket up high. Contrast this with soccer, in which people can make do with fairly simple equipment for playing (shirts thrown down on the ground to be used as the goals, socks stuffed with old newspapers for the ball, etc.).

The Third World

The left has long insisted that it is the champion of the Third World. It constantly talks about Third-World poverty, about American cultural imperialism, and about postcolonial culture.

However, when it comes to the sports played in the Third World, the American left has no interest. It has no interest in soccer played in most of the Third World or in cricket played in south Asia. At best, it has some marginal interest in baseball played in Central America. But beyond that, its interest in sports in the Third World is entirely nonexistent. During the Nineties, there were a number of important soccer victories by African nations (such as the victory of Cameroon over Argentina in the World Cup of 1990). These were declared by their participants to be victories "for the entire Third World." But the American left didn't care. They never even noticed.

Distributive Justice

Distributive justice is one of the more important themes of leftists. How goods and privileges get distributed is important for leftists because leftists believe it ought to be done as equitably as possible. Though many leftists of late have abandoned economics for identity politics, even those who are more interested in identity politics are still interested in the issue of distributive justice. Poverty, after all, is a consequence of the wrong economic and social policies, and identity leftists are not uninterested in the evils of poverty.

So, it is a mystery then why no leftists (aside from Brent Staples) ever complain about the distribution of action with the ball in baseball or football. It is perfectly obvious that these distributions are unequal and that nothing can justify them. For those who are strict egalitarians, no inequality is ever justified, yet such American leftists have never condemned baseball. Other liberals or leftists are willing to allow some inequalities under certain conditions, but again I have never seen such people justify the inequalities of baseball.

Hating America

One of the more prevalent themes of today's leftists is that of hating America. One can see it in a previous topic, cultural imperialism, for leftists identify certain things with America, such as fast food restaurants, which it then can't stand seeing spread elsewhere. But it is much more widespread than that. During the Vietnam War, leftists typically referred to our country as "Amerika," the German spelling being intended to illustrate some resemblance between our country and Nazi Germany. Of course, the comparison is ludicrous. But what is more ludicrous is the way that these people, who profess to hate America, also love American sports and hate foreign sports. Why not call baseball, football, and basketball, not American sports, but Amerikan sports? Somehow, today's leftists cannot bring themselves to do that. These three sports have become sacred cows for the left, and they couldn't possibly impugn them in this way.

Such people are even willing to put up with the playing of our national anthem at every one of our sporting events. I have attended sporting events in several other countries, and one thing that struck me was that national anthems were rarely played. The game simply started at the scheduled time. It was only when teams from two countries were involved that a national anthem was played. If it was between two teams in the same country, there was no reason to do so. Because so few American leftists have bothered to see soccer games abroad, they have never noticed this sort of thing and so are unaware of it. Consequently, they patiently abide the playing of the Star Spangled Banner when one would expect them to protest against it. This is especially odd given that such people would happily burn the flag that is being honored.

And speaking of burning our flag, let me note that while our leftists are quite happy to burn our flag, if you ask them to burn their baseball paraphernalia, you will see a different response.

Citizens of the World

Some American leftists are so embarrassed by our country that they prefer to think of themselves as citizens of the world rather than as citizens of America. It goes without saying that they generally pay no attention to and are ignorant of the sports being played in the rest of the world. To what extent are they truly citizens of the world?

Hate Speech

Leftists have insisted that certain forms of speech count as hate speech and so deserve to be banned, in spite of the First Amendment. They even consider it a form of violence (although clearly hate speech and physical violence are two very different things). Some leftists have even declared certain areas hate-free zones.

Of course, what they are thinking of when they condemn hate speech is speech that is derogatory toward blacks, women, and homosexuals. Other groups aren't included. Not even Jews are included, even though that would have been unthinkable forty years ago. But if Jews aren't included, you can bet that other groups aren't, either. For example, those of us who are the wrong size for football and basketball cannot count on any help from the left if we are subjected to verbal attacks on our size. It is true that hate speech of this sort seldom occurs, but that is mostly because our sports environment is so relentlessly sizist that it doesn't need to be said. Yet occasionally it does get expressed, as in the following: "Why is it always up to me to point these things out? They've given the Heisman Trophy to another pixie." These words appeared in a sports column of the *Chicago Tribune*.[14] How did the left respond? They said nothing. Is it the case that there are no leftists in Chicago? Hardly, because that is where the leftist magazine *In These Times* is published, but apparently none of them noticed this blatant exercise in sizism. And not only was the statement derogatory, it was not even about someone who was truly small. One can only imagine what the columnist would say about someone who was truly small.

In addition, when I was playing intramural soccer, occasionally people driving by in cars would shout out their windows, jeering at us for playing such a stupid sport. And down through the years there have been many letters to the editor that expressed hatred against soccer and the idiocy of foreigners for accepting such a sport. I've never heard any leftist complain about the hatred that we soccer fans have to put up with. Not once. Not even when it spills over to include people of the Third World. As with many themes the left promotes, the one condemning hate speech and hate itself is pure hypocrisy.

Listening to Other Voices

Listening to other voices has been one of the catch-phrases of the left, especially among feminists. They insist that their own voices were squelched for many centuries, but that we would be better off if we were to listen to all voices, especially those voices that we haven't heard from.

Naturally, listening to other voices hasn't included listening to us soccer fans (to say nothing of cricket and rugby fans). The fact that we don't have much of a voice in our media has never bothered Americans leftists, despite their pious pronouncements about listening to other voices. It is just one more example of leftist hypocrisy.

Gender Equality

The concept of gender equality has been applied to sports in this country by feminists, but their application has been rather peculiar. Basically, what feminists are up against in our schools are two facts: the most dominant sport is football, and football has no female equivalent. This isn't true of many other sports. Men's basketball can be balanced by women's basketball. Men's baseball can be balanced (perhaps) by women's softball. Men's soccer can be balanced by women's soccer. Even men's rugby can be balanced by women's rugby. But for football there is no female equivalent because hardly any women want to play football. There just is no women's football, which puts feminists in a bind.

This situation can of course be dealt with in several ways. One such way is to choose a women's sport which won't also be a men's sport. Some schools have chosen field hockey as the sport in question, and there is a good deal of logic in this choice because, whereas in some parts of the world field hockey is played by men, that isn't true in America. By contrast, American women have been playing field hockey for many years. Nevertheless, choosing field hockey to achieve gender equality isn't exactly going to work because – let's face it – football is so dominant in men's sports that to have gender equality any female sport used to balance it would also have to be just as dominant in women's sports, and field hockey just doesn't have that position of dominance for women.

An even worse option is to choose some sport other than field hockey to emphasize for women. My own alma mater, the University of Minnesota, chose this regrettable course of action by making soccer into a women's sport, but not a men's sport. But if using field hockey to balance football was somewhat problematic, using soccer is even more so. Soccer is by no means the dominant sport among women in America, not in the way that football is for men. In addition, soccer is played just as much, if not more, by men than by women. The result is that we can now talk about a distinct hierarchy among athletes at Minnesota. At the top of the hierarchy are the big men who are big enough to play football. Somewhere below them are the women who are allowed to play soccer. Below these women are those of us men who aren't allowed to have a varsity sport that favors people our size. Obviously, there are some major problems here.

But there is one option that would solve the whole problem quite nicely: *Dump football.* Yes, dump football. Dump football and replace football with men's and women's soccer teams. If soccer is too much of a wimp sport for you, then use men's and women's rugby teams. But whichever you choose, dumping football has to come first because it is the sport of football that fouls everything up for those who want gender equality. Now dumping football, once looked at in this way, is so obviously the right choice that it is hard to believe that no one has ever suggested it before, yet no one to my knowledge has, at least among leftists. Consider the various proposals that leftists have made during my lifetime:

(1) Nationalizing all industry.
(2) Socializing medicine.
(3) Turning America into a communist country.
(4) Allowing women to fight in combat.
(5) Replacing the current army with an all-women's army.
(6) Eliminating the army altogether.
(7) Having a negative income tax, which would mean that the poorest people would get money from the government instead of having to pay money in.
(8) Soaking the rich.
(9) Allowing homosexuals to marry.
(10) Eliminating the institution of marriage altogether.
(11) Eliminating the death penalty.
(12) Eliminating prisons.
(13) Making spanking a crime.
(14) Refusing to ever discipline one's children.
(15) Allowing abortion on demand.
(16) Making hate speech a crime.
(17) Eliminating all motorized vehicles.
(18) Returning us to a hunting-and-gathering society.

All of these are quite radical proposals, some extremely radical. Some have actually been instituted, but when they were first suggested, they were almost impossible to imagine. Making radical proposals that would turn society upside down is what the left is known for, yet it is clear that there are *some* radical proposals that even America's leftists cannot stomach. Demanding that football be eliminated from our schools is so radical that not even the most radical of radical feminists can contemplate it, not even for the sake of gender equity in sports. Of course, I admit I haven't read everything that every leftist has ever written and for all I know some feminist has said this at one time or another. However, if someone did say it, that person was probably ignored because otherwise there would by now be a knot of feminists chanting outside every college football game demanding that this sport be dumped. Since this has never happened, I take it that dumping football is an idea that is too radical *even for people who wanted communists to take over this country*. Again, we see that retaining American sports is one of the American left's most cherished values, as cherished as leftist principles.

Media Lies

One of the big themes for us protesters back in the Sixties was the lies we continually found in the media. We would stage a huge protest with many thousands of people, and the media would underestimate how many people had been there. Or they wouldn't even report it. Even today, leftists are suspicious of the media, which is why they have developed their own alternative media.

But when it comes to sports, the alternative media of this country are worthless for dealing with the mainstream media's lies. Here is an example of what I mean. One of our news magazines once referred to Michael Jordan as "the most recognized black man on the planet."[15] Almost nothing I had ever read about sports in Africa or anywhere else outside the United States indicated that this was true. The only exceptions to this were what I had read in *American* sources, but I didn't trust them. The further I went from American sources, the less they talked about the importance of basketball and the more they talked about the importance of soccer, so I was quite suspicious of this claim.

Just to make sure, however, I went to the University of Minnesota campus, approached blacks I suspected of being from Africa, and gave them an informal poll. After first verifying that they were indeed from Africa, I then asked the following question: "Who is the most recognized black person in the world?" The answers were varied, but most chose Nelson Mandela. No one chose Michael Jordan. I prodded several people by suggesting Michael Jordan, but they all said very bluntly, "No!" One man said, "Michael *Jackson*, yes. Even people in the most remote villages of Africa have heard of Michael Jackson, but Michael Jordan? No." I won't say that I talked to a representative sample of Africans, but then I was also relying on everything else I had learned about Africa after having involved myself in soccer. Everything I had read, ignoring American sources, indicated that soccer was king in Africa, which meant that it was unlikely that a mere basketball player would achieve the sort of fame in Africa that he had achieved in the United States. My sample merely confirmed what I felt I already knew.

Now this is the sort of media lie that leftists love to expose, a lie that is based on American arrogance. But as far as I know, no leftist did expose this lie, the reason being that it was a lie that they themselves believed. Accordingly, their own media, the alternative media, didn't expose it. Face it, the alternative media is afraid of alternative sports.

Censorship and the Arts

Some years ago public funding for the arts became a hot issue. It exploded into the ordinary person's consciousness when it became known that certain very controversial artworks had been made with public funds. The outcry that this generated was vilified by leftists, who insisted that to refuse government funding for such progressive artworks was censorship.

Now most of us, when we think of censorship, think of works of art, literature or music which are censored as being subject to a government *ban*. We don't count it as censorship merely because the government refuses to fund a project. After all, many of us have projects that *we* would like to have funded. Maybe we even think of them as artistic, for example, an oddly shaped addition to the house. Yet, if the government refused to fund it, we wouldn't call it *censorship*. Or if we did, we would rightly be derided by others. Only the left considers a refusal to fund as out-and-out censorship.

The justification for this odd, tortured use of ordinary language is that those artworks were "progressive." That is, they were promoting the left's agenda, and because they were doing that, they deserved to be funded. After all, such works will one day be wholly revered once those loutish people on the right are vanquished (or so the thinking goes). Meanwhile, the best we leftists can do is to say that such works represent the cutting edge, the avant-garde, and to demand that they be funded.

Against this nonsense, first of all, is that leftists make mistakes just like everyone else and there is no guarantee that even leftists of the future will agree with us on art. More important is the censorship in connection with foreign sports. For example, certain movies never make it to America. For a long time the movie *Fever Pitch* never made it to America, despite the fact that it starred Colin Firth, who had become famous playing Mr. Darcy in the BBC/A&E production of *Pride and Prejudice*. Eventually, the movie came to New York and perhaps other big cities, but what about those of us in small-town America? Why aren't there government funds available so that movies like this can be distributed here? Isn't this censorship?

Still another point in connection with this topic is funding for NPR. Its defenders claim that it is serving people who aren't served by commercial radio, and that therefore the rest of us should subsidize their listening habits. What they *don't* say is that not everyone who isn't served by commercial radio is served by NPR. I learned very quickly that NPR had little interest in doing anything other than supporting the sports status quo, so I stopped listening. PBS, it is true, was willing to broadcast *Soccer Made in Germany*, for which I was very grateful. But they stopped showing that nearly thirty years ago.

The fact is that the people served by NPR are asking the rest of us to subsidize their narrow interests. If I have to spend a lot of my own money to fuel my interest in soccer, why shouldn't they spend a lot of their own money to fuel their interest in folk music, opera, and other unpopular forms of music?

The last point I want to make is that many artists say that the purpose of art is to shock or challenge us. The phrase they use is *épater les bourgeois*, "shock the bourgeoisie." Yet, one has to wonder about such a statement when one sees artists ignoring many opportunities to shock and challenge people in our society. The typical way that artists shock and challenge is by creating art that denigrates the mainstream's religious views. But the mainstream is much less rigid about religion today than it was when I was a kid. The number of people who need to be shocked about religion is much smaller now than it was then.

By contrast, the number of people who need to be shocked about sports is very high. Moreover, attacking the mainstream's views on sports seems desirable, given the many instances of unfairness that they encapsulate, which would make such art progressive. Plus, these sports are in effect our civic religion. Yet, how many of the works that get funded these days attack our sports? I know of none. How many attack institutional sizism? I know of none. How many attack the prevalence of white pitchers in baseball? I know of none. How many attack the xenophobic hatred of the average American sports fan for foreign sports? I know of none. What is progressive, it turns out, is defined rather narrowly, and since that is true, then all government funding of "progressive" art should be abolished.

It should be clear that the progressives in sports aren't the artists or anyone else on the left. The progressives are the people I kept seeing at soccer games: the young people from the suburbs, the people in R.O.T.C., and the people in fraternities and sororities. It is true that they aren't as progressive as I'd like them to be. They don't complain about institutional sizism. But at least they show up at the games.

Forget *épater les bourgeois*. *Épater les artistes* is more like it.

Appropriation

Many leftists complain about the appropriation of something by one group that was actually invented or developed by another group. For example, some artworks are now said to be by women painters which were formerly said to be by men painters. Why the change? Originally, it was not clear who had done these artworks, but since they were exceptionally good, they were thought to have been done by men because, of course, women would not have been good enough to paint them. With less prejudiced thinking, that sort of reasoning has come to be seen as dubious, and so the evidence has been re-examined. Lo and behold, the evidence suggests that women had painted them and not men. Likewise, some forms of music were taken over, and so appropriated by whites, that were originally invented by blacks (for example, rock and jazz). The same can be said for certain types of dancing (for example, swing dancing).

But the left is not above doing its own appropriating. This happened in 1999 after the U.S. women's soccer team won the third Women's World Cup. Of course, the U.S. women had won the *first* Women's World Cup as well, but since that event had received very little media attention, there was no felt need by feminists to appropriate it. But the third World Cup was a different matter. The large number of young girls who showed up at the games forced the national media to pay attention, and that forced the feminists of my generation into a dilemma: obviously, they wanted to be attached to this wonderful event somehow, and just as obviously they had done little or nothing to deserve to be attached to it. For what had they done? They had enrolled their daughters on soccer teams, it is true, but so had many other people, some of whom had no strong leanings towards feminism. Moreover, those other people had probably started to do this *before* the feminists had done it. Certainly, I have never seen any evidence that enrolling one's daughter on a soccer team was something started or promoted by the leading feminists of my generation. So, those feminists were forced to think up something else, and what they said was that they had worked to pass Title IX legislation that allowed girls to be treated as equals in sports in our schools. That was all they could think of.

What wasn't ever said in the media, either by the dominant liberal media or by the right-wing media (that is, *The Wall Street Journal*, the *National Review*, and so on), was that Title IX did *not* count as doing very much to get us to the excitement of the third Women's World Cup. To brag about having supported Title IX is a little like bragging that you ran the first hundred yards of a marathon, when obviously there were so many other people who had run so much farther. In fact, supporting Title IX may not count for anything at all, for the Title IX legislation was passed at a time when virtually no one in this country was thinking of soccer. It was passed before I myself got involved, and I got involved before most of the people who are involved in it today got involved. That means that the Women's World Cup was an unintended result of Title IX legislation.

Any feminist who bristles at what I have been saying should ask herself the following: Did you join a soccer team back in the 1970s? Did you watch any women's soccer games before this World Cup? Did you read any books about soccer, especially soccer as it exists in other countries? Did you spend a great deal of money trying to learn about the world of soccer the way I did, on magazines, a shortwave radio, trips to other countries, and so on? If you did, fine, but I reckon that you are an exception, because most feminists I know from my generation wanted to have nothing to do with soccer.

Anyway, what exactly did Title IX legislation accomplish? It allowed schools to have girls' teams. But I have been arguing that sports don't need the schools in order to thrive. It all could have been done with privately-owned clubs. Why depend on schools at all? This sort of appropriation was completely worthless.

Then again feminists at least had the wit to *attempt* to appropriate the success of the U.S. women. Other leftists did not even bother to do that much. Neither *The Nation* nor *In These Times* said anything about the Women's World Cup, despite the fact that it made the cover of *Sports Illustrated* and our three news magazines (*U.S. News and World Report*, *Newsweek*, and *Time*). The further to the left one went, the less likely it was that one found anyone who wanted to talk about it, except for the feminists, and what they said was laughable.

Hegemonies

Leftists talk a great deal about hegemonies, that is, people or organizations that have a great deal of power to influence what is said and thought in our society. So, they have decried the hegemony of males, the hegemony of whites, the hegemony of capitalists, and so on. But one could just as well talk about (and decry) the hegemony of American sports over foreign sports, the hegemony of the big and tall in our schools' sports programs, and so on. Needless to say, leftists never want to talk about those hegemonies.

International Consensuses

The last theme of the left I want to talk about is that of an international consensus. This has been used by our more leftist judges in explaining their opinions. They have searched to see what judges in other countries have said about a topic, and finding an international consensus, they have alluded to it in writing up their opinions.

Of course, it goes without saying that these same leftist judges ignore any international consensuses about sports. International sports wouldn't even be possible without some sort of consensus among different countries about what sports to play and what rules to play by, so there have to be international consensuses about sports. International soccer, for example, is the result of a consensus going back more than a century, and this is reflected in the fact that FIFA, the international organization governing soccer, was founded in 1904. Of the international consensuses discovered by our judges, are there any that go back that far? Are there any that even go back half that far?

These, then, are some of the many themes that leftists promote these days. I concede that not all leftist themes have some implication for sports, for environmentalism generally does not. But I believe I have said enough to show that sports intersects with many of the left's themes and ideas and also that the left is guilty of massive amounts of hypocrisy.

Endnotes

1. *Independent* June, 28, 1996. Cited in *The Oxford Dictionary of Quotations* (1999)
2. Cited in Paul Gardner, "Soccer, American Style," *New York Times Magazine* (May 4, 1975), p. 15.
3. See David L. Andrews, Robert Pitter, Detlev Zwick, and Darren Ambrose, "Soccer's Racial Frontier: Sport and the Suburbanization of Contemporary America," in Gary Armstrong and Richard Giulianotti, *Entering the Field: New Perspectives on World Football* (Oxford: Berg, 1997), 261-281.
4. May 17, 1987.
5. Strictly speaking, basketball was invented by a Canadian living in the United States. This doesn't negate the point I am making.
6. *The Kenyon Collegian*, Feb. 7, 2002, p. 8.
7. Russell Kirk, *America's British Culture* (New Brunswick and London: Transaction Publishers, 1993), p. 90.

8. Lawrence E. Cahoone, "Introduction," *From Modernism to Postmodernism* ed. Cahoone (Blackwell, 1996), p. 16.
9. *Times of London*, May 9, 1992, p. 12.
10. John D. Caputo, "The Good News about Alterity: Derrida and Theology," *Faith and Philosophy* 10 (1993), 453.
11. Unfortunately, the website that I found this on no longer exists.
12. Minneapolis *Star-Tribune*, May 30, 1998, pp. A1 and B1.
13. Minneapolis *Star-Tribune*, June 2, 1998, p. A16.
14. December 5, 1988, sec. 3, p. 1.
15. *U.S. News & World Report*, March 24, 1997, p. 50.

Chapter 12
The Reactionary Left

What exactly is the left's problem? Why do they find it so hard to get over what seems to be a simple and simple-minded prejudice? In the last chapter I pointed out that there were about forty different themes that are part of leftist ideology these days that ought to be pushing leftists away from this prejudice, yet they cling to it. Why? During the Sixties, I noticed that when young leftists were introduced to a new cause, they almost instantly became converted. But today, any attempt to get leftists to see any sort of injustice or prejudice other than the ones they can already see is impossible. I'm always being told that what I am saying is unimportant.

Yet, for leftists to say that some issue is unimportant is strange and idiotic, because the left already used that response against feminism, and it ended badly. I started college in 1969, and the current wave of feminism was just beginning to get going. Naturally, everyone on the right was virulently against feminism, but what about the left? *Nearly every leftist said that feminists' concerns were unimportant.* (And the ones who didn't say this were almost always the younger ones.) Young people today may find this hard to believe, but I was there, and I heard it. Feminists were told by the other leftists that their concerns were totally unimportant compared with the concerns of workers, blacks, Vietnamese peasants, and so on. By the time I had graduated, the your-concerns-are-not-important response was slowly being replaced by acceptance, and now feminism is so accepted that it is hard for people who didn't live through this period to imagine that it ever happened.

Anyway, the business of this chapter is to try to explain a similar reactionary attitude among leftists towards soccer and related issues. Why haven't American leftists recognized any of the rather obvious points I made in the last chapter? Why weren't they willing to critique our sports as I did in Chapter 10? Let me suggest several explanations, none of which is right, except for the very last one.

(1) "Leftists think of sports as they do religion, the opiate of the people."

Most of the leftists I have known have been sports fans. (As always, I'm talking about American leftists here.) As Katha Pollitt's remark in Chapter 9 shows, many leftists are dyed-in-the-wool baseball fans. There may be a few who think of sports as the opiate of the people, but they are few and far between.

(2) "Maybe soccer prejudice runs very deep, deeper than any prejudice against blacks or women."

This is an explanation I would have accepted if I hadn't seen so many people in the center and even on the right overcome their soccer prejudice.

(3) "Everyone uses logic, but it is actually used as a sort of afterthought to justify what people really want or believe. People really run on emotions, and most American leftists had fond feelings towards American sports but no feelings at all towards soccer."

There is something to be said for this. In particular, American leftists seem especially fond of the story of Jackie Robinson and how he became the first black to play major league baseball. But other people have had these same warm and fuzzy emotions about American sports, and they managed to switch over to soccer.

(4) "For every question of the form 'Why don't they do X?,' the answer is always, 'Because of money.'"

This simply isn't true in this instance. Money, or rather the lack of it, wasn't the reason why the left failed to support soccer or failed to condemn institutional sizism or failed to be critical of American sports. Money wasn't the issue at all, and it never is when ideological principles are at stake. Anyway, it wouldn't have cost the left much of anything to do what I wanted them to do. How much money does it cost to write a letter to the editor of a newspaper to complain about institutional sizism? The cost is minimal. And how much does it cost to complain about our sports? Nothing. Of course, it might have cost something in terms of intangibles like lost friendships, but that is a different matter.

No, the left's failure was not caused by lack of money.

(5) "Fighting against the American sports establishment is a daunting task. It would be difficult enough to get a small college to abandon or de-

emphasize football and basketball, but imagine trying to do this for a large university such as the University of Michigan. This would be so difficult that most leftists didn't even want to try."

I never saw any evidence that leftists even considered trying it or that they wanted to try it. Anyway, the problem with this explanation is that leftists have never shirked from a battle. During the Sixties, leftists happily fought against the military-industrial complex. A little thing like a sports establishment wouldn't deter them.

Besides, activism in favor of soccer is pretty easy: just go to the games! And write a letter to *The New York Times* demanding more coverage of soccer. How hard can this be?

(6) "The Old Left paid little attention to sports because it was the opiate of the people, while the New Left wanted to stay in touch with the masses by paying attention to their passions. Since soccer has been championed in America by mostly upper-middle class suburbanites, the New Left had no reason to pay attention to this new sport."

Yet, such an explanation misses something vital. First of all, soccer in America isn't championed *entirely* by suburbanites. There have been plenty of Latino immigrants in America who love soccer, and every leftist ought to know that soccer is supreme in most of Latin America, Africa, and the Middle East (as well as Europe, which they generally prefer to the U.S.). Why would anyone who wanted to remain close to the masses *and* who wanted to be in touch with the cultures of the Third World ignore soccer?

(7) "Soccer has a reputation for mindless violence, and leftists avoided it for that reason."

It is true that soccer does have this reputation. However, it has that reputation, not in the foreign media, but in the *American* media. Within soccer-playing countries, its reputation is quite different. Since most leftists are suspicious of America's media, so suspicious that they developed an alternative media, there is no obvious reason why the left should have believed what the American media was saying about soccer.

Along the same lines, leftists in this country seem to imagine that the only people in foreign countries who support soccer are thugs and reactionaries. But that simply isn't true, anymore than it is true that our sports are supported only by that sort of person. Again, there is no good reason for the American left to be uninformed on this topic.

(8) "There is a tradition in America of not politicizing sports. We like to keep sports and politics separate."

That is true enough, but the left has never paid any attention to any other tradition that it didn't itself invent. So, why pay attention to this one? Anyway, in recent years the left has politicized sports to a limited extent. They have been pushing for gender equality in sports in our schools.

(9) "Sports just aren't important enough for the left to do anything about them."

But sports are apparently important enough for the left to push for gender equality in sports. Anyway, this is the argument that was used on feminists by leftists back in the late Sixties, as I've already mentioned.

Another point to consider is that people who commit themselves to a principle commit themselves to whatever is derived from that principle. As I argued in the last chapter, supporting soccer (or at any rate, being critical of our sports) fits in well with leftist principles. One way to test whether someone is committed to a principle is to see how they react to an application of that principle that goes beyond what they are now saying. If they are genuinely committed to that principle, they will be committed to its new application, but if not, then they won't be.

Finally, anyone who demands that others give up what they have strong emotional feelings about, such as a white-dominated society or a male-dominated society, had better be willing to give up those traditions about which they themselves have strong emotional feelings. For the fact is that leftists haven't been utterly indifferent to all sports. Instead, they have been very fond of our sports. Accordingly, they should have been willing to do what they demanded of others: to give up what they were emotionally attached to for the sake of social justice and their other principles. Given the emotional attachment of many leftists to our sports, saying "It's not important to change things" sounds too much like "It's important *not* to change things."

(10) "Even though things like institutional sizism are obvious once someone points it out to you, they are quite invisible beforehand, even though they are all around us. Similarly, fish are not supposed to be aware of water, even though they live in it."

True enough, but noticing these invisible social injustices is supposed to be a leftist specialty. There are many things I now notice that I wouldn't have noticed before, if it hadn't been for leftists who pointed them out to me. Why, then, haven't the other leftists noticed institutional sizism?

(11) "Leftists overcame their prejudice against soccer. It is just that they never became excited about it. They are indifferent."

I'm not buying this. I never saw much evidence for it, plus it doesn't explain why the left remains uncritical of American sports.

(12) "The left was worried that if soccer became big in the United States, then that would be one more way in which America would dominate the Third World."

There isn't the slightest reason to accept such an explanation. Lots of American leftists don't even seem to know that soccer is big in the Third World, an ignorance on their part for which there is no excuse. Anyway, if the left did have such worries, I would have noticed them, and I never heard anyone expressing such sentiments. The obvious time during which such sentiments would have been expressed was after the victory of the U.S. women in 1999, but I heard nothing. To the extent that American leftists commented on this victory, they seemed pleased by it because it represented a victory for women.

(13) "We on the left are powerless, so it doesn't really matter what we support."

This is nonsense. The left has plenty of power. The left has enormous amounts of cultural power. It is true that it hasn't had much political or economic power in recent decades, but its cultural power over the last few decades has been simply enormous. Basically, leftists run our media and our schools. (Anyone who doesn't believe this should look at conservative blogs and see how frustrated the conservatives are about this situation.) Anyway, if it doesn't matter what leftists support, does that mean it doesn't matter if a person refuses to support gay marriage or abortion?

Finally, leftists individually have the power to avoid being hypocrites. As I mentioned above, activism in favor of soccer is pretty easy. Go to the games. Plus, if you are the letter-writing type, write a letter to your favorite newspaper (*The New York Times*) demanding better soccer coverage. How difficult can this be?

(14) "You are just a privileged white male, so you're concerns cannot have any importance for the left."

When I started college, I was 5' 9" tall and I weighed 130 pounds. I was too small or short for the two dominant sports in our schools, football and basketball. I do not call that being privileged.

(15) "Aren't foreigners being xenophobic in not paying attention to our sports?"

But why should they pay attention? If our sports were generally popular throughout the world, then that would make sense. But as they are mostly confined to the U.S., then there is no more reason for them to pay attention than there is for us or anyone else to pay attention to, say, Ireland's sport of hurling.

Anyway, this is beside the point. What other people do or don't do shouldn't affect how a principled person acts.

(16) "The fact is that the left gets around to liberating people in terms of the importance of the issue. If you look at the history of these things, you will realize that the left first focused on workers, then blacks, then women and gays. The left will eventually get around to dealing with things like institutional sizism."

If this were true, one would expect them to acknowledge at least occasionally that institutional sizism is wrong, but I never hear this from leftists. No, leftists won't get around to dealing with institutional sizism until they are dragged kicking and screaming to the issue.

(17) "The fact is that while the left is critical, it is never self-critical. And that leads leftists to make many mistakes."

Unfortunately, this was the only explanation I could come up with that satisfied me. I was completely befuddled by the curious mix of the progressive and the reactionary among my fellow leftists. I had never read anything that led me to expect such a phenomenon. I had never read anything which would have predicted it. But once I saw it, I began to see it in many other places. Here are some of the examples I found:

(A) The abolitionists in America were extremely radical concerning the issue of abolishing slavery, but they shied away from the idea of treating blacks as the social equals of whites.[1]

(B) During the French Revolution, the wealthiest members of the Third Estate wanted to get voting rights for themselves, but not for *others* in the Third Estate. The French Revolution had been inspired by many calls for equality during the eighteenth century, with the result that power was seized upon by many different groups in succession. But no matter which revolutionary group was in power, there was always a group to the left of them that wanted rights spread to more parts of society than they did.

(C) As the bourgeoisie liberated itself from feudalism, it exploited the proletariat.

(D) Those who attempted to extend voting rights to all adult males generally had no interest in extending the vote to adult females.

(E) Wealthy and middle-class women in the nineteenth century who worked to get women the vote had little interest in helping lower-class or black women. In fact, some feminists back in the 1920s were part of the Ku Klux Klan.[2]

(F) Early labor unions excluded blacks.

(G) The liberation of India from British rule didn't mean the end of the caste system.

(H) The old left as it existed prior to the 1960s was concerned almost exclusively with the workers, and the leftists of that period were often quite homophobic, which led the French thinker and homosexual Michel Foucault to leave the Communist Party.[3]

(I) The internment of Japanese-Americans in World War II was supported by Earl Warren and the Communist Party.[4]

(J) Academia today is dominated by liberals and leftists, but these people couldn't cope with the sudden academic jobs crisis of the 1990s. When some young academics who were teaching assistants at Yale went on strike and tried to form a union, older leftist academics acted in a thoroughly reactionary way. As one person has put it:

> Sara Suleri, a brilliant postcolonial critic… urged disciplinary action against one of her teaching assistants…. Nancy Cott, a widely admired labor historian, spoke out against the union, and David Brion David, a distinguished historian of slavery, sought college guards to bar his union-identified teaching assistant from entering the room where undergraduate final exams would be given.[5]

This account has all the more validity in that it comes from another leftist academic, Cary Nelson, who was one of the few to notice that something was terribly wrong.

Thus, we see that for centuries people who have been progressive in some way have also been reactionary in some way, too. But why?

The only explanation I could find that covered *all* of the cases I have given is simply that leftists are critical, but never self-critical. Accordingly, they will see some type of social injustice and work very hard to eliminate it, but will fail to see other sorts of social injustice. This is particularly evident in the first example I gave, which I learned about from Louis Menand in his book *The Metaphysical Club*. Menand is quite adamant that the abolitionists were extremely radical about ending slavery, but at the same time hadn't thought much about what would happen to blacks after they were freed and so weren't too interested in their social equality. Another example in which leftists didn't think critically is that of communism, in which it seemed as if a great deal of effort by leftists was put forth to deal with the economic problems of the exploited worker, but almost no effort was put into dealing with how to equitably distribute power in the "worker's paradise." Accordingly, my explanation for the curious juxtaposition within leftists of extreme radicalism on many issues with reactionary views on foreign sports makes the most sense and has historical precedents. If the leftists of my generation had been self-critical, they would have listened to me or they would have discovered institutional sizism on their own. I concede that this explanation doesn't explain why any *particular* type of blindness by leftists will occur. It just says that examples of blindness are likely. In view of that, I have to say that the behavior of my fellow leftists with respect to foreign sports is to some extent still a mystery to me.

However that may be, the next chapter is my own exercise in being self-critical.

Endnotes

1. See Louis Menand, *The Metaphysical Club* (Farrar, Strauss and Giroux, 2001), ch. 1, especially, for example, pp. 9 and 15.
2. See Kathleen M. Blee, *Women of the Klan: Racism and Gender in the 1920s* (University of California, 1991), p. 6: "Some of the women I interviewed who participated fully and enthusiastically in the Klan, expressing few regrets, were active in progressive politics, favoring peace and women's equality in the decades after the Klan collapsed."
3. Didier Eribon, *Michel Foucault*, trans. Betsy Wing (Harvard Univ. Press, 1991), p. 56.
4. Christopher Hitchens, "Obon Jour," *Slate*, Aug. 3, 2009.
5. Cary Nelson, *Manifesto of a Tenured Radical*, p. 143.

CHAPTER 13
Being Hard on Soccer

As I argued in the last chapter, leftists here in America failed to take to soccer or to become critical of our sports because they failed to be self-critical. People who fail to be self-critical often fail to notice important problems. They make allowances for and have emotional attachments to practices or ideas long after others have realized that they belong in the dustbin of history. They can, as the Bible says, see the mote in another's eye but not the beam that is in their own. Since this is a book on soccer and not leftism generally, this is not the place to recount how the left has made it hard for itself by failing to be self-critical. But in the spirit of being self-critical myself, I want to be critical of soccer and those connected with it.

Let me start with myself. Initially, I imagined that the sports environment of a country like Brazil represented an ideal. Brazil has soccer for the average-sized person, and it has basketball for the tall. It wasn't until I became self-critical that I was willing to acknowledge that this leaves out the very short and small, because even though soccer is much kinder to the undersized than basketball and football are, it still doesn't represent all that could be achieved along these lines. I don't know what sport could be added here that would make up this deficit, but at least I am now aware of the problem.

In addition, in complaining about the situation that we soccer fans have here in the United States, I was never willing to acknowledge that some have it worse. Anyone who is a cricket or rugby fan has it much worse than we soccer fans do. Rugby is almost never on television, while cricket is simply never on television, and as a school sport cricket is nowhere close to being accepted, while rugby is in the shadow of soccer in this respect.

My apologies to all of America's rugby and cricket fans for overlooking their plight.

Here's another error I made in the past. I'm quite critical of our newspapers' sports sections, which seem to think that this is still the 1950s when baseball, football, and basketball ruled all. There are important straws in the wind, with the existence of some young people following nothing but soccer, and I've long thought that newspapers ought to reflect this reality. However, I have to admit that there are other young people who represent different sorts of change. These are the ones who engage in those activities spotlighted in the X games, or else those who follow NASCAR. The existence of such people proves that there is a diversity in our sporting environment far beyond that of what is shown in our newspapers.

The next topic I want to take up deserves a long section all its own. In Chapter 5 I argued that soccer is not boring, and in particular it is not boring despite its lack of scoring. However, I will admit that soccer could use some more scoring. In saying this, I am not admitting that I find soccer boring when there is little scoring. Instead, I find it frustrating. So let me talk about how soccer could have more scoring, and how it could do this not by enlarging goals or changing the rules but simply by training in different ways.

The first topic to discuss is shooting at goal. Shooting at goal would seem to be a fairly simple task. One aims, one shoots, and that's all there is to it. Nevertheless, even at the top levels of the game today players seem unable to avoid having many, many shots go high and wide. I don't think it was as bad thirty years ago as it is today. It seems that back then players could shoot on goal reasonably well, but that may be bad memory on my part. But here are some examples of what I mean. One shot in particular, the penalty kick, is too often missed these days. The best example is the miss by Italy's Roberto Baggio that lost the 1994 World Cup. In the 1998 World Cup England crashed out because of a missed penalty kick. The person missing the shot later admitted that he hadn't taken a penalty shot since he was a kid. And Holland hadn't practiced for penalty kicks, either, according to David Winner,[1] and as a result suffered for it.

These stories are incomprehensible to me. Penalty kicks should almost always be successful, but for that to happen the players do need to practice. There's simply no excuse for a player in a World Cup match not having taken a penalty kick since he was a kid. If the players practice penalty kicks, then they can be successful about ninety percent of the time (according to the very first soccer book I read back in the early 1970s). This is because

Soccer, the Left, & the Farce of Multiculturalism

if it is placed in any corner of the goal with a reasonable amount of force, then the goalie cannot get to it without cheating (that is, by moving too soon). Blasting a ball into a corner should be within the capabilities of any professional. Shouldn't it? Yet many today seem incapable of doing it. Because of this, they try to use *guile*. But if you use guile, then you can't count on being successful ninety percent of the time. Perhaps seventy percent, if that much, but certainly not ninety percent. I have watched penalty kicks very closely for the last decade, and it's discouraging to see how often goalies make saves these days. This isn't because goalies have gotten much better, but because the shooters seem to have gotten worse. They just can't seem to blast it into a corner. Every single save I've seen was of a shot that was nowhere near a corner. Back in 1970, an Austrian author, Peter Handke, wrote a novel called *The Goalie's Anxiety at the Penalty Kick* (later made into a movie), but today it seems that the anxious person is the shooter rather than the goalie.

I confess to being somewhat obsessed with shooting because it was something I worked on and which helped me to become a more effective player when I played intramural soccer as a grad student. I became much better at shooting than at anything else. People who watched me dribble or attempt to control the ball automatically rated all my skills at a fairly low level. They weren't expecting me to score against them. But then I would, simply because my shooting was accurate.

Some professionals have figured this out. The great Hungarian star Ferenc Puskas said that he and the other Hungarian forwards would spend an hour after practice every day taking shots from various angles. And it helped because he scored some fantastic goals. Later on he became a manager in Greece, and he said that his players didn't bother with that extra practice. Their scoring was unexceptional. I also have to mention Gerd Müller. His shooting wasn't necessarily accurate, and he himself admitted that he didn't know where the ball was going when he took a shot. But I mention him simply because he is an example of someone who could score goals even when his other skills were just average. Anyway, my main complaint is that players seem incapable of avoiding high and wide shots.

At some point, perhaps in the 1960s, shooting began to deteriorate.[2] The average score in earlier decades of the twentieth century was something like 4-2. But then shooting seemed to deteriorate. Or else referees began to favor the defenders. Or maybe something else changed. Whatever it was, once it became more likely that the average score would be, let us say, 2-1, the worse it was when a goal was scored that didn't deserve to be scored. When goals came fairly frequently, as in a 4-2 game, a single goal didn't mean very much, but in a 2-1 game, a single goal meant more. The result was that the pressure increased on the referee not to allow a bad goal. The resulting pressure meant a further favoring of the defenders, till the average score dipped to 1-0, at which point a bad goal almost represented a political crisis. Once these changes got going, soccer began a sort of death spiral.

Perhaps the reason that referees began to protect the defenders is a change in manners. Whereas an earlier generation of athletes might have simply shrugged off an undeserved loss as one's fate or as a trial to be overcome by a show of good character, the attitude more and more transformed into something else, that an undeserved loss should be protested against as loudly and vociferously as possible, that one ought perhaps even to go so far as to sue referees for bad calls (as I've heard of recently), that one ought to install automatic replay cameras to provide a second opinion from that of the referee (though how the poorest countries will be able to afford something like this is not explained). When every important decision gets argued, it is much easier for the referee *not* to call a dubious penalty than to call one. The reason is simply that when you *don't* call a penalty, play goes on and the players are ultimately too busy to protest. But let a referee call a dubious penalty, and he or she will immediately be surrounded by angry players from the defending side denouncing the decision.

If the problem in this instance is due to the slow loss of the idea that character is important, then the solution is to regain that idea. Admittedly, bringing back the idea that character is important is something that goes way beyond soccer. However, maybe soccer is where it should be started. And if things changed because of a deterioration in shooting prowess, then that needs to be improved. And improving shooting isn't hard. It simply takes a little bit of extra practice. It shouldn't be beyond the abilities of the top professionals to take a penalty kick and have it skim one of the posts as it goes into a corner. Players at that level of the game who can do phenomenal things with the ball should find this quite easy. The fact that they now cannot shows that the training needs to be changed.

The same thing can be said about corner kicks or any dead-ball situation. It is easy enough to shoot astray during ordinary play, when one has a microsecond to set up, aim, and take a shot. But with a dead-ball situation, it should be easy to shoot accurately. It should be easy to take aim and shoot, simply because one has so much time, comparatively speaking. Yet even at the highest levels of play, corner kicks are placed too close to the goalie. Better training seems to be the answer, or at least part of the answer.

Better training would, I think, make players better able to take penalties and corner kicks. Taking penalty kicks is so very important because a penalty kick is practically a free goal, so doing it well would seem to be important, too. Furthermore, what I noticed during my own playing time was that the accurate shooting I developed for taking a penalty carried over to regular play. Think about it in this way. If you have five shots in a game, then if only one shot is on goal, you will score at most one goal (ignoring deflections). But if your shooting is accurate enough that four of those five shots are on goal, then you have increased your chances of scoring a goal by a factor of four. Someone once pointed out that most goals get scored when the shooter is just a few yards from goal. That means that to score a goal a team has to get in quite close, which means a great deal of control and dominance over the other team. But you can change all this by shooting accurately from further out. If you can shoot accurately from further out, your team doesn't need to get in so close to goal, which in turn means it can score even when it is not doing so well. I've watched soccer for many years, and during the last decade or so I've watched carefully what happens in a 1-0 game. Typically, the team that lost had many chances to score a goal, but its shots were generally poorly aimed. If all those shots had been on target, they might have gotten a tie or even a win. There is no good reason why professionals should be shooting poorly, but they do and it is frustrating to watch.

Since I have broached the topic of character, I need to talk about diving. Many soccer haters talk about diving and how ridiculous it is, and they have a point. However, it is not as big a point as they think it is. When I first got involved, diving (for the purpose of getting the referee to give your team a penalty kick) was not much of a problem. It began growing, however, and it seemed to reach its height during the World Cup of 1994, which sadly was the one held here in America. Since then, the soccer establishment has tried to deal with the situation by instructing referees to give yellow cards to anyone who they think has dived rather than suffered a foul. Of course, the soccer haters are quite unaware of this and still talk as though things were as bad as they were back in 1994. Nevertheless, it is a problem. But is this a soccer problem? That is, this may be a problem of our era rather than a problem of soccer. Our era is an era in which character just doesn't seem as important as it once did, so diving becomes acceptable, to some degree. On the other hand, if players hadn't made things difficult for themselves by becoming less adept at scoring, this whole business might not have happened. That is, because scoring is so low, getting a penalty becomes hugely important, so the temptation to take a dive is high. When scoring is more frequent, a single penalty doesn't mean as much, so the temptation is lower. In any case, I'd like to think that diving is a temporary problem.

Another problem related to scoring concerns fast breaks. I was familiar with these from watching ice hockey: the two-on-one breaks, the three-on-two breaks, the three-on-one breaks, and so on. They didn't always deliver what we fans wanted, namely a goal. But they sometimes did, and even when they didn't, the important thing was that they were always *exciting*.

In soccer, however, fast breaks often dissipate into thin air. They simply vanish into nothingness. Three people, let us say, are bringing the ball down the field against two defenders. At some point when they get in or near the penalty area, the ball will be passed to whichever of the three is furthest out on the wing, and that person will fail to take advantage of an opportunity to either shoot or cross it. They find themselves blocked by a defender, so they pass the ball *backwards* to someone who wasn't even part of the break. That person will pass the ball still further back, or if not that, they will fail to pass the ball forward. And just like that, the fast break has disappeared into thin air. The ball is now thirty or more yards from the goal, when just moments before it had been less than twenty. Even worse, the advantage in numbers has been lost because the opponents who were caught upfield have had a chance to get back into the play. Sure, the attacking team still has possession, but it would be worth it, perhaps, to lose possession if that meant an exciting shot on goal.

I don't know what the answer to this is, and I leave it to others to figure out. I don't know how often fast breaks are even practiced by teams. Maybe all it takes is practice. Maybe, too, there is something wrong with passing it to the wing when the ball is in so close. Maybe the winger shouldn't be so far out. Maybe the person who makes the pass to the wing lacked the imagination to follow through with the break; passing to the wing often seems to be the answer when nothing else comes to mind. Then again, I don't know that passing it to the wing is the problem. Maybe that is the symptom that I have seen and the real cause is elsewhere, because maybe the fast break had already dissipated by the time it was passed to the wing.

Anyway, this is something that soccer players need to think about and work on.

Another mistake that players make, or perhaps it is the managers who encourage it, is to constantly choose low-percentage tactics. When the goalie gets the ball, he or she can throw it to a defender or blast it up field. It *seems* more exciting to blast it, but the problem is that it has much less chance of actually reaching a teammate. During the years I was following the Minnesota Kicks in the old NASL, I began to take note of what percentage of times the ball actually ended up in the possession of a teammate when the goalie punted, and it was very low, as little as ten percent of the time. That's not very good. But even if it is as high as fifty percent, a simple throw to a defender means retaining possession ninety percent of the time. It is true that the other team probably knows this and so will try to prevent it. Nevertheless, I've seen it work often enough. A simple fake by the goalie is enough to get an opponent going the wrong way, but I seldom see this used.

The same thing can be said about long passes versus short passes by the other players. A long pass can look spectacular, but it often goes to the opposition or else is received in a space that is not very advantageous. A short pass may be the better option. Likewise, what I said earlier about players not practicing their shooting entails that a shot on goal by someone who hasn't practiced shooting will be a low-percentage play. So long as players get only one out of five, say, of their shots on goal, instead of three or four out of five, their chances for scoring will be small.

Another problem is that there are many games that could have been more exciting, but for the strange decisions of the managers. When the United States defeated England back in the 1950 World Cup, England's best player, Stanley Matthews, wasn't playing. He was sitting on the bench. In the 1938 World Cup, Brazil's Tim didn't get to play in the semi-final because he was being "saved" for the final. As a result, Brazil didn't make it to the final. Twenty years later, it took a delegation of players to get Garrincha into a starting position, so that Brazil could win its first World Cup. In Euro 2000, Michael Owen wasn't allowed to play the full ninety minutes in England's games, although he had done so back in 1998 in the World Cup. Apparently, it was felt that he was too young.

Another problem in soccer is the racism that afflicts those in Europe who seem to feel that Africans can't play as well as Europeans can, although this has been disproved many times. The reason given is always the same, that during the World Cup such African nations do not do as well as expected. The obvious bias here is that we have no idea how European teams will do when the World Cup is held in Africa. When the World Cup was held in the United States, we saw for the first time many countries playing in a more or less neutral venue, for it was the first time that the tournament had been held in neither Europe nor Latin America. Our World Cup showed that Nigeria could hold its own against Europeans. Likewise, the 2002 World Cup showed that many countries not previously thought of as very capable (such as South Korea and the U.S.) were in fact fully capable of advancing.

Another problem that has been suggested to me is that despite my claim that in soccer, players are treated as equals, there is a hierarchy. People on defense seem to be undervalued in comparison with people on offense, plus they have pressures that the offensive players don't have. If they make a mistake and a goal is scored, they will be crucified by the media, while none of their best exploits mean as much to the average fan as a goal does. First, let me say that the defensive players get more protection from the referee than the offensive players do (as I've just been saying). Secondly, this objection is ameliorated by the fact that there are systems of play, such as the clockwork orange of the Dutch, in which the positions aren't so rigid as they are in other systems. The defensive players can wander up to the forward position and score goals, while the offensive players may find themselves forced to defend. But thirdly, I will admit the justice of this objection. In response, let me say that for right now, there is nothing better in existence. The hierarchies in baseball and football vastly exceed those in soccer. Basketball probably has the same problem to a lesser degree, as do all goal sports, but it has a severe height problem that means it is morally inferior to (that is, less inclusive than) soccer. Cricket seems to have a hierarchy like baseball's, only less pronounced. But it still doesn't quite achieve what soccer achieves. Rugby can be seen as the socialist version of football in that it distributes the action much more equitably, but it tends to favor large people. For the average-sized person, soccer still does a better job than these other sports at treating people right.

Another objection is this: "You have complained about the nationalism of American sports fans, who prefer American sports to the sports played by the rest of the world. But how is this different from the nationalism of soccer fans, who prefer their own national team?"

Obviously, people in soccer who are ready to riot (or even go to war) when their national team loses are acting poorly. But in general, soccer fans aren't so rigidly nationalistic. Many non-Brazilians admire Brazil's style and players. Ditto for Holland's style and players. Moreover, American sports fans are nationalistic in this same way, come Olympics time. They may favor the basketball team and individual American athletes rather than the soccer team, but they clearly favor Americans. Anyway, as 9/11 showed, we need to learn more about the rest of the world, and hiding our heads in the sand by following only American sports isn't the way to do this. Whether one rigidly supports America's team over others or not, following soccer brings one in contact with other countries.

Another problem is possible brain damage from heading the ball. People have been discussing this problem for many years, and I believe no firm conclusions have been reached. However, results I have seen lately confirm my own experience, that it is not heading the ball that is the problem. It is two heads colliding that is the problem. And that can be dealt with by extending the dangerous-play rule. (I don't know exactly what details this would entail.) Many purists won't like it, but we do need to protect people.

In this chapter, I have so far avoided talking about problems with the way soccer is administered, which ought not to count against the sport of soccer itself. However, I do need to mention a few such problems. First is the disastrous demise of the women's league here in 2003. As the 1999 women's World Cup showed, women and girls will come out in large numbers to soccer games, if the occasion is right, for they came out by the tens of thousands for that event. With that in mind, it ought not to be too hard to get 15,000 young girls out to a soccer game once a week. Yet, that didn't happen. The average attendances were much lower than that. Why?

I have to put it down to bad management or a bad strategy. Either tickets were priced too high, or the marketing was poor, but somehow the many young girls in those areas that had a team simply weren't showing up. And when it became clear that the league was going to go out of business, the heads of the league made a push for getting lots of corporate sponsors – and why should corporations provide help given that attendances were so low? – when they should have been making a push for a large number of season tickets to be sold for the next season. Once you've sold lots of season tickets, the corporations will follow without too much begging. I saw what the Minnesota Kicks did to attract huge crowds. They had inexpensive tickets that were made even more inexpensive by a student discount. Most of all, they had free parking.

The teams in the men's league ought to think about trying this tactic, too.

The second example is simply the way that soccer is promoted here in America. The underlying idea seems to be to say, "Soccer is just like America's sports," to which the obvious response by the soccer haters is, "We've already got three of those and we don't need another." I would say instead, "Look at what soccer has that our sports don't have." Using the current strategy, the powers that be have instituted an all-star game because that is what baseball and basketball have. But soccer just doesn't need an all-star game. That concept is for those sports where there is very little international action. We in soccer don't need an all-star game because we get to see the best stars play in competitions like the World Cup. Why bother with an all-star game when you can have a World Cup? Instead of having an all-star game, we should promote as heavily as possible the open-cup competition that we already have. I've always made a point of going to such games when I can, just to support them as much as possible, and the reasons for this are, first, that it's a very democratic and appealing competition and, second and even more important, that the other sports don't have it. I have whenever possible taunted the soccer haters by asking them, if their sports are so great why they don't have an open-cup competition. They are usually flummoxed by this idea.

The idea that we should show that soccer is just like our sports has led to the rise of soccer as a school sport, just like football and basketball. And does this give us the wonderful pyramid of teams that England has? Of course not. The result is that those who play soccer in college find themselves with few options once they graduate, which is no better than football or basketball. The American Jay DeMerit found himself in this situation when he graduated from college a few years ago and was not drafted by any of the top pro teams. But he was able to go to England (due to having a Danish grandfather, according to Wikipedia) where he joined a ninth tier team. He quickly moved up the ranks and has now played for the U.S. men's national team. DeMerit's story is a Cinderella story, but one shouldn't forget that the reason he had to go to England to play in the first place was that there are so few teams here in the U.S., and there are few teams here because we have adopted the college model that we are familiar with rather than the private-club model that the rest of the world is familiar with.

It is pointless to promote soccer as though it were just like our sports, because sports fans here already have three such sports. But soccer has things that those sports don't have. It has World Cups. It is in the Olympics. It has national teams that players can aspire to join and that the rest of us can root for. It has open cups, so that the lower-ranked players can try to match their skills against the pros. It is both a spectator sport and a participation sport. It is easily played by both men and women. It is a cheap sport, which allows for a proliferation of teams even in the poorest of countries. It can be played at the highest levels by people of average size. These are the points that soccer's promoters here in the U.S. should be focusing on rather than trying to make soccer seem just like our sports.

My final example of an administrative problem in soccer is the downside of what I have been promoting: soccer sponsored by private clubs rather than by schools. I admit that the tendency under this system is for the teams at or near the top to stay at or near the top. Bayern Munich is always at or near the top of Germany's Bundesliga. Real Madrid is always at or near the top of La Liga in Spain. And so on. I admit that here in America the college draft allows our Major League Soccer (MLS) to avoid this since the worse teams get the best draft picks, just as the NFL and NBA do with their college athletes, and this allows the worse teams eventually to rise (assuming they play their cards right). Accordingly, my own team, the Columbus Crew, went from being the worst MLS team in 2007 to being the champion in 2008. This would be unheard of in the European leagues. (It is strange that this socialistic system exists in America rather than Europe.) Naturally, some may not see this as a defect. I live in central Ohio, where The Ohio State University football prevails. Every year Ohio State is not only at or near the top of the Big Ten, but is also at or near the top of the national rankings. My neighbors seem to think this is an inviolable right of theirs. Meanwhile, my own alma mater, the University of Minnesota, generally languishes at the bottom. (Not that I care.)

Are these dynasties good or bad? I think they are bad, but obviously some people think otherwise. Evidently, this is a subjective matter, so I'm not going to say much more about it. In Europe the whole business is ameliorated by the promotion-and-relegation system that relegates bad teams from the top tier to the second tier and allows the best teams of the second tier to be promoted to the first tier. Under this system even a giant like Manchester United has spent time in the second tier. However, such a system works tolerably well in the small and densely-populated countries of Europe, but it may not work here. What I mean is that if one's team is relegated to the second tier and one still wants to see top-flight soccer, one can do so fairly easily since a top-flight team is probably a short train-ride away. (I've taken trains to games myself in England, and I've seen plenty of boys and young men on these trains who were obviously going to the same game I was going to.) Here in the U.S., however, with our vast spaces and comparatively sparse population, this system won't work so well. Relegating a team in my hometown of Minneapolis would mean a long trip for those wanting to see the best teams play. I don't now have any solution to this problem.

Let me leave the administrative problems of soccer and talk about something related: how the game is televised. Initially, soccer presented a huge problem for television stations that wanted to televise the games. This was because soccer has no natural breaks during its play, so there was no easy way to insert a commercial. I admit that our sports have it easy in this regard, for baseball, football, and basketball all have so many breaks that it's easy for a station to break away for a commercial. With soccer, it isn't easy at all. Various methods have been tried down through the years to deal with this problem. I think the worst was during the World Cup of 1990, when the station in question actually went away from the play to show commercials, which seemed to last forever. Other solutions seem to work better, such as continuing to show the game, but in a reduced space on the screen while a commercial takes up the rest. What is disappointing, though, is that what should be the solution, namely cable television, isn't. What I mean is that back in the 1960s, when we first began hearing about "pay" TV, it was touted as a medium that wouldn't have commercials. And if it didn't have commercials, then naturally cable stations would have no problem with televising soccer. We all know, of course, that cable TV has commercials. Anyway, the problem seems to have been solved to the satisfaction of those channels that televise soccer.

Let me now talk about a certain segment of America's soccer fans. These are the snobs who think the local league is not good enough for them and so refuse to go to the games. This happened with the old NASL, and it's now happening with the current MLS. The obvious problem here is that there is no reason to believe that the level of play is going to get any better, unless lots of people support soccer by showing up at the games. That gives the teams more money, and with more money they can pay the players more, which gives a greater incentive to highly gifted athletes to make soccer their sport of choice. Otherwise, why should they bother? Why play soccer when they can make more playing one of our other sports? Yes, it's a sacrifice an American soccer fan has to make to go to games that aren't up to the level of the games in Europe, but that is our situation right now. It won't change much if people don't go to the games.

Another problem has been bad analyses of soccer's situation. Some fans got it into their heads during the old NASL days that the reason that soccer wasn't really making it in the U.S. was because the teams consisted mostly of foreigners. When the league died, these fans felt vindicated. What these people are ignoring is that some soccer fans didn't care if the teams were mostly foreign – the Minnesota Kicks drew huge crowds, for example – plus the teams of the MLS are mostly American and soccer still isn't really making it here. It's still very much a second-class sport.

Another idea is that we American soccer fans must make some kind of accommodation to the preferences of the vast majority of American sports fans if we want to draw in other Americans. And so we have had to put up with overtimes since Americans supposedly don't like ties. Never mind the fact that people who are indifferent to soccer are probably not going to be enticed in large numbers simply because there are no ties in our game. The real problem with not having ties is that it means overtime must be scheduled, and for televised games, overtime can cause headaches. And since soccer is a low-scoring sport, it is very likely that a game will end in a tie, so overtimes will be common. All this means that to get a soccer game televised, the league must arrange for a two-and-a-half hour time slot instead of a two-hour time slot. And if that extra half-hour isn't filled, then the station in question must fill it with something that isn't scheduled, which means it won't be watched. Or it must gamble that there won't be an overtime, in which case should the overtime occur, they must delay what is scheduled. And how will those other fans feel about soccer when their beloved baseball or football game is delayed by a soccer game? Soccer in America already has enough problems. Let's not add to them. So, it was a great move by the MLS commissioner, Don Garber, to eliminate overtimes. It is all the more impressive since Garber doesn't even come from a soccer background.

Let me talk about one last problem with the actual playing of the game. I want to talk about size in soccer. I've been promoting soccer as a sport that privileges those of average size in contrast with football and basketball, which privilege the big and the tall. Nevertheless, there may be a problem even here. In 1958, Pelé played for Brazil's national team, even though he was a mere 5' 9" and weighed 130 pounds. Twenty years later, Diego Maradona, who was a little shorter but somewhat heavier than Pelé, was not allowed to play for Argentina's team because he was thought to be too small. Had soccer evolved in the direction of football? Perhaps not. Today, we have America's DaMarcus Beasley, who is even smaller than Pelé, but who nevertheless plays professional soccer. Still, there is a tendency to prefer bigger players. Recently, Paul Gardner has talked about this issue. He pointed out that in the 2006 World Cup Argentina's team could have included "a quartet of highly skilled attacking players – Lionel Messi, Carlos Tevez, Javier Saviola and Sergio Aguero – all of whom were decidedly on the short side, with an average height of around 5-foot-6."[3] However, Argentina's manager decided against using them all at once, and so that talent was wasted and perhaps as a result, Argentina was eliminated. Gardner goes on to rail against such attitudes and how shortsighted they are. If putting all of them on at once had led to problems, then everyone would have said it was because they weren't big enough, but the elimination of Argentina when they weren't used was not blamed on their not being used. (Similarly, René Higuita of Colombia played a goalie/sweeper position, and he was quite good at it, but one loss against Cameroon in the 1990 World Cup, in which he was dispossessed of the ball far from goal, was enough for everyone to decide that the goalie/sweeper position was a bad idea. Never mind that if it had been that bad, Colombia would never have made it to the World Cup.)

Nor is it merely the managers who are at fault, for since referees tend to favor the defenders these days, that means that the highly skilled players up front, who are often small, are at a big disadvantage and are likely to be injured more often than one would like. Of course, as I've been saying, if the level of scoring were to return to what it once was, then referees would feel less inclined to favor the defenders, and that would encourage the highly skilled, who are often undersized.

While time will tell if soccer is headed the way of football in privileging the big, the continual emergence of brilliant but undersized players like Pelé, Maradona, and Messi means that such a tendency will have tough sledding.

Endnotes

1. David Winner, *Brilliant Orange*, p. 150.
2. I am making this claim partly on the basis of Pelé's autobiography (assisted by Robert L. Fish), *My Life and the Beautiful Game* (Doubleday, 1977), Appendix III. That appendix lists the scores in every game Pelé

ever played in, and it is instructive to examine the scores of the first hundred games he played in versus the scores of the last hundred (with Santos). One thing that can be said is that the first hundred had exactly one scoreless tie, while the last hundred had eight.

3. Paul Gardner, "A Triumph for the Snow White Formation," *Soccer America* Online, March 30, 2009.

Chapter 14
The Farce of Multiculturalism

Multiculturalism in this country is a farce. Unfortunately for leftists, there is no way to soften this assertion and at the same time be realistic. Multiculturalism is a farce in the same way that a law-and-order campaign would be a farce if it focused primarily on pickpockets while ignoring murderers and rapists, for the way in which Americans are least multicultural – that is, the way in which they are least respectful of other cultures – concerns the sports of those other cultures, yet our multiculturalists have utterly ignored this. In fact, they themselves are not respectful of those sports, so it's as if in the law-and-order campaign the police who went after the pickpockets were themselves murderers.

When I first conceived of this book, I had planned to bash American society from a leftist point of view for its prejudice against soccer. But eventually I realized that this wasn't honest. While it's certainly true that the mainstream of American society is prejudiced in this way, I had to acknowledge that the people who were overcoming that prejudice weren't my fellow leftists but instead were in the middle or even on the right. (And when leftists have overcome it, it is because they were younger.) It is perfectly possible today to have a leftist professor bash a conservative student for not being respectful of other cultures, even though the student pays attention to international soccer while the professor knows nothing about it. Multiculturalism is primarily an educational movement, but it may be the most farcical educational movement ever in our history. Not even the most ardent supporter of multiculturalism can legitimately claim that this movement has done anything to deal with the traditional American prejudice against foreign sports, and multiculturalists from the

Sixties are as a rule just as prejudiced against such sports as the average American is.

None of this does much credit to leftists, who like to think of themselves as the best, the brightest, and the most progressive. It is sad but true that they harbor hidden prejudices and hatreds, and it is possible that future generations will wonder why dealing with this was such a problem for them. When faced with a challenge to their claims to be open-minded, they turned out to be closed-minded. When confronted with the sports of the "Other," they went scurrying back to the safety and familiarity of America's sports. While demanding that our schools be inclusive, they have ignored the obvious way in which they are not inclusive (in terms of sports that exclude on the basis of size). While pushing for the questioning of everything, they just couldn't bring themselves to question our hatred of soccer, our devotion to our own sports, and the importance of privileging the big and tall in our schools. And so on. And they did this all to themselves. No one stuck a gun to their heads and demanded that they continue to be prejudiced against foreign sports.

It's very easy to be open-minded about something when everyone around you is open-minded about that thing. It's quite different when everyone around you is narrow-minded or if in fact only one unimportant person is telling you to be open-minded. American leftists obviously have deep and warm emotional ties to our sports, while having no emotional ties to foreigners' sports. They meant nothing to us. Our parents probably told us that they were dumb. They were not just foreign, but alien to our sensibilities. Nor is reading the histories of such sports comfortable since no or few Americans were involved. But so what? Getting over such feelings of unease is what the left demands that everyone else do in other circumstances. White racists had deep and warm emotional feelings about a society in which whites were on top. And male sexists had deep and warm emotional feelings about a society in which men were on top. The left didn't care about their deep and warm emotional feelings at all, and just told them to get over it. Yet, when I told leftists to get over their deep and emotional feelings about American sports, they couldn't handle it. Even in the most progressive circles, it is still permissible to dump on soccer.

It is typical for Sixties leftists (as well as some younger leftists) here in America to be utterly oblivious to anything remotely connected with foreign sports. Accordingly, they first heard of Lynne Truss when she wrote a book on punctuation in 2006, but I had first encountered her in the late 1990s when she was writing a quirky soccer column in the (London)

Times. They know Nick Hornby as the author of *High Fidelity* or perhaps *How To Be Good*, but never as the author of *Fever Pitch*. And the movie version of *Fever Pitch* that they are familiar with is the American version, which is about baseball, rather than the original British version, which is about soccer. And they know the star of the British version, Colin Firth, as Mr. Darcy from the BBC miniseries *Pride and Prejudice*, but not also as the crazed Arsenal supporter in *Fever Pitch*. They had never heard of David Beckham before the movie with his name in it came out. They travel to foreign countries (generally Europe rather than Latin America) and pay no attention to the sports there, though occasionally they are taken unawares when sporting events that they knew nothing about suddenly cause noise and traffic disruptions around them. They think soccer is all about riots and is supported only by hooligans, having no notion that foreign leftists whom they respect love soccer or cricket. They imagine that they are the only Americans who know what's going on in the rest of the world, but they are much less knowledgeable than they think they are. They are unfamiliar with famous teams like Manchester United, and are at sea with abbreviations like QPR, WBA, and lbw, to say nothing of nicknames like Bafana Bafana. They know nothing about sports in the rest of the world – they have no inkling of the existence of England's pyramid – and their critical abilities are in abeyance on the topic of sports. Even their language is laced with metaphors from our sports ("getting to first base," "hitting a homer," "slam dunk"), while similar talk by foreigners they don't understand ("scoring an own goal," "keeping a clean sheet," "hitting for six"). In Chapter 6 I mentioned an opinion piece in the *Wall Street Journal* that marveled that even though Barcelona had staged the Olympics, it seemed like a sporting backwater. I pointed out how loony this was, given the actual situation in Barcelona. So, how many leftists of my generation would be able to make this criticism? Almost none, because they have no idea what is going on in sports in Barcelona or elsewhere (unless of course it is a sport that our Sports Establishment approves of, like tennis or skiing).

Even worse, they are silent when other Americans rant against soccer. Here is a rant I encountered recently:

> Americans hate soccer with a passion. We will always insult it no matter what. We will always question the masculinity of the millions who play it and the billions who watch it. Nothing will change that. We are superior because we are American. Our sports are superior,

foreign sports are inferior. This is the mindset that no matter what you soccer fags think will never change. America's culture and sports dominate the world. Soccer is inferior, for weak people of lesser physical and mental stature to Americans. Soccer sucks. Soccer is the most effeminate, unmanly/un-American, pansy foreigner thing ever. As the great patriot Frank Hill said, "Soccer was invented by European ladies to keep them busy while their husbands did the cooking." No real man (i.e. American white nonHispanic male) would ever dream of even thinking of soccer without telling others how much soccer sucks and how it's a pansy sport played only in Europe by sissy French and that it's inherently more boring than real sports like baseball, football and NASCAR.[1]

We soccer fans are constantly having to put up with talk like this, while the left remains silent. But anyone with the least little bit of intelligence would notice when perusing this comment that it is filled with racism, sexism and homophobia. Yet, the left remains silent.

I had hoped to learn from my fellow leftists. I come from a lower-middle class background and so couldn't easily travel to other countries the way that wealthier people could. There were many questions I had, and there was no one available to answer them. If I wanted to find out about, say, cricket in south Asia, I couldn't go there and ask questions, nor were there many people to ask when I first got interested. Nor were books of any use. Americans who traveled there never talked about cricket, while foreigners who did talk about cricket assumed a background knowledge of it that I lacked. I was hoping that other leftists would be able to enlighten me, but they couldn't because they were so prejudiced. Instead, I am constantly having to enlighten them about what is going on in sports in the rest of the world

Likewise, trying to understand the soccer culture of England was daunting at first. Americans who talked about sports over there assumed that it was structured roughly as our sports were structured, while English writers writing for American soccer fans like me weren't aware that we had no idea that there could be anything like the huge pyramid of teams or the FA Cup. It took me a long time and lots of reading to figure these things out. Sometimes the vocabulary was different. For example, "nonleague" means semipro, but this isn't obvious. (It might equally refer to some new league that has just sprung up, like arena football). Likewise, it took a while to figure out that "hockey" meant field hockey and not ice hockey.

And today there is the term "Championship Final," which sounds to us like Super Bowl or World Series, but which in fact is a game between two teams in the second division which are trying to gain promotion to the top division.

I'm not going to say all that I could say about how I felt about the left's failure to be open-minded about soccer, but I can't pass over it, either. At first, I was puzzled by the left's inactivity, then I felt increasing disdain, and finally a great anger. I felt betrayed. I had turned away from the views of my conservative parents and toward the left during the late 1960s, and I had done so because of the hypocrisy I had perceived on the right. Subsequently, I had participated in countless demonstrations, marches, and even a riot. I had written letters to the editors of various newspapers complaining about the right, I had voted for leftist candidates, I had done nearly everything the left wanted me to do.

But eventually I realized that the left was hypocritical, too. I thought I could trust these people, but I couldn't. I thought I knew them, but I didn't. I had never signed a formal contract with the left, but it seemed that there had been a tacit one. The left had said that it attacked social injustice wherever it existed, and I said I would become a leftist and support its causes. But later on it seemed that they had broken that contract. They had no interest in fighting institutional sizism, or even acknowledging it. Likewise, they assured me that they were open-minded and that conservatives weren't, but that turned out to be false, too.

I had no more use for the left (that is, as it currently exists). It seemed strange that I should be fighting against the left to make soccer popular, but that was the way things turned out. The people who always claimed to be standing up for the "little guy" had no interest in standing up for those of us who were, literally speaking, little guys. The Marxists had done nothing about institutional sizism. Neither had the Leninists. Nor had the Stalinists, the Trotskyites, the Maoists, the Pol Potists, the socialists, the environmentalists, the feminists, the black liberationists, the gay liberationists, the postmodernists, nor any other leftist group I could think of. None of them had done anything about institutional sizism. None of them were even willing to acknowledge that it was unfair. Since they refused to act, I had no further use for them.

I couldn't even count on foreign leftists who loved soccer. They had no interest in the plight of us soccer fans here in America. They apparently never chastised their American leftist cousins for being such reactionaries about soccer. Instead, they worried about a problem that didn't exist, namely the exclusion of inner-city blacks from our soccer teams. *Everyone in America knows that inner-city blacks don't care about soccer.* What they care about is basketball. But while everyone in America knows this, somehow foreign leftists don't. Foreign leftists were just as worthless as American leftists were.

Let me hasten to point out that I tried to get through to my fellow leftists. I talked to people and wrote letters to famous leftists, but it was no use. Their hearts just weren't in it. Oh, to be sure, one might be able to persuade an individual here and there. But my generation was made up of millions of people, and one couldn't get through to that many people one person at a time. The frustrating thing was that sometimes I would see a new idea get a small amount of publicity, but because it resonated so well with other leftists, it would flash through the entire left and be espoused by every leftist in a few months. But for other ideas, that didn't happen. I thought the article by Brent Staples in *The New York Times Magazine*, which was entitled "Where Are the Black Fans?" and which took some shots at baseball along leftist lines, would have been a wake-up call for my generation. But it wasn't. Despite the fact that it was published in a very prestigious and widely read publication, no one responded.

What was frustrating about all this was the enormous cultural power that the left had and still has. When I had protested against the Vietnam War, I had thought of us leftists as powerless. But once I got onto a different side, I realized how much power the left had. *And none of it went to help soccer or to overcome institutional sizism.* I wanted to read about Third-World soccer in leftist magazines like *The Nation*, but I was never able to. I was hoping they would pick up the slack exhibited by the mainstream media and provide coverage of international soccer. But they never did. Obviously they hated the sport. Ditto for all the other leftist magazines (with the exception of the *Village Voice*, which occasionally had an article about soccer).

Meanwhile, I was also playing soccer, generally with people from other countries (mostly the Middle East and Africa). I interacted with these people frequently and became familiar with their ways. Eventually, I was able to travel to the Third World, but prior to that the many people I played with and against down through the years represented the Third World for me. By contrast, my fellow leftists have a more theoretical view of the Third World. It is true that some have traveled there and have met people from the Third World, but most leftists I know were like me before I got involved in soccer: we didn't know anyone from the Third World or else we knew one or two such people. These really weren't enough to be able to form any sort of basis for knowledge of what they were like, which is why I say that this is a theoretical view of what these people are like. For example, after 9/11 I talked to a leftist about Muslims, but she admitted that she had never actually known one. This is inexcusable. I played with and against many Muslims down through the years. Similarly, before I got involved in soccer, I knew very little about Brazil, but once involved and after taking some time to learn some Portuguese, my knowledge increased by a vast amount.

All of this contributes to what I think of as my multicultural education. I could have gotten involved in softball or throwing a frisbee around the way so many other people my age did, but if I had I wouldn't have met any foreigners, I wouldn't have been impelled to look at foreign media and learn the rudiments of foreign languages, and I never would have ended up traveling to places like Brazil. Moreover, since we are a Third-World country in terms of soccer, getting involved when I did was quite informative since there is virtually no other way that America counts as a Third-World country. I feel sorry for those leftists who didn't get this education and who didn't take the route I took, because it was so enlightening, but then they absolutely refused to take that route, and the reason they refused to take it was sheer prejudice on their part. And since it was prejudice, I can't feel too sorry for them. Meanwhile, who were the people besides me who were overcoming this prejudice? Why, it was the people who came of age during the Seventies. This group has to have modesty as one of their most distinctive attributes, because I have never once heard anyone in this group brag about this, even though it is worth bragging about. But they don't do so, perhaps because our culture is so dominated by the mindset of the Sixties that it just never occurs to them that it would be worth doing.

Likewise, younger leftists are more likely to take to soccer, but their thinking is also dominated by Sixties thinking, and so they never condemn their prejudiced elders, they never notice the institutional sizism, they never ask why we play baseball rather than cricket, and so on.

So, what does multiculturalism as it now exists entail? Does it entail that an American who is a multiculturalist will learn the rules of soccer and cricket? No. Does it entail that they will know particular facts about the worlds of soccer and cricket? No. Does it entail that they will stick up for those sports when other Americans bash them? No. Does it entail that they want our students to learn about these sports in school? No. Does it entail that they want them to get more coverage in our media than they now do? No. Does it entail that they have any respect for these sports? No. The conservative writer Mark Steyn has sneered at multiculturalism, saying that it doesn't entail that one needs to know any particular facts about other cultures. "All it requires is feeling good about other cultures," he complains.[2] But when it comes to sports, multiculturalism doesn't even make that minimalist demand. In America, one can bash foreign sports and still be considered a multiculturalist.

So, I now offer a challenge to this country's multiculturalists: What does multiculturalism demand of the American sports fan? If it is nothing, then multiculturalists need be no different from the average American sports fans in being ignorant, prejudiced, and arrogant. If it is something, then what is it? And why have so many multiculturalists in America wanted to do nothing? Multiculturalism has to entail something about sports, but what exactly is it?

It's now time to deal with some loose ends. I know that some people are going to ask me, "So what do you think of bullfighting?" The meaning of this question is simply that if I, as a multiculturalist, insist that other multiculturalists respect soccer and other foreign sports, then I must respect bullfighting and other practices that most Americans rightly abhor. However, though I am a multiculturalist in a weak sense, I am not a multiculturalist in the strong sense in which most leftists today are multiculturalists. That sort of multiculturalism seems insane to me, for it says that we as leftists want other Americans (and Westerners) to respect all other cultures, even those that hate leftism or parts of leftism. (And there are plenty of cultures like that.) That to me is utter madness. It is self-destructive.

No, for me multiculturalism means something weaker. It means informing oneself about other cultures partially because it makes good sense to do so (in terms of defense or business dealings) and partially because they may have practices that we would find congenial. When one does this, of course, one will find many practices we would not find congenial, but the point here is to cut through the prejudice of the average American who thinks that everything about America is superior. There will be some practices that we will find congenial and which are superior to what we are doing. The soccer environment of England, with its open cups and its pyramid, is one example. Bullfighting is an example of a practice we would not find congenial. It will also happen that we will find practices that, though, congenial, will not work here. I look wistfully at the system of promotion-and-relegation that England has, but it simply won't work here. It works in England because England is a small country that is densely populated. If you live in England and your region's team gets relegated and you still want to see top-flight soccer, that is no problem. A team in the top division will probably be close enough that one can drive or take a train to it. This just won't work in here in the U.S. with the large distances between big cities. There are also other practices that seem silly to adopt. I don't feel the slightest inclination to call a field a "pitch." On the other hand, the foreign practice of reporting scores by giving the home team first rather than the winner makes sense.

Another point I want to clarify is that while in this book I have made myself look like an expert on foreign sports, that isn't exactly true. I know vastly more than the average American about foreign sports, but probably vastly less than the foreigner who is steeped in those sports. Truth be told, I probably know less than the average ten-year-old in England. I could easily make a "multicultural sports quiz" that most Americans would fail, but a true expert could make one that I would fail. I'm saying this now just because I know that hostile people will be peppering me with questions like, "Who won the FA Cup in 1934?" or "When was Flamengo founded?" And I'm saying right now that I probably will not know the answers to such questions.

Another issue is whether multiculturalism should deal with sports at all. People have said to me that it isn't in fact about sports, so what I'm saying is irrelevant. This is just silly. Once one promotes a principle or project that is general rather than specific, one has to accept where it leads, even if it leads in directions one doesn't like. Libertarians who are against government interference in business ought to be against government bailouts. And pacifists who are against all wars ought to have been against Saddam Hussein's war against Kuwait. Demanding that Americans respect other cultures is something general and not specific, and it can lead in all kinds of unexpected directions. Sadly for those leftists who want to remain prejudiced, it can lead to demands that they themselves respect other cultures' sports. Finally, what is the point of leaving sports out of multiculturalism? Sports are as much a part of a culture as its music, literature or dance. In fact, throughout most of the world, the sports sections of newspapers encompass many more pages than are devoted to those three. Moreover, sports will touch people who aren't touched by literature, for example, since even the illiterate can enjoy sports though they can't read their culture's literature. Leaving sports out of multiculturalism is just special pleading by the prejudiced.

I've also heard leftists say that *they* aren't prejudiced against soccer. And that may be true. Nevertheless, the leftist reaction to soccer falls far short of my expectations (set out in Chapter 1). Merely being unprejudiced is just one small step along the way. For that matter, I had a letter published in the *Times Literary Supplement* once in which I complained that leftists like Noam Chomsky, Susan Sontag, and Gore Vidal had never shown any interest in soccer.[3] In response, I received a postcard saying that both Sontag and Vidal were soccer fans. The postcard seemed to be signed by Howard Zinn, but I couldn't swear to this since it was so scribbled. But in any case, I never received any postcards from either Sontag or Vidal, so I don't know if what the postcard-writer was saying was correct. But suppose they were soccer fans. Why didn't they write against the American prejudice against soccer? Their fandom (if it exists) did nothing to educate their fellow Americans. And to all those leftists out there who are supposedly soccer fans, Why no letters to *The New York Times* demanding better treatment of soccer in their sports pages? And why did you fail to be critical of our sports?

Another reaction seems to be that prejudice against soccer is such an insignificant sort of prejudice that it shouldn't really count against the left. But prejudice is prejudice. If you want to be unprejudiced, then you are committed to being unprejudiced in every possible way, including against foreign sports. More to the point is that, as I just implied, getting over one's prejudices is just one part of what is going on. Being critical of our sports is another. The fact that our two main school sports, football and basketball, exclude as much as a third and maybe even half of the male portion of the student body should be cause for concern, shouldn't it? And if not, why not? Moreover, sports aren't insignificant, as I've just been arguing. It has its own daily section of the newspaper. More important is that while for my generation overcoming soccer prejudice seems quite minor, that doesn't mean that future generations will feel the same way. A generation gets judged not just on its accomplishments, but also on its failures. It gets judged on its failure to do things it should have done, and it gets judged even more harshly on its failure to see things. What for my generation is a blind spot may not be a blind spot to future generations, and they may shake their heads with amazement that my generation never even noticed institutional sizism.

Finally, it looks very bad for leftists to have been outdone in open-mindedness by frat boys.

Another issue is media coverage of sports. I think it is ridiculous that progressive newspapers are really no different from conservative newspapers in the sports that they cover. (Compare the *Washington Post* with the *Washington Times*, for example. There is no difference between them.) I will be told that progressive newspapers are merely reflecting the interests of their readers. However, many progressive newspapers have taken up the cause of gays and lesbians, for example, even though many of their readers (or potential readers) dislike this immensely. So why shouldn't progressive newspapers be willing to take up the cause of soccer? Many of the readers of progressive newspapers have asked me to make sacrifices in the name of progressiveness. Why shouldn't I be allowed to ask them to make sacrifices, too? Soccer, as I've been arguing, is more progressive than our sports. It is more inclusive than football and basketball, and it is more egalitarian than baseball and football. It should get more coverage in a progressive newspaper than our sports. If that makes some progressives unhappy, so what? Why should a progressive like me reading a progressive newspaper have to go elsewhere to read about a progressive sport?

Another response is to acknowledge what I've said, but to insist that this isn't the time to be bringing these issues up because there's so much else that needs to be done and the sports stuff all needs to go on the back burner. Of course, having it on the back burner is better than not having it on any burners, which is its status now, but still, think about this response in comparison with, say, feminism. How did feminists respond to talk like this? They rejected it completely. Instead of acknowledging that women's concerns were less important than the concerns of the workers, the Vietnam War, and so on, they made a systematic search through history and condemned even the most progressive thinkers of the past, if they did not live up to today's feminists' standards. Why should we soccer fans put up with mere back-burner status for our concerns?

There have also been leftists who have nitpicked at one or another point that I have made. Baseball fans in particular seem absolutely convinced that somehow baseball is the divine pastime, and leftist baseball fans are no different from any others. Yet, for the leftist baseball fan this nitpicking is quite contrary to their normal behavior in other areas. When they have reached a conclusion, they don't like it at all when the conservatives nitpick away at what they are saying. They believe that they are speaking about the essence of the matter and that nitpicking doesn't change the fundamentals.

Mostly, though, these people are showing that in spite of their belief that we should question everything, they just cannot bring themselves to question our sports.

I've also been told that my evidence is just anecdotal and therefore can be dismissed. This seems to be a common and easy way to dismiss just about anything, if there hasn't been a rigorous study for it. Yet, it is too easy. Surely, it would be greatly to the credit of someone living a few hundred years ago to have accepted the anecdotal evidence of a few escaped slaves on how horrible the institution of slavery was rather than waiting for a study of it. Wouldn't it? The better way to dismiss me is to show that in fact that I am ignoring a great deal. But am I ignoring a great deal? One columnist with whom I sparred insisted that her father had come of age in the 1960s but that he had played soccer professionally and that he was a leftist. Therefore, I was wrong. And similarly Franklin Foer has claimed that it was parents like his who were to the left of center who got the current American interest in soccer (such as it is) started. Both of these are anecdotal evidence, too, and they seem much more limited than the anecdotal evidence I used, namely because both seem to be generalizations on a single example. I tried to use as much evidence as possible, relying on studies if they were available, but mostly relying on what people in many places throughout the country said and did. If, for example, someone wants to claim that sports have been a strong part of the multicultural movement here in the U.S., fine. Let them trot out their evidence for it. I have seen nothing along these lines, even though I was constantly looking for it. And let me observe that while I was looking for it, I desperately wanted to find it. I found next to nothing, however. While I occasionally found leftists who were soccer fans, I can only remember twice during the last thirty years when liberals or leftists brought up institutional sizism in our schools. That just isn't good enough.

Some are going to get heavily involved in some foreign sport like team handball, just to show that they aren't prejudiced against foreign sports. Now to some degree that is laudable, but it misses the point. There has never been any prejudice in this country against team handball, not to the extent that there has been against soccer and cricket. I remember watching a broadcast of team handball during the 1984 Olympics and being struck by how the American announcers were quite intrigued with the sport. So getting involved in a foreign sport that has never elicited any prejudice from Americans isn't being as open-minded as one could be. And of course by itself such involvement is still failing to be critical of our sports.

Some will pick up on a stray comment I made in Chapter 1 and decide that all sports invented by dead white males should be ignored, including soccer. There are several problems here. The first is whether such a person is truly sincere. After all, are they willing to come out and denounce *our* sports for this? If not, then this is just a ruse. Second, it is too easy. Instead of taking the time to do the hard work of overcoming a prejudice, one simply develops a grudge against it of another sort. It's as though someone who was prejudiced against blacks because he thought they were stupid decided, after being harshly criticized for this, that he didn't like them because they were too athletic. Is this really overcoming a prejudice? Third, soccer is a very progressive sport and has spread to most parts of the world, particularly the Third World, so denouncing it because it was invented by dead white males means, at the very least, saying that you don't respect other cultures. It also means being cut off from much of the world. But finally, while baseball fans insist, despite the facts, that baseball is an American invention, soccer fans have always had the opposite impulse, for they have insisted that soccer has roots in many cultures. Its rules may have been codified by the English in 1863, but similar games can be found in ancient Greece and Rome, in China, and so on.

Mostly, I expect a lot of silence. When Cary Nelson criticized his fellow leftist academics for squashing a graduate student union (an event which I mentioned back in Chapter 12), the left reacted with nothing but silence, and Nelson's observations seem all but unknown to everyone. So, it is possible that leftists will simply keep silent about my criticisms, too.

Finally, there will be responses based on a too casual reading or thinking about what I am saying. This seems inevitable when anyone writes any polemical tract. People misunderstand, and leftists are no exception to this rule. I've been told that I am saying that the left is to blame for the plight of soccer here in America. No, I'm not saying that (not exactly, anyway). I'm not saying that the prejudice against soccer and other foreign sports was begun by leftists. (At least, I found no evidence for this.) Nor am I saying that leftists are to blame for the continuation of this prejudice, if that is supposed to mean that they and they alone are to blame, for there are plenty of others who are to blame. What I am saying is that they are *partly* to blame. But more than that, I am saying that they should have been the first ones to overcome this prejudice, instead of which it was other people who were in the middle and on the right who did this. Along similar lines, I imagine some will think I'm saying that all conservatives have overcome this prejudice, when in fact I am saying that only some have. There will probably be other misunderstandings, but it is impossible to anticipate everything in advance, so I will say no more.

These are the responses I'm expecting from leftists, who are like anyone else in not liking criticism. I don't expect many to admit outright something like, "You're right. We blew it big time." But as time goes on, and more and more young people figure out that soccer offers opportunities that our sports don't offer, my generation's pathetic showing will look more and more feeble, until someday people will look back in wonder at such blindness. Now some are going to decide that since it's too late to show their open-mindedness, there's just no point in doing so at this late date. Nevertheless, that's the wrong attitude to take. Here is one thing today's leftists can do. In an earlier chapter I mentioned the irritating and smug newspaper articles I have seen warning us whites about the coming colored majority in places like California. Since many of the people making up this new majority are Latinos, and since many Latinos are soccer fans, I pointed out that these articles ignore the increasing role that soccer will play in such places. Eventually, schools and the media are going to have to make decisions about sports, such as, Do we continue to treat soccer with contempt, or do we yield? Just as important is what role the left will play in this drama. Will it continue to stick to the soccer-doesn't-really-belong-here attitude that it shares with most of America, thus pitting itself against the wishes of a lot of brown-skinned people, or will it be at the forefront of change? So far its attitude has been a reactionary one. Will it continue in its reactionary ways or will it become a progressive agent of change?

How will I know things have changed and that leftists have finally gotten on board? Recall the list of my expectations in Chapter 1. When some of these actually come to pass, I will know that things have changed. Also, I will know it when the *New York Times* treats soccer as the equal of our sports. When some leftist professor writes about his or her experiences on the back pages of the *Chronicle of Higher Education*. When *The Nation* apologizes for its past hatred of soccer. When soccer bashing is no longer acceptable among the left. When leftists become bothered by institutional sizism. When those on the furthest fringes of the left start moaning about the hegemony of American sports in our schools. When leftists stop talking of baseball as the divine pastime and start talking of it as inconsistent with leftist principles. And so on. When these things start happening, I will know that a corner has been turned and that leftists are finally starting to wake up to the consequences of their stated beliefs. In the more immediate future, let me note that "Archbishop Desmond Tutu believes the 2010

World Cup is a good chance to demonstrate the gains South Africa has made since the end of apartheid. 'This thing is as important as Obama getting into the White House,' he told reporters Friday at the South African Embassy in the German capital. 'For people of color everywhere, it would lift them.'" This is from the Associated Press for July 17, 2009. Does his announcement mean that multiculturalists here in the U.S. will encourage their students to watch the 2010 World Cup? Probably not. Not even a Desmond Tutu can cut through leftist prejudice.

So, what exactly has soccer prejudice among America's leftists gained them? Nothing of value to the left. They got to participate in America's sports, but those sports aren't exactly close in spirit to leftist values. They shared with other Americans traditions that other Americans revere, but then leftists aren't big on tradition anyway. Meanwhile, look what they lost. During my years as a grad student, I seldom left my hometown of Minneapolis, but I nevertheless got to mix with people from many different countries. As I said earlier, it was my multicultural education. Soccer is an international language, and playing in games with people from various parts of the Third World brought those places closer to me than merely reading about them would have done.

And when I finally got to travel to soccer-playing countries, I had pleasant experiences related to soccer. Here is one. I was staying at a hotel in Cairo a couple years ago, and once when I went into one of its cafes, I noticed that on the TV there was a soccer game between two Egyptian teams, so I sat down to watch. There were no other patrons there besides me, so the staff were all watching the game as well, and they were so pleased I was watching it with them that they offered to buy me a drink. I protested because, after all, I was the (comparatively) rich American, while they were poor, hardworking Egyptians. But they insisted. "Please, you must allow us this. It is our pleasure," one of them said. Afterwards, I thought about this incident and decided that they were pleased because foreigners weren't likely to watch an Egyptian soccer game. Most foreigners in Egypt were from Europe and so probably looked down on Egyptian soccer, while the few Americans who were there weren't likely to watch, either. Since I'll watch just about any game, I was perfectly willing to watch an Egyptian soccer game, but in their eyes, I was a rarity.

Not only did my fellow leftists, by ignoring soccer, miss out on meeting many foreigners in America and having pleasant experiences with foreigners in their own countries, they also missed out on enjoying a progressive sport. Soccer is a mostly egalitarian sport, in terms of shared action on the field. Yet, this shared action still allows for large amounts of freedom to the players (regarding whether to dribble or pass, where to dribble and whom to pass to, and so on), unlike the sports of football and baseball, most of whose players are very much constrained in terms of their actions. Soccer is also for average-sized people, unlike basketball, which privileges the tall. Furthermore, it is a cheap sport, so the Third World generally loves it. And even countries that are small in population (like the Netherlands, Sweden, and Uruguay) still manage to do well in it. In most places it is known as the people's sport. Adding all this up entails that soccer is a leftist dream come true. Why would America's leftists not want to participate in this dream? By refraining, they have only made themselves look intolerant and closed-minded. What a horrendous and ugly stain on their reputation. And what's worse is that they were outdone in open-mindedness by frat boys. Is this really a legacy that leftists are proud of?

To end this long rant, all we soccer fans have ever asked for is open-mindedness. Soccer would have many more fans here in America if all the people claiming to be open-minded were truly open-minded. It's not that I expect everyone who is truly open-minded to become a soccer fan, but I at least expect some support from them against the intolerant, and I expect some demands from them that soccer get more respect in our newspapers. Likewise, if all the Anglophiles had been soccer fans, that would have helped tremendously, though in fact such people seldom have been. Ditto for those who claim to be Europhiles or multiculturalists or cosmopolitans. Soccer should be more popular than it is, and while today's leftists, Anglophiles and so on, cannot be blamed for starting the prejudice, they can be blamed for not doing anything to eliminate it.

To leftists and everyone else in America, all we soccer fans ask is that you give soccer a fair shot, the same fair shot that you gave our sports when you were young.

Endnotes

1. From http://www.epltalk.com/aninterviewwithstevenwells/4242?disqus_reply'6052778#comment6052778 I have cleaned up the grammar.
2. "It's the Demography, Stupid," *New Criterion* vol. 24, Jan. 2006, p. 11.
3. *Times Literary Supplement*, Jan. 31, 2003, p. 17.

Index

A

Abati, Reuben 228
Affirmative action 217 ff.
African Cup of Nations 167
Aguero, Sergio 264
Anglophiles 19, 128, 282
Appropriation 238 ff.
Austen, Jane 103, 151, 199

B

Bafana Bafana 269
Baggio, Roberto 252
Barcelona, soccer in 80, 90, 269
Barzun, Jacques 74
Baseball, critique of 175 ff.
Baseball, popularity of 26-27
Basketball, critique of 182
Bat-and-ball sports 43
Beasley, DaMarcus 22, 185, 264
Beckham, David 6, 84, 199, 269
Bernstein, Carl 211
Best, George 64
Blair, Tony 86
Blee, Kathleen M. 250
Bradman, Donald 88, 89
Brain damage (from heading) 259
Bullfighting 8, 98, 201, 274

C

Cahoone, Lawrence E. 242
Camus, Albert 79
Caputo, John D. 242
Censorship 237

Chadwick, Henry 132
Chilavert, José Luis 171, 184
Civic religion and sports 117, 238
Cricket 2, 3, 5, 7, 8, 21, 22, 25, 26, 37, 41-50, 57, 58, 60-63, 66, 69, 73, 76, 78, 86, 88-90, 93, 94, 102, 103, 108, 109, 111, 115, 120, 125-35, 137, 138, 146, 149, 151, 159, 160, 168, 171, 172, 175, 181, 182,185, 188, 204, 207, 208, 214, 218, 220, 223, 227, 231, 233, 251, 252, 258, 269, 270, 273, 278
Cruyff, Johan 90, 163, 185
Cultural imperialism 228 ff.
Cultural relativism 229 ff.

D

Dead white males 218 ff.
Deford, Frank 70
DeMerit, Jay 260
Derrida, Jacques 6, 226
Diversity 220 ff.
Diving in soccer 255 ff.

E

Eastaway, Robert 120
Eco, Umberto 89
Eribon, Didier 250
Exceptionalism, American 142 ff.
Exclusion 213 ff.
Expectations for leftists, my 4-5

Exploitation of school athletes 190 ff.

F

FA Cup 31-35, 37, 41, 83, 114, 199, 270, 275
FA (Football Association) 27
False consciousness 192, 215 ff.
Farce, multiculturalism as 3, 8, 222, 267 ff.
Fast breaks (two-on-one, etc.) 256 ff.
FIFA (Fédération Internationale des Football Association) 49, 76, 168, 241
Firth, Colin 6, 87, 237, 269
Fish, Robert L. 264
Foer, Franklin 21, 100, 278
Football, critique of 183 ff.
Football, difficulty of playing informally 30 ff.
Football, social costs of 194
Foreign languages 153 ff.
Foucault, Michel 249
Frank, Anne 78
Fraternities and sororities 1, 11, 13, 14, 16, 17, 164, 172, 238, 277, 282
Freyre, Gilberto 59
Friedel, Brad 22

G

Gaedel, Eddie 179
Garber, Don 263
Gardner, Paul 64, 241, 264
Garrincha (Manoel Francisco dos Santos) 64, 185, 257
Gender equality and sports 233 ff.
Gingerrich, Owen 140
Goal-line sports 43
Goal sports 42

Goodwin, Danny 72
Grace, W.G. 78
Greer, Germaine 201

H

Handke, Peter 253
Hate speech 232 ff.
Havelange, João 168
Hegemonies 240 ff.
Hellerman, Steven L. 70, 142 ff.
Henry, Thierry 223
Higuita, René 184, 264
Hill, Frank 270
Hitchens, Christopher 250
Hornby, Nick 27, 71, 86, 87, 96, 169, 269
Hostile environments 216 ff.
Howard, Tim 33
Hume, David 58
Hunter, Bob 72

I

Immigration 227 ff.
Incuriosity 223 ff.
Individualism, and baseball 108 ff.
Institutional sizism 186-9, 191, 193, 196, 198, 207, 210, 211, 215, 216, 217, 233, 238, 244, 246, 248, 250, 271, 272, 273, 276, 278, 280
International consensuses 240 ff.
Iron Curtain of Sports 50, 75, 91, 92
Isolationism, cultural 151 ff.

J

Jocks, comparing English and American 34 ff.
Jordan, Michael 236

K

Keegan, Kevin 86
Keillor, Garrison 6-7
Khumalo, Doctor 170
Kicks soccer team, Minnesota vii, 15, 16, 17, 22, 90, 92, 164, 170, 257, 259, 263
Kirk, Russell 221
Kissinger, Henry 20
Knickerbocker Base Ball Club 126
Kuper, Simon 121, 122, 173, 201

L

Lacrosse 5, 21, 22, 42, 57, 185, 219, 220
Landry, Tom 20
Ledbetter, Bonnie S. 148
Left-handers in baseball 177 ff.
Lever, Janet 9, 28, 111, 112, 171, 212
Levine, Lawrence W. 166
Lies, media 236 ff.
Lifestyle, sport as a 36, 38, 67
Listening to other voices 233 ff.

M

Magath, Felix 22
Mandela, Nelson 89, 170, 201, 223, 236
Maradona, Diego 75, 185, 263, 264
Marginalization 214 ff.
Markovits, Andrei 70, 142 ff.
Marylebone Club 133
Matthews, Stanley 64, 257
McBride, Brian 22
McIlvanney, Hugh 89, 157
Menand, Louis 249
Merrill, Christopher 23
Messi, Lionel 264
Metric system 141, 143 ff., 152 ff.
Michener, James 8, 18, 43, 81, 93, 98, 101
Milbrett, Tiffany 185
Miller, Charles 139
Müller, Gerd 253
Multiculturalism 221 ff., 267 ff.

N

NASL (North American Soccer League) 6, 90, 228, 257, 262, 263
NBA (National Basketball Association) 28, 33, 38, 40, 77, 113, 183, 189, 190, 193, 261
NCAA (National Collegiate Athletic Association) 39, 79-80, 206
Nelson, Cary 148-9, 249, 279
News and American cultural isolationism 155 ff.
NFL (National Football League) 29, 32, 34-38, 40, 91, 189, 190, 193, 261
North, James 171-2
Novak, Michael 109, 125
Ntsoelengoe, Ace 170

O

Olympics 15, 36, 44, 47 ff., 53 ff., 67, 75, 76, 80, 82, 90, 91, 93, 94, 103, 115, 195, 197, 259, 261, 269, 278
Open-cup tournaments 31-34, 38, 67, 114, 260, 261, 274
Open-mindedness 1-3, 9, 11, 12, 16, 21, 148, 163-5, 171-2, 207 ff., 223, 268, 271, 278, 280, 282

"Other," leftist reaction to sports of 17-8, 225, 268
Otherness 224 ff.

P

Paglia, Camille 9, 171-2
Pelé (Edson Arantes do Nascimento) vii, 15, 19, 48, 59, 64, 75, 84, 99, 113, 169, 185, 192, 208, 209, 263, 264
Penalty kicks 252 ff.
Peters, Tom 165
Politicization of sports 202
Pollitt, Katha 170, 244
Postmodernism 226
Poverty and sports 230
Prejudging soccer 72 ff.
Privileging 210 ff.
Puskas, Ferenc 87, 253
Pyramid of soccer teams, England's 27 ff., 73, 75, 260, 269, 270, 274

Q

Questioning everything 13-16, 50, 148, 175, 204 ff., 268, 278
Quintessentialism in sports 94 ff., 108 ff., 138

R

Racism 177, 180, 186, 211 ff., 223, 257, 270
Ralbovsky, Martin 121
Rebels and rebelling 206 ff.
Robinson, Jackie 212, 244
Role models 215
Rounders 43, 91, 102, 126, 132-3
Rote, Kyle, Jr. 19
Rowling, J.K. 36
Rugby 5, 17, 21, 26, 35, 38, 40, 41-5, 47, 57, 58, 60, 61, 63, 66, 73, 83, 88, 91, 101, 102, 108, 111, 113, 118, 126, 135 ff., 145, 171, 184, 233, 234, 251, 258

S

Saviola, Javier 264
Schlosser, Eric 200
School sports, critique of 186 ff.
Self-esteem 214 ff.
Sensitivity training 216 ff.
Shackleford, Todd 40
Shindler, Colin 122
Shortwave radio 20, 158-9, 240
Sizism (see institutional sizism)
Smith, Red 77
Social injustice 209 ff.
Spalding, Albert G. 132
Spencer, Benjamin 148
Staples, Brent 177, 203, 211, 231, 272
Status quo 203 ff.
Stenvig, Charles 20
Stereotypes 96-100, 208-9
Steyn, Mark 274
St. George Cricket Club 126, 134
Sub-alterity 224

T

Tendulkar, Sachin 188
Tevez, Carlos 264
Third World, soccer in and the left 230 ff.
Thurber, James 195
Tibballs, Geoff 32
Tim (Elba de Pádua Lima) 257
Tolerance 207 ff.
Tolstoy, Leo 141
Tradition 203 ff.

Truss, Lynne 28, 268
Tutu, Archbishop Desmond 280
Tygiel, Jules 133-4

V

Veeck, Bill 179
Vidal, Gore 165, 276

W

Walzer, Michael 165
Weiland, Matt 200
West, Brian 197
Wheatcroft, Geoffrey 89
Whitsitt, Sam 146 ff.
Will, George 117, 203

Wilsey, Sean 200
Wilson, Harold 201
Winner, David 95, 201, 252
World Cup (cricket) 168
World Cup (soccer) 19, 20, 23, 36, 38, 47-50, 70, 75, 76, 84, 85, 87, 88, 89, 94, 95, 98, 99, 100, 106, 114, 116, 118, 119, 160, 168, 171, 185, 209, 218, 231, 239, 240, 252, 255, 257, 258, 259, 260, 261, 262, 264, 281

Y

Young, Dick 70